THE JEWISH TEMPLE

This book uncovers the meaning and significance of the Jewish Temple and its Service during the last centuries of its existence. The non-biblical sources indicate that the Temple and its rites were seen as holding the universe together, providing order and meaning in a world which could otherwise easily lapse into chaos.

The author offers a careful analysis of surviving accounts of the Temple and its Service. All the central texts are provided in translation, with a detailed commentary. While descriptions of the Temple and its Service are available, discussions of the meaning of these things are less easily found. This study clearly illustrates how the Temple was seen as a meeting point between heaven and earth, its Service being an earthly representation of heavenly reality. Jews regarded the Temple Service therefore as having significance for the whole created world. *The Jewish Temple* offers a valuable collection of materials both for those looking for an introduction to the topic and for the scholar interested in grasping the meanings beyond the texts.

C. T. R. Hayward is Reader in Theology at the University of Durham. He has published translations and commentaries on major texts of Jewish Bible exegesis and is the author of *Jerome's Hebrew Questions on Genesis* (1995).

THE JEWISH TEMPLE

A non-biblical sourcebook

C. T. R. Hayward

London and New York

First published 1996
by Routledge
11 New Fetter Lane, London EC4P 4EE

Simultaneously published in the USA and Canada
by Routledge
29 West 35th Street, New York, NY 10001

Typeset in Garamond by RefineCatch Limited
Bungay, Suffolk

Printed and bound in Great Britain by
Mackays of Chatham PLC, Chatham, Kent

British Library Cataloguing in Publication Data
A catalogue record for this book is available from the British Library

Library of Congress Cataloguing in Publication Data
The Jewish Temple: a non-biblical sourcebook / [edited by] C.T.R. Hayward.
    p. cm.
Includes bibliographical references and index.
    1. Temple of Jerusalem (Jerusalem)—History—Sources. 2. Greek
literature—Jewish authors—History and criticism. I. Hayward, Robert,
1948– .
BM655.J49   1996
296.4—dc20   96–12157

ISBN 0–415–10239–1
0–415–10240–5 (pbk)

This book is dedicated to

Sheridan Gilley

and

Linda Munk

in thanksgiving for their friendship

Benedictus es Domine Deus patrum nostrorum
et laudabilis et superexaltatus in saecula.
Benedictus es in templo sancto gloriae tuae
et superlaudabilis et supergloriosus in saecula.

CONTENTS

PREFACE

In 1990, along with other colleagues in the Department of Theology in the University of Durham, I was invited to take part in a symposium on the theme of the New Jerusalem held at and organized by the Theological Faculty of the University of Aarhus. This invitation carried with it a request that I produce a learned paper, and it therefore encouraged me to undertake detailed work on a text which had long held my interest. The fiftieth chapter of ben Sira's Wisdom presents the modern reader with one of the very few surviving eye-witness accounts of the Service of the Jerusalem Temple as it was in the days when the Second Temple still existed. Furthermore, a glance at that chapter shows how well disposed was ben Sira towards the Temple and its Service. As my work progressed, it became clear to me that ben Sira had chosen his words with great deliberation, and that attention to the biblical and traditional backgrounds of the words and phrases he had employed revealed an astonishingly rich and varied understanding of the significance of the Temple and its rites.

Study of ben Sira inevitably led to concern with other non-biblical texts favourable to the Jerusalem Temple in the days of its Service: hence this book. It is a pleasure to be able to thank those who have helped me as I wrote it, most especially all my colleagues in the Department of Theology for providing me with space and time to complete the basic research. My colleagues in Old Testament studies Tony Gelston and Walter Moberly have, as ever, been generous in their helpful comments. Loren Stuckebruck has taken a keen interest in this project, and I am grateful for his expert advice on many points. I am also indebted to Carol Harrison, Jimmy Dunn, and Sheridan Gilley among my colleagues, and to Daniel

Williams among our undergraduates. Defects in the work are my responsibility, not theirs.

Finally, thanks are due in full measure to the library staff who have facilitated my research, not least the staff of the Durham University library, who are unfailingly helpful and unsparing with their time. The final stages of this book were completed while I was resident in the University of Toronto during my research leave, and I must end by offering special thanks to the librarians of Knox College and Trinity College in that University for their generous assistance.

C. T. R. Hayward
College of St Hild and St Bede
University of Durham
Feast of St Peter's Chair at Rome 1996

ABBREVIATIONS

PRIMARY SOURCES (EXCEPT PHILO'S WORKS)

Ant.	Josephus, *Jewish Antiquities*
b.	Babylonian Talmud, ed. L. Goldschmidt, *Der Babylonische Talmud*, 9 vols (Martinus Nijhoff: Haag, 1933–1935). Followed by name of Tractate.
B. Bat.	*Baba Bathra*
Bek.	*Bekhoroth*
Ber.	*Berakhoth*
CD	Damascus Document
Cont. Ap.	Josephus, *Contra Apionem*
Erub.	*'Erubin*
FT	Fragment Targums of the Pentateuch, cited from M. L. Klein, *The Fragment Targums of the Pentateuch According to their Extant Sources*, 2 vols (Biblical Institute Press: Rome, 1980)
FTP	The Fragment Targum according to Paris MS 110
FTV	The Fragment Targum according to Vatican MS Ebr. 440
Giṭṭ.	*Giṭṭin*
Ḥull.	*Ḥullin*
jer.	*Jerusalem Talmud*
Ker.	*Keritoth*
Ket.	*Ketuboth*
LAB	Pseudo-Philo's *Liber Antiquitatum Biblicarum*
LXX	Septuagint
m.	Mishnah. *Shisha Sidre Mishnah*, ed. H. Albeck and H. Yalon (Dvir: Jerusalem, 1958)

Meg.	*Megillah*
Mekh.	Mekhilta. *Mekhilta of Rabbi Ishmael*, ed. J. Z. Lauterbach, 3 vols (Jewish Publication Society of America: Philadelphia, 1933–1935)
Men.	*Menaḥoth*
Midd.	*Middoth*
Ned.	*Nedarim*
Pes.	*Pesaḥim*
PJ	Targum Pseudo-Jonathan
PR	*Pesiqta Rabbati*, ed. M. Friedmann (Vienna, 1880)
PRK	*Pesiqta de Rab Kahana*, ed. B. Mandelbaum, 2 vols. (New York, 1962)
PRE	*Pirqe de Rabbi Eliezer*, English translation by G. Friedländer, *Pirke de Rabbi Eliezer* (London, 1916)
QH	Qumran Thanksgiving Hymns
Qidd.	*Qiddushin*
QS	Qumran Community Rule
QTemp.	Qumran Temple Scroll
Rab.	*Rabbah*, indicating *Midrash Rabbah*. For the Hebrew text E. E. Hallevy, *Midrash Rabbah*, 8 vols. (Tel-Aviv, 1956–1963) has been used. English translation in H. Freedman and M. Simon, *Midrash Rabbah*, 9 vols. and index (Soncino Press: London, 1951)
Shab.	*Shabbat*
Sheq.	*Sheqalim*
Sanh.	*Sanhedrin*
Sifre	*Sifre on Numbers*, ed. H. S. Horovitz, *Siphre D'be Rab* (Jerusalem, 1966) *Sifre on Deuteronomy*, ed. H. S. Horovitz/L. Finkelstein (New York, 1969)
Soṭ.	*Soṭah*
Sukk.	*Sukkah*
t.	*The Tosefta*, translated J. Neusner, 5 vols (Ktav: New York, 1977–1981)
Ta'an.	*Ta'anith*
Tanḥ.	*Midrash Tanḥuma*
TN	Tarqum Neofiti
TO	Targum Onqelos
War	Josephus, *The Jewish War*

yer.	Jerusalem Talmud. *Talmud Yerushalmi* (Pietrokov and Wilna editions, rep. in 7 vols; Otzar Ha-Sepharim: New York, 1959)
Zeb.	*Zebaḥim*

PHILO'S WORKS

De Agr.	*De Agricultura*
De Conf. Ling.	*De Confusione Linguarum*
De Cong.	*De Congressu*
De Ebr.	*De Ebrietate*
De Gig.	*De Gigantibus*
De. Mig. Abr.	*De Migratione Abrahami*
De Mut. Nom.	*De Mutatione Nominum*
De Op. Mun.	*De Opificio Mundi*
De Plant.	*De Plantatione*
De Post.	*De Posteritate Caini*
De Praem.	*De Praemiis et Poenis*
De Sac.	*De Sacrificiis Abelis et Caini*
De Sob.	*De Sobrietate*
De Somn.	*De Somniis*
De Spec. Leg.	*De Specialibus Legibus*
De Virt.	*De Virtutibus*
De Vit. Cont.	*De Vita Contemplativa*
De Vit. Mos.	*De Vita Mosis*
Leg. All.	*Legum Allegoria*
Quis Heres	*Quis Rerum Divinarum Heres sit*
Quod Deus	*Quod Deus Immutabilis sit*
QE	*Questions on Exodus*
QG	*Questions on Genesis*
Quod Omnis	*Quod Omnis Probus Liber sit*

SECONDARY LITERATURE

Bib. Zeit.	*Biblische Zeitschrift*
CBQ	*Catholic Biblical Quarterly*
CRINT	*Compendia Rerum Iudaicarum ad Novum Testamentum*
HTR	*Harvard Theological Review*
HUCA	*Hebrew Union College Annual*
IEJ	*Israel Exploration Journal*
JJS	*Journal of Jewish Studies*

ABBREVIATIONS

JSJ	*Journal for the Study of Judaism in the Persian, Hellenistic and Roman Period*
JSS	*Journal of Semitic Studies*
PIBA	*Proceedings of the Irish Biblical Association*
RQ	*Revue de Qumrân*
SJOT	*Scandinavian Journal of the Old Testament*
VT	*Vetus Testamentum*
ZNW	*Zeitschrift für die neutestamentliche Wissenschaft*

PRIMARY SOURCES AND REFERENCE WORKS

PRIMARY SOURCES

In addition to the editions of ancient primary texts detailed at the beginning of each section, the following critical editions have been used.

1 Masoretic Text (MT)
Biblia Hebraica Stuttgartensia, ed. K. Elliger and W. Rudolph (Deutsche Bibelstiftung: Stuttgart, 1967–1977).

2 Septuagint (LXX)
Septuaginta, ed. A. Rahlfs, 2 vols (Württembergische Bibelanstalt: Stuttgart, 1935).

3 Vulgate (Vg)
Biblia Sacra iuxta Vulgatam Versionem, ed. R. Weber, 2 vols. (Württembergische Bibelanstalt: Stuttgart, 1969).

4 Targum Onqelos (TO)
The Bible in Aramaic, vol. 1: *The Pentateuch According to Targum Onkelos*, ed. A. Sperber (Brill: Leiden, 1959).

5 Targum Neofiti (TN)
Ms. Neophyti 1, ed. A. Díez Macho, 5 vols (Consejo Superior de Investigaciones Científicas: Madrid and Barcelona, 1968–1978).

6 Targum Pseudo-Jonathan (PJ)
Targum Pseudo-Jonathan of the Pentateuch: Text and Concordance, ed. E. G. Clarke, W. E. Aufrecht, J. C. Hurd, and F. Spitzer (Ktav: Hoboken, 1984).

7 Fragment Targums of the Pentateuch (FT)
The Fragment Targums of the Pentateuch According to their Extant Sources, ed. M. L. Klein, 2 vols (Biblical Institute: Rome, 1980).

8 Syriac Version

The Peshiṭta Version (United Bible Societies: London, 1979).

REFERENCE WORKS

The Jewish Encyclopaedia, ed. I. Singer, 12 vols (Funk & Wagnall: New York, 1901–1906).

Encyclopedia Judaica, ed. C. Roth, 16 vols (Keter: Jerusalem, 1971–1972).

The Anchor Bible Dictionary, 6 vols, ed. David Noel Freedman (Doubleday: New York, 1992).

INTRODUCTION

One of the best known sayings in Rabbinic literature is attributed to a high priest, the Zadokite Simon the Righteous, who remarked that the world stands upon three things: the Torah, the Temple Service, and deeds of loving kindness (*m. Abot* 1:2; cf. *PRE* 16:1; *b. Meg.* 31b; *Ta'an.* 27b). The maxim refers to the Temple in Jerusalem, restored by Zerubbabel ben Shealtiel and Joshua ben Jehozadak (Hag. 1:2, 2:2–9; Ezra 3:2) after the Babylonians had destroyed Solomon's renowned building (the First Temple). Commonly known as the Second Temple, this sanctuary was dedicated in 515 BCE, and only a few years before its destruction at the hands of the Romans in 70 CE had been greatly embellished and effectively rebuilt by Herod the Great (see Josephus, *War* I. 401; *Antiquities* XV. 380–402, 410–423; John 2:20). For Simon's statement to make sense, the Temple and its Service must not only have been highly esteemed in themselves, but also have been considered to possess profound significance, even by Jews who compiled the Mishnah, the earliest surviving Rabbinic text, long after the destruction of the sanctuary in 70 CE. It would not be unreasonable, therefore, to suppose that in the days when the Temple stood and the Service was being offered day by day, there would have been those who made it their business to reflect upon the inner meaning of the Temple and its rites, and to convey those thoughts to generations yet to come.

The period of the Second Temple did indeed produce writers who, in their several different ways, pondered the inner significance of the Jerusalem Temple and its Service. Their works were not included in the Hebrew Bible, and therefore are generally not quite so well known as the biblical traditions about the Temple and the

1

sacrifices offered there. This study is concerned only with these authors, most or all of whom would probably have had direct or indirect experience of worship in the Temple. Among them we find Flavius Josephus, who was of priestly family, and Jesus ben Sira, himself possibly a priest, whose original Hebrew work was put into Greek by his grandson. The author of the Jubilees wrote at a critical period in the history of the Temple Service, and was determined to underscore for his contemporaries its supernatural dimension. Two people wrote in praise of the Temple apparently with a non-Jewish readership in mind: the author of Aristeas was almost certainly a Jew, while the identity of the man called Hecataeus of Abdera remains open to doubt. Philo of Alexandria is famous as a philosopher of the Jewish Diaspora. Resident in Egypt, he expounded the scriptural laws relating to the Temple in treatises which could be read by anyone familiar with the Greek tongue. They convey a whole world of hidden significance to be discerned by the lover of Wisdom. Finally, the curious work called *Liber Antiquitatum Biblicarum*, which was once wrongly attributed to Philo's authorship, displays an interest in the meaning of Temple and sacrifice which in some respects is quite distinctive and unusual. Assuming that 'Hecataeus' wrote at the end of the fourth century BCE, this survey extends from that time down to the end of the first century CE with the writings of Josephus and the *Liber Antiquitatum Biblicarum*.

These texts have been chosen, first, because they purport to speak, and speak well and at some length, of the Temple in Jerusalem. We shall not be concerned directly with writings which refer to the Jerusalem Temple only in passing, or offer brief remarks of a purely descriptive character. Thus I Enoch 89:73, which refers to the Temple under the symbol of a tower, although of great interest in its own right, in actual fact tells us little of the significance of the Temple Service. A recent discussion of it can be found in D. Bryan, *Cosmos, Chaos and the Kosher Mentality* (Academic Press: Sheffield, 1995), pp. 71–74, 179; and the provenance of the tower symbol is discussed in my article 'The Jewish Temple at Leontopolis: A Reconsideration', *JJS* 33 (1982), pp. 432–433. Similarly, we read in 1 Macc. 1:21–23 (cf. 2 Macc. 5:15–16) how Antiochus IV seized the golden altar of incense, the great candlestick, the table of the Bread of the Presence and its vessels, and other sacred objects and removed them from the Temple; but nothing is there said of what they might have signified for the

Service of the sanctuary, and in consequence they receive no comment here.

The Jerusalem Temple was revered by the vast majority of Jews in the land of Israel and in the Diaspora as the one legitimate sanctuary required by the commandments of the Torah (e.g., Deut. 12:5; 16:2; 26:2). The texts examined in this book assume without further ado that such is the case; and, as we have remarked earlier, it is this Temple which will claim our attention. There were, however, temples which rivalled that in Jerusalem, the most famous being the sanctuary in Shechem to which the Samaritans owed allegiance (see Josephus, *Ant.* XI. 306–312, 321–324; XII. 254–258). This temple on Mount Gerizim (Har-Gerizim), offering apparently a complete sacrificial Service based on the Torah of Moses, proved something of a provocation to the priestly authorities in Jerusalem. Its importance can be gathered from ben Sira's outburst at the conclusion of his poem in praise of Simon the Zadokite (50:25–26), and it receives attention in the commentary on those verses.

Yet another temple rivalling that in Jerusalem was built in Egypt sometime around the mid-second century BCE by a son or grandson of Simon the Zadokite (see Josephus, *War* I. 31–33; VII. 420–436; *Ant.* XII. 387–388; XIII. 62–73, 285; XIV. 131–132; XX. 235–237). The Simon referred to here was the man ben Sira had described in his Wisdom book, about whom we shall hear a good deal in the following pages. This son or (much more probably) grandson of his, commonly known as Onias IV, constructed a shrine at Leontopolis which remained in operation until its closure by the Romans in 73 CE. That this was no minor project is demonstrated by Rabbinic writings, which voice their concern about it long after its demise (see, for example, *m. Men.* 13:10; *t. Men.* 13:12–15; *b. Men.* 109 ab; *Abodah Zarah* 52b). As the commentary in the following pages will show, it is not unlikely that this Egyptian Jewish shrine was opposed by ben Sira's grandson, who lived in Egypt and translated his grandfather's work into Greek. Aspects of his translation suggest that he may have been keen to distance himself from the sanctuary at Leontopolis and numbers of Jews who supported it.

It was not necessary for Jews who rejected the legitimacy of the Jerusalem Temple to construct rival sanctuaries to display their opposition to the latter and its priesthood. The Jews who settled at Qumran on the shores of the Dead Sea from around the mid-second century BCE onwards differed sharply from their co-religionists in matters concerning the Temple, the laws of purity governing it and its Service, the calendar, and a host of other fundamental commandments. They did not, however, build a sanctuary, but understood their own society or Union as having the effect of a temple (see, for example, 1QS 8:4–12), atoning for the land with good deeds and prayer which for them took the place of sacrifice. They did not, however, abandon the idea of a temple building. On the contrary, they had quite definite notions of the form the temple building should take according to law, and equally clear understandings of what sacrifices should be offered in it, at what time, and by whom. Their plans for this 'correct' and legitimate temple fill some sixty-six columns of the Temple Scroll (11Q Temp.) which for the most part, however, has little to say about what the meaning and significance of the service to be offered in this ideal sanctuary might be.

Mount Gerizim, the Qumran Union, and Leontopolis will appear from time to time in the following pages, and in consequence they receive brief attention here. In an inquiry into what the Service of the Jerusalem Temple might have signified, however, it is necessary to focus upon people and writings which were favourably disposed towards it, and to attempt to glean from their often allusive and oblique statements some sense of the meaning of the rituals which were carried out day by day, year by year in that place. With these writings and other contemporary evidence before us, it is possible to offer a reasonably accurate *description* of what the Temple in Jerusalem may have looked like, what was the appearance of its furnishings, how its priests were organized, and how the sacrificial Service was ordered. The monumental two-volume work of T. A. Busink, *Der Tempel von Jerusalem von Salomo bis Herodes. Eine archäologisch–historische Studie unter Berücksichtigung des Westsemitischen Tempelbaus* (Brill: Leiden, 1970, 1980) explores the buildings which made up the Temple complex, their architectural form and dimensions throughout the period of the Temple's existence, and the fashion of the interior furnishings and appurtenances. The ceremonial duties of the priests and forms of the rites which they carried out are also reasonably well known. Schürer's *History of the Jewish People in the Age of Jesus Christ*, rev. and ed. by G. Vermes, F. Millar, and M. Black, (Clark: Edinburgh, 1979), vol. 2, pp. 237–313, provides an excellent account of these things, as well as a description of the Temple buildings in which they took place.

For descriptions of the Temple and its rites, the reader is referred to these work, and others listed in the comprehensive bibliographies which they contain.

Much less has been written, however, on what the ancient writers who speak of the Temple and its Service thought about the meaning and significance of the things they describe. With the exception of Philo, who delights in suggesting highly wrought, multi-layered, and sometimes inconsistent meanings for the various elements which make up the Temple Service, the ancient authors themselves are somewhat reticent about these things, and this reserve on their part has undoubtedly had its influence, not to say impact, on modern examinations and analysis of the Temple Service. Reticence, however, need not be taken for complete silence. The *significance* of the Temple and its Service is often revealed to us not in some direct and obvious fashion, but by hint and allusion, and by the intelligent and highly nuanced use of Scripture and tradition. Most of the authors examined here were more than familiar with the Hebrew Bible, either in its original language or in Greek translation (the so-called Septuagint, LXX). Almost all of them were Jews (Hecataeus of Abdera, or the person who passes under that name, may be an exception), no doubt aware in varying degrees of the extra-biblical traditions of the Jewish people. Since the Temple was one of the central pillars of Jewish religious life, it is impossible to imagine that the learned and pious did not reflect on its inner significance. Should they have sought to commit their thoughts on these things to writing, it is reasonable to assume that they would have looked to the language of Scripture and tradition for an appropriate means of expression.

This book seeks to investigate afresh writings which may convey something of what the Jerusalem Temple Service meant to Jews of Second Temple times who supported it and held it in high regard. Each individual text will be examined separately. Except in the case of the Jubilees, where the translation of R. H. Charles is used, fresh translations into English are provided, along with a basic commentary on each text which seeks to elucidate the significance which the Temple and its rites may have held for the author. The several texts are analysed one by one, and no attempt has been made to impose on them an artificial unity, or to force them into a preconceived mould. Their different and differing concerns will, it is hoped, be evident from the commentaries. None the less, certain themes turn out to be shared by two or more texts; and in this

Introduction an attempt will be made to give something of an overview of the main understandings of the Service as they emerge from the individual writings. Since the commentaries to each text set out the details on which particular appreciations of the text are based, those details will not be repeated here, and the reader is referred to the body of the book.

THE STABILITY AND ORDER OF THE COSMOS

Liber Antiquitatum Biblicarum, one of the most recently written (mid-to late first century CE) of the texts examined here, directly associates the Temple Service with the continuing stability of the contemporary order of the world. Other texts, as will be seen presently, are aware of this association, but express their perceptions using different language. For the author of *Liber Antiquitatum Biblicarum*, however, the sacrifices offered in the Temple at the time when he wrote are in direct continuity with the sacrifice offered by Noah. For this author, Noah represents all humanity: he is a kind of second Adam, the second originator of the human race as a whole, all other human beings descended from Adam having perished with the Flood. His is the first sacrifice of the new order of the universe after the Flood, and it elicits from God a covenant made with Noah (and, since he will be the father of all future generations, with the whole human race) that the world will not again be destroyed by flood; that it will remain stable, the seasons and days succeeding one another regularly and in due order; and that it will be fertile, fructified by life-giving (not destructive) rain to provide food for all human creatures and animals. The rainbow is the memorial of this covenant, and its appearance results in a response from the inhabitants of the world: they offer sacrifice.

When the author of *Liber Antiquitatum* tells of Moses' reception of Torah with its commandments about the sanctuary and its service, he is careful to refer back to Noah's sacrifice and the covenant then established. The order of things which was then granted to all humanity in the person of its common ancestor is now, with the gift of Torah to Moses, firmly anchored in Israel, which is represented as a great vine linking the abyss or underworld, earth, and heaven. The orders which Moses receives about the Temple and its sacrifices, the feasts and the offerings, are given to him direct from God: the author strongly implies that these are heavenly things which he is to replicate on earth. From this point on, *Liber Antiqui-*

tatum understands Israel as vine, Temple, and sacrifice as one great continuum uniting the whole universe, heaven, earth, and abyss, and assuring the order of creation. This order, however, is for a strictly defined period of time, of days and seasons as we know them, of days and seasons regularly and predictably recurring as they were promised to Noah. Those times and days and seasons will be 'changed' in the coming order of things, when God will raise the dead and judge the world. The sanctuary and service of those days will be different from the one known to the writer of *Liber Antiquitatum Biblicarum*.

From the first quarter of the second century BCE we encounter in the Wisdom of Jesus ben Sira, chapter 50, an understanding of the Temple Service which has points of contact with that just described. In particular, the high priest Simon, as he offers (most probably) the daily burnt offering of a lamb, is directly compared with the rainbow, the sign of God's covenant with Noah; he is also compared with sun, moon, and a star of light, the very celestial bodies which Ps. 148:3 commands to praise God because 'he has made them *stand* for ever and ever'. Ben Sira's expression of these things is, however, quite different from that of the author of *Liber Antiquitatum*: he resorts to a complex and subtle use of words and phrases derived from the Hebrew Bible to express his thoughts. Most important is his comparison of the high priest, as he carries out the Service, with trees and flowers which themselves are compared with Wisdom elsewhere in his book. The point is conveyed that in some measure the high priest represents, even embodies Wisdom as he carries out his sacrificial duties in the Temple; and this Wisdom, whom ben Sira personifies as a grand lady, is none other than the principle on which the universe is founded and which continues to order it.

The Greek translation of ben Sira's work by his grandson repays careful analysis: the words which he chooses for his version of his grandfather's work may be intended to heighten and strengthen the notions of order and stability which ben Sira regarded as characteristic meanings of the Temple Service. Both grandfather and grandson compare the officiating high priest with celestial bodies, and build up a picture of the Service as uniting the earth with heaven in some mysterious way: this, too, speaks of order, of all created things conspiring in unison in the worship of the creator. Particularly instructive, however, is the grandson's rendering of 50:19, which suggests that the high priest's completion of the Service after all due ceremonies have been discharged is somehow analogous to God's completion of the work of creation at the beginning.

Jubilees, too, is concerned with the Temple Service as a power for stability and order; yet the emphasis in this writing differs somewhat from those examined so far. As is well known, this book promotes a particular calendar, and is determined to ensure that Israel's Temple worship takes place on earth on the correct days and at the correct times. Although the sacrifice of Noah is as significant for Jubilees as it is for the author of *Liber Antiquitatum*, the former is more concerned than the latter to emphasize the necessity of harmony and union between earth and heaven in matters of worship. The stability and order of the world are inextricably linked with Israel's duty and privilege of observing all the laws of the Service in tune with the heavenly ministers of God, the highest angels. These carry out their service at set times, observing the festivals in heaven: only Israel, of all people, keeps these festivals and performs this service on earth. But all must be done on earth in union with heaven, if God's intended order of things is not to be undermined.

THE TEMPLE AS SYMBOLIC OF THE COSMOS

Closely related to the preceding discussion is an understanding of the Temple and its furnishings as symbolic of different parts of the universe, a point of view characteristic of Josephus, Philo, and some later writers referred to in the commentaries. Thus Josephus can state that the tripartite division of the sanctuary corresponds to the sea, the earth, and the heavens; both Philo and Josephus relate the seven lamps on the candlestick to the seven heavenly bodies (sun and moon and five planets); and for Josephus, the twelve loaves of the Bread of the Presence represent the Zodiac and the twelve months of the year, while the altar of incense symbolized that all things came from and belonged to God. Both writers offer symbolic explanations of the high priest's vestments, whereby these are held to represent various parts of the cosmos. As we try to show in the commentary, both authors appear on occasion to be dependent on earlier Jewish tradition which had already adopted a cosmic interpretation of the Temple and its furniture.

In general, Philo's explanations are more elaborate than those of Josephus, who nevertheless speaks in general of the Temple Service as 'cosmic worship' without further elaboration or definition. Philo leaves his readers in no doubt of the universal significance of the Temple service, and he explains this in several ways. First, the worship of the Temple is offered not just for Jews, but for the whole human race. This notion is implicit in ben Sira's portrayal of the high priest Simon as a kind of modern representative of Adam, the ancestor of all people. Jubilees, too, had regarded Adam as a priest; and in view of what has been said above about the significance of Noah and his sacrifice for earlier writers such as ben Sira and the author of Jubilees, Philo's blunt statements that the Jewish Service is offered for all humanity should come as no surprise. The Service is also offered for the universe itself: as far as Philo is concerned, the universe is indeed a Temple. Logically, therefore, the Temple constructed by Israel at God's command, being a copy of a heavenly reality, is a copy of the universe in all its manifold parts and divisions, representing all that has been created.

Compared with earlier writers, however, Philo and Josephus are much clearer in their articulation of the cosmic meaning of Temple matters, and express themselves at far greater length on the subject. It is quite possible that both men were motivated by the need to offer an apologetic for Jewish religion, and found in the cosmic, universal aspects of the Temple Service a useful response to Gentile misunderstandings or calumnies. The commentaries below single out possible instances of apologetic as they occur; but it will be appropriate here to give a few representative examples. Philo, often reiterating that Temple worship is offered for all people, focuses attention on the sheaf offered at Passover (*De Spec. Leg.* II. 162–167). The Jews, he says, offer this in thanksgiving to God on behalf of everyone: this thanksgiving, a religious obligation binding on all men, is shirked by most; but the Jews undertake it for all, and thereby give the lie to those who accuse them of hatred of the human race. An older apologetic stance, associated with Greek-speaking Jews such as Eupolemus and Artapanus, appears when Philo demonstrates that Moses, in ordering the golden candlestick, knew the theory of opposites long before the time of Heracleitus (*Quis Heres* 213–214). Josephus' concern to defend Judaism against calumny appears in his explanation of the meaning of the Temple veil, which represents heaven without depicting the creatures of the signs of the Zodiac (for Jews do not worship animals, *War* V. 214), as well as in the statement that sacrifice is offered to produce a state of moderation in the offerers (*Cont. Ap.* II. 195).

These forays into apologetics, however, depend on, rather than create, the understanding of the Temple and its furniture as representing parts of earth, heaven, and underworld. The biblical notice that God ordered Moses to make the sanctuary and its furniture according to a pattern which He Himself showed to Moses (Exod. 25:9, 40; 26:30) were enough for the ancient exegetes to conclude that the buildings and furniture of the Temple were in reality replicas of heavenly things. Thus time and again ben Sira's description of the Service evokes scriptural verses which speak of the heavens where sun, moon, and stars are fixed, performing the creator's will (Isa. 40:26; Ps. 147:4) in heaven as the high priest does on earth. The stars and planets, however, are not the only inhabitants of the heavens: the angels dwell there too, servants of God, ready to do His bidding, serving Him day and night (Isa. 6:2–3; Ps. 103:21; Dan. 2:10). To these we must now address ourselves.

THE TEMPLE AND ANGELIC WORSHIP

As already noted, Jubilees strongly emphasizes the harmony which should exist between Israel's worship on earth and the service of the highest orders of angels in heaven. Fundamental to the thought of this writing, however, is the striking notion that Israel has been 'written into' the very order of creation itself, specifically with reference to the observance of the Sabbath. The privilege of observing this most holy day along with God is reserved to Israel, and to the angels of the presence and the angels of sanctification. Each week, therefore, when Israel keep Sabbath on earth, it is in union with the highest angels that they do so, and for a space of time heaven is represented on the earth. More than this, however, is granted to Israel. Her priests are the earthly counterparts of the angels in heaven: this is stated plainly at Jubilees 30:14; 31:15. The first of these verses indicates that the worship of the angels and of the earthly priests is 'continual'. Here we encounter a reference to the twice daily sacrifice of lambs in the Temple which the Bible orders (Exod. 29:38–42) as *tâmîd*, 'continual, perpetual'. Jubilees offers a highly complex interpretation of this sacrifice, in which the earthly ministers correspond to angelic servants of God in heaven.

What Jubilees must imply in all this is that the appearance of the Temple Service, as it proceeds step by ordered step, corresponds visually (at least in some sense) with the service of the angels in heaven. What the earthly priests experience is thus something of the heavenly ritual. This observation, as we suggest in the commentary on Aristeas, may help to explain a puzzling feature of that writing, namely the assertion that the Temple Service took place in silence. No other writing from second temple times known to me makes any such statement; and it is quite unlikely to correspond to historical reality. It is suggested here that the writer was acutely conscious of the Service as a replication of heaven on earth, the priests representing the angels. Amongst some Jews, in particular those at Qumran, it was believed that the angels offered to God silent worship: this belief, coupled with biblical words commanding silence before God in His Temple (Hab. 2:20), may have led the author radically to expound the earthly Service as a great offering in a profound silence fitting for the presence of God. It is noteworthy that this author brings his description of the Service to a close with emphasis on what was seen: the high priest, fully vested and bearing on his forehead the golden plate inscribed with the Divine Name comes into view as if from another world. But the writer remains tantalizingly allusive; and the commentary given below attempts to be duly cautious in its final evaluation of what Aristeas is saying.

In heaven, the angels worship God in His role as king: he sits enthroned, while His ministers, the heavenly creatures, stand ready to do His will (1 Kings 22:19; Dan. 7:10). The concept of God's kingship is inseparable from His authority over the angels who perform His Service in heaven; and it cannot be divorced from His presence in the earthly Temple, which is a replica of heaven. The Service carried out there is the fulfilment of the royal commands of the king to his earthly subjects, the Jewish people. This fundamental idea underlies all the writings examined here, although it is mostly taken for granted. Ben Sira, however, in particular chooses to bring it to the fore and to articulate it with great care. He does this first by making it clear that the Temple belongs to God as king (Hebrew ben Sira 50:2, 7) and by his use of the title Most High, 'elyôn, to speak of God (Hebrew ben Sira 50:14, 16). This title, 'elyôn, is used of God specifically as king in Ps. 47:3; not only that – as 'elyôn, God is proclaimed as utterly superior to all other heavenly beings, angels, or supernatural creations (Pss. 82:6; 97:9).

This state of affairs has two important consequences. First, the God worshipped in the Jerusalem Temple is the creator of the whole universe: He stands supreme as king over even the highest supernatural entities. When Philo and Josephus later come to speak at length about the *universal* character of the Temple service, this fundamental belief of their predecessors in Judaism underlies all they have to say. To dispel any doubt about this, we may turn to the Greek translation which ben Sira's grandson made of his grandfather's poem. Here the title Most High is introduced in verses where his grandfather had not used it (50:7, 19, 21), along with the divine designation 'the King of All' (50:15). This last title appears also in Jubilees (e.g., 22:10; 30:19) to single out the unique creator God of Judaism from the many deities of the Gentiles. It is not difficult to appreciate how such emphasis on God as king and creator relates to other aspects of the Service so far described.

Second, God's Name is resident in the Temple, which is the place where He has made His Name dwell. This is a biblical commonplace (e.g., Deut. 12:5), as is the intimate association between God's kingship and His Name (e.g., Zech. 14:9). At least one of the texts we examine states that the universe was created by means of God's Name (Jubilees 36:7). It is this Name which the heavenly beings praise: the song of the seraphim recorded in Isaiah 6:2–3 is perhaps the best known example of this heavenly worship. On earth, however, the Name of God may be uttered only in the Temple worship. For those who experienced the Service directly, the Name would be heard proclaimed in the blessing spoken aloud by the priest at the conclusion of the sacrifice, and it would form the climax to the impressive and awe-inspiring ceremonies of the day. The utterance of the Name, redolent of the Lord's kingship, means that the worshippers must behave as in the presence of a king, prostrating themselves: ben Sira expounds this portion of the Service in some detail. But the high priest himself bears the Name inscribed in letters on his golden head-dress; and the Bible, in ordering the priests to bless Israel, says that thereby they put God's Name upon the people (Num. 6:27; cf. Deut. 28:10).

This inevitably leads us back to the angels, who praise God's Name and do the will of God whose kingship is so bound up with His Name. What they do in heaven, as we have seen, is ideally to be replicated on earth. The high priest, bearing the Divine Name on his forehead, recalls the angel who went before Israel in the days of desert wanderings after the Exodus, of whom God said 'My Name is upon him' (Exod. 23:21). By virtue of the priestly blessing, Israel has the divine Name imposed upon her – in the Temple Service. God's Name indicates above all His presence with Israel; and where God is present as king, He must of necessity have attendant ministers. The angels will not be strangers, then, to the earthly Temple, which is an open door to heaven for its earthly ministers. Aristeas appears to assume as much, the spectacle offered by the Service being definitely *other-worldly*. In different language, ben Sira points to a similar assessment of the Service. Neither writer, however, is as clear as the author of Jubilees, for whom the Temple Service properly performed should join earth and heaven in perfect harmony. Philo, too, is no stranger to this idea, as the commentary will show.

INVOCATION OF THE LORD ON ISRAEL'S BEHALF

Since the Name of God is present in the Temple, priests and worshippers are able to 'call on the Name of the Lord', to 'invoke' God to elicit his mercy and blessing for Israel. The invocation of God may be accomplished in different ways; and some of our texts indicate the importance of 'memorial' in calling God's attention to Israel. The Bible itself speaks of certain elements of the Service as constituting a memorial for Israel: most striking is the statement of Exod. 28:12, 19 that the names of the twelve tribes engraved on precious stones set in the high priest's breastplate effect a memorial for Israel. Israel is by this means brought directly into God's presence, as the high priest, fully vested, performs the Temple Service. The point is graphically illustrated by ben Sira, who extends the idea of memorial beyond the biblical data to include the sound made by the bells on the fringes of the high priest's robe as he walks in the sanctuary (45:9): the engraving of the names on the breastplate, ben Sira suggests allusively, is also the work of God Himself (45:11). We find a similar stress on memorial in *Liber Antiquitatum Biblicarum*, which makes the Feast of Unleavened Bread into a memorial, and, in a somewhat obscure passage, elaborates on the meaning of Rosh Ha-Shanah as a day of memorial for the world celebrated by the Jewish people (*LAB* XIII. 4, 6). For the author of this work, the rainbow granted after Noah's Flood is a 'memorial' whose appearance calls forth sacrificial offerings (IV. 5); and other such 'memorials' are noted and discussed in the commentary.

The Temple Service, with its invocations of God's Name by means described here, seeks to obtain for Israel God's *mercy*. This is explicit in ben Sira 50:19, where the Most High is tellingly designated 'the Merciful One' to whom the prostrated people present their petitions in prayer. Philo's exegeses of the various sacrifices, as a glance at the commentary will show, take for granted the belief that they call forth God's mercy for His people, and, given Philo's universal understanding of the Service, for the whole human race. The notion of God's mercy in all likelihood underlies what Josephus says (*Cont. Ap.* II. 197), that the sacrificial Service is intended to ensure that we may receive, accept, and keep the good things which God has granted. The discerning reader may also perceive in the attitude of Jubilees a sense of God's mercy called forth in the service of the sanctuary. This work expresses more clearly than some of the other texts examined here the atoning effects of worship, and the gracious gift from God of blood to effect such atonement in sacrifice. This is, perhaps, the greatest of all signs of God's mercy made plain by the Service.

The atoning properties of blood are further elaborated by Jubilees in its account of Noah's first sacrifice after the Flood, where this is tied to the covenant sealed between God and Noah, and to the future daily lamb offerings of the Temple Service (Jubilees 6:1–19). This complex of ideas brings to the fore the covenant as a focal point of divine mercy; and other writers of Second Temple times discover covenant, in one guise or another, coming to expression in the Service. Here we might note how ben Sira's description of the Temple Service reaches its climax in a prayer that God confirm for the high priest the covenant made with Phinehas (50:22–24; cf. Num. 25:10–13), having strongly implied in the preceding poem that the high priest, in carrying out the Temple Service, may realize some aspects of the ancient royal covenant with David (see especially commentary on 50:6–7; 45:15). For *Liber Antiquitatum Biblicarum*, too, the covenants which God made with Noah and with Moses stand as the foundation of the Temple Service, and *ipso facto* are recalled as each day the round of ordered sacrifice continues.

Ben Sira's highly wrought descriptions of the sacrificing high priest also indicate that the latter stands before God as representative of Israel, whose prayers and petitions he brings into the house of the Great King, God Most High. His juxtaposing of the high priest with Adam, expounded in the commentary on 50:1, strongly suggests that ben Sira took the high priest as a latter-day representative of Adam; and that the Service, therefore, was offered for the whole world. This, as has been seen, was a notion

Philo appreciated and developed: both Israel and the world are represented before God in the Temple which is a copy of the universe. Given the times in which he lived, the author of Jubilees is understandably less concerned about the Gentiles; but by associating the sacrifices and festivals observed in the Temple with significant events in the lives of the patriarchs, he ensures that Israel in the shape of her pious ancestors is for ever in God's sight. A glance at the commentary will show how the first celebrations on earth of (for example) the Festivals of Weeks, Tabernacles, and Unleavened Bread are tied to important developments in the unfolding story of God's dealings with the fathers of Israel. In this way, it is inevitable that each occurrence of a particular feast will bring the appropriate patriarch to mind, so that not only Israel recalls her righteous fathers, but God Himself has their righteous deeds in mind. To obtain God's remembrance, Israel of the writer's time thus presents her Service to God as it were *along with* the memorials of the righteous patriarchs, whose deeds and dispositions Jubilees calls on its contemporaries to emulate.

LIGHT

In what is possibly the oldest writing surveyed here, Hecataeus of Abdera singles out as a distinctive feature of the Temple the burning of a light which never went out; he offers no direct clue to its possible significance. Philo speaks at length about the seven-branched candlestick with its seven lamps, and attributes several possible meanings to these things (see commentary on Philo, pp. 123–127). Josephus also briefly expounds his understanding of the lampstand (e.g., *War* V. 217), and further uses the imagery of the sun's brilliant light to expound the significance of the high priest's ephod and the golden head-dress on which is illuminated the Name of God (*Ant*. III. 184–187). The imagery of light is perhaps found at its most intense in *Liber Antiquitatum Biblicarum*, where a non-biblical tradition concerning twelve precious stones yielding a light of unparalleled brilliance plays an important role (*LAB* XXVI).

This last writing insists that God is entirely light and has decorated His house with precious stones (XII. 9). The light-giving stones which He has ordered to be placed in His earthly dwelling will be joined by others at the judgement day to provide light for the just (XXVI. 13). In the meantime, the precious stones are to be placed in the Ark of the Covenant, and give out a light like that of

15

the sun diffused over all the earth (XXVI. 15). The writer refers these matters to Solomon's Temple, and presents himself as writing at a time before that building was set up. His meaning, however, is not obscured: God intended that the Temple built by Solomon should be a source of light for the earth. Possibly lying behind this is a particular understanding of the scriptural verse referring to God: 'For with Thee is the source of life: and in Thy light we shall see light' (Ps. 36:10).

Such a point of view is not explicit in the writings of our other authors, who none the less draw freely on the imagery of light. Even without close reading of the texts, the splendour and magnificence of the Service as described by ben Sira and Aristeas leaves the reader with an impression of a rite suffused with heavenly radiance. Philo's evocation of God as supreme source of light to which all virtuous souls aspire pervades his account of the candlestick and the high priest's breastplate; and Josephus, as we have seen, has the Name of God, the sign of Divine Presence, borne majestically by the high priest in rays of brilliant golden light. Different emphases on light, then, may be found in the individual authorities; but at the root of all their thoughts lies the ancient biblical tradition of God's presence in the Temple defined as 'glory', a dazzling radiance manifesting God's companying with Israel (see especially Lev. 9:4, 6, 23; Num. 14:10).

THE TEXTS CONSIDERED IN THIS BOOK

The reasons for the choice of particular texts have been set out above. Each individual writing is provided with an introduction, providing information about the author, the provenance and date of the text, and bibliographical information for further study. These introductions are followed by a translation of the text: the source of the text in its original language is given in notes to the text, which follow the translation. These also deal with problems in the manuscript sources and, where necessary, set out reason for the adoption of particular readings. In the case of Jubilees, however, the translation is not mine, but that of R. H. Charles, *The Book of Jubilees* (Black: London, 1902). Then follows the commentary on the text, to which is appended, in most instances, a brief summary of the author's thoughts on the significance of the Temple and its Service.

In this way every effort has been made to allow the texts to speak for themselves. It should be apparent, however, that some of them share common concerns: the similarities between ben Sira and the Jubilees in understanding particular details of the Service, for instance, should be apparent to any reader, as will certain shared concerns of Jubilees and the *Liber Antiquitatum Biblicarum*. It might be argued that all the writings surveyed here implicitly share a common understanding of the Service inherited from a tradition older than any of the individual authors, which each has fashioned under the influences of their respective times and concerns. Substantiating such an argument, however, would require analysis of biblical texts from the Second Temple period relating to the Service, as well as detailed study of documents from the Dead Sea caves. These things are beyond the limits set for this book, although the commentaries included here may give hints how a study of this kind might begin.

1

HECATAEUS OF ABDERA

Josephus informs us (*Cont. Ap.* I. 183) that Hecataeus of Abdera was a Greek philosopher who lived in the days of Alexander the Great and Ptolemy I (Soter) son of Lagus (*c.*367/6–283/2 BC), and goes to some lengths to demonstrate that such is the case (*Cont. Ap.* I. 184–185). Certainly this Hecataeus wrote a book on the history of Egypt, incorporating references to the Jews, which Diodorus Siculus (died *c.*20 BC) used as a source for his historical writings (XL. 3). Josephus (*Cont. Ap.* I. 183) does not refer to his Egyptian History, but states rather that Hecataeus wrote another book specifically about the Jews. From the latter he quotes substantial portions (*Cont. Ap.* I. 185–204), including a description of Jerusalem, the Temple, observations on its cult, and a note on the priests. It is these sections alone as preserved in *Cont. Ap.* I. 187, 197–199, which are here under consideration. Other material attributed to Hecataeus falls outside the scope of this study.

If Hecataeus was truly the author of the writings which Josephus reproduces, we have before us one of the oldest surviving descriptions (outside the Bible) of the Jewish Temple and its Service, most unusually written by a non-Jew. For these reasons alone, such information should occupy a special place in any account of the Temple and its rites. The question whether these fragments are authentic, therefore, is a matter of great moment: it is also far from simple. They are considered first in this book because the balance of probability suggests that they are genuine, for the most part the work of Hecataeus, and therefore written in the late fourth or early third century BC. None the less, since their authenticity is so keenly disputed, a brief summary of scholarly opinion is desirable.[1]

Already in the second century AD, Origen (*Contra Celsum* I. 15) records that Herennius Philo expressed doubts about the work *On the Jews* attributed to Hecataeus, saying that if Hecataeus had been the author, he had been influenced by Jewish propaganda.[2] Josephus (*Ant.* I. 159) ascribes yet another book to Hecataeus, entitled *On Abraham*: this work is now almost universally regarded as inauthentic, and suggests that other *spuria* may have been passed off in the name of Hecataeus.[3] The fragments are also said to contain anachronisms. Thus, in the material translated here, we read of a high priest Ezekias (*Cont. Ap.* I. 187) otherwise unattested in Josephus' list of high priests, and of tithes given to the priests (*Cont. Ap.* I. 188) rather than to the Levites, a practice best attested in the Maccabean period (Judith 11:13; Jubilees 32:15). In fragments other than those given below, we read of Jewish resistance to the death when their laws are attacked by foreigners (*Cont. Ap.* I. 191), which recalls the period of the Maccabean revolt. Further, Hecataeus is said to have praised Jews for destroying Babylonian pagan altars and temples (*Cont. Ap.* I. 192–193), a strange sentiment in the works of a Gentile; and he reports an otherwise unknown award by Alexander to the Jews of the land of Samaria as a reward for their loyalty (*Cont. Ap.* II. 42–43).[4]

All these points, however, can be countered. Thus Herennius Philo does not actually state that *On the Jews* is spurious; and Gentile writings favourable to Jews were known in the late fourth to early third centuries BC.[5] Neither is it logical to argue that because *On Abraham* is inauthentic, *On the Jews* must also be spurious. A coin from Beth-Zur, of late Persian or early Greek vintage, has the name Hezekiah inscribed in Hebrew, suggesting that this man was of noble lineage; and it should be noted that the term 'high priest' need only signify 'member of a high priestly family'.[6] On the tithes, we simply do not know when the custom changed whereby they were given to priests rather than Levites. Nor can it be asserted that Jews did not suffer for their laws before the days of the Maccabean revolt; the biblical book of Esther indicates persecution in the Persian period. The praise of Jews destroying heathen cult sites, and the grant of Samaria to Jews by Alexander, may derive from Jewish sources; but these notes could have been inserted into the genuine text of Hecataeus by a pious Jew.[7]

In short, it would appear that the case against the authenticity of fragments of Hecataeus' *On the Jews* remains unproven. None the less, since the matter is so finely balanced, it is appropriate to record datings of the fragments given by three representative scholars who regard them as spurious. Thus, with regard to the fragments translated here, Wacholder[8] suggests that their author was a Jew, probably a priest of Jerusalem, writing around 300 BC. Walter posits two men, Pseudo-Hecataeus I and II, the first of whom penned *On the Jews* probably around 100 BC, very likely in Alexandria.[9] Finally, we may note Holladay's arguments for a date in the first half of the second century BC, the author working either in Palestine or Egypt.[10]

TRANSLATION OF FRAGMENTS OF HECATAEUS OF ABDERA PRESERVED BY JOSEPHUS, *CONTRA APIONEM* I. 187; 197–199

187   Of these, he (Hecataeus) says, there was one Ezekias a high priest of the Jews, a man about sixty-six years of age, great in esteem among his fellow countrymen and not un-intelligent of soul; he was still competent in speech, and in matters of business he was skilled more than any other. Yet he says that all the priests of the Jews who receive the tithe of the revenue and administer the affairs of the community are around 1,500.

197   For while there are many fortresses and villages of the Jews throughout the country, there is one strong city of about fifty stades' circumference which around 120,000 men inhabit; and they call it Jerusalem.

198   And here, almost at the middle of the city, is a stone-enclosed precinct, the length about five plethra, and the breadth about one hundred cubits, having double gates. In this, there is a square altar composed of unhewn, undressed stones collected together. Each side is twenty cubits, and its height ten cubits. Now alongside it is a large building where there is an altar and a lampstand; both are golden, and their weight two talents.

199   Upon these is an inextinguishable light both night and day. There is absolutely no statue or votive offering; nor is there any plant of any kind at all such as a sacred grove, or anything of such a kind. And priests spend their time in it night and day, performing certain purificatory rites; and they drink absolutely no wine at all in the temple.

NOTE ON THE TEXT

The Greek text translated is that given by H. St J. Thackeray in
Josephus, vol. 1: *The Life, Against Apion*, Loeb Classical Library (Harvard University Press: Cambridge, Mass., 1966).

COMMENTARY

187   As was noted earlier, a silver coin of the later Persian or early
Hellenistic periods discovered in excavations at Beth-Zur is inscribed with the name Hezekiah, along with another word, in
Hebrew script. The coin is thus roughly contemporary with the
reign of Ptolemy I, when Hecataeus of Abdera was writing. Most
students of the coin interpret the second word as Hebrew *yhd*, to
give the sense 'Hezekiah of Judah', indicating no doubt a man of
some importance: possibly he was the Ezekias referred to here, or
one related to him.[11] The description of him as high priest need
not indicate that he had occupied the office of high priest, but
simply that he came of a family related to the members of the high
priesthood.[12]

According to biblical law, the tithe was given first to the Levites,
who themselves were to render a tenth of the tithe to the priests
(Num. 18:21, 25–29). This practice was still current in the time of
Nehemiah (Neh. 10:37–38) and the writer of Tobit 1:6; but Judith
11:13 and Jubilees 32:15 attest a change of practice, whereby the
tithes are given to the priests in the first instance, the custom which
obtained in the time of Josephus (*Ant.* XX. 181; 206–207; *Vita* 63,
80). The Talmud ascribes this change of practice to Ezra (*b. Hull.*
131b; *Ket.* 26a), thereby indicating its antiquity; but in truth, we do
not know exactly when the change of custom took place. The fact
that Jubilees records it without comment, however, suggests that
the change in the law was uncontroversial for the writer of that
book: this probably means that it took place long before the Maccabean revolt.[13] Furthermore, even if the law had not been
changed by 300 BC, the pagan Hecataeus may not have been aware
of the precise distinction between priests and Levites.[14]

The priests rule the Jewish community, says Hecataeus: this was
indeed so, and its significance in relation to the Temple Service was
later (*c.*190 BC) explored in some detail by Jesus ben Sira. Hecataeus
is quoted by Diodorus Siculus (XL. 3:5) to the effect that priests
rule the Jewish state.[15] But the number 1,500 is very small, when set

alongside the biblical evidence for priestly numbers in early Second Temple times (Ezra 2:36–39; 1 Chr. 9:13), the evidence of Aristeas 95 discussed below, and Josephus (*Cont. Ap.* II. 108).[16]

197   Hecataeus refers to 'fortresses', *ochurômata*, already a feature of the Judaean countryside in the earliest Maccabean times (e.g., 1 Macc. 4:61; 5:9, 11; 9:50) and before.[17] But Jerusalem was the only strong city (*polis ochura*);[18] *ochura* indicates a city which is firm, stout, and lasting, and was used by LXX to indicate the might of the Canaanite cities captured by Israel (Num. 13:29; Deut. 3:5). Fifty stades is around six miles, which Hecataeus gives as the city's circumference: this seems large, since Josephus (*War* V. 159) puts it at thirty-three stades. The size of the population, too, is probably inflated.[19]

198   The Temple was not actually in the middle of the city, and Hecataeus qualifies the location slightly.[20] His description of it as an enclosed precint, *peribolos*, recalls two other descriptions. Greek ben Sira 50:2 speaks of repairs to 'the high underwork of the enclosed precinct of the Temple', and seems to have external building work in mind: nothing in the original Hebrew corresponds exactly to what the Greek translator has written. Aristeas 84 used *peribolos* to describe the three enclosed areas which make up the Temple site proper: see also Philo, *De Spec. Leg.* I. 71, who describes the outer *peribolos* as being strong (*ôchúrôtai*). Josephus (*Ant.* XV. 418) also designates the Court of Women a *peribolos*. Hecataeus, then, seems to be giving a general external description of an enclosure or large court he estimates as 500 feet in length and 150 feet wide.[21] For the double gates, see also Philo, *De Spec. Leg.* I. 71 and Greek ben Sira 50:2.

The altar of burnt offering Hecataeus calls *bômos*, which LXX uses often to speak of the pagan altar (e.g., Exod. 34:13; Num. 23:1–2, 4, 14; Deut. 7:5; 12:13) and 'high place', the similar-sounding Hebrew *bâmâh* (Hos. 10:8; Amos 7:9; Isa. 15:2; Jer. 7:31; 31:35). But it should be noted that Greek ben Sira 50:12, 14, uses this word of the altar in the Temple, as does Josephus (*Ant.* III. 149) of the altar of burnt-offering in the Tabernacle. The altar is square (*tetragônos*), as described in LXX Exod. 27:1. Its stones are unhewn (*atmêtoi*; cf. LXX Exod. 20:25, *ouk . . . tmêtous*, and Philo, *De Spec. Leg.* I. 274), further qualified as 'undressed', *argoi*, stones on which no human art has been expended. The dimensions of the altar correspond to those of the bronze altar of burnt offering in Solomon's Temple according to the Chronicler (2 Chr. 4:1).

The Holy Place itself he calls a building, *oikêma*, a word never used by LXX to speak of the Temple. It is, however, used by Herodotus (*Histories.* VIII. 144) as a general word describing a shrine or chapel. Hecataeus notes the presence there of an altar (again styled *bômos*), the altar of incense, and a lampstand, *luchnion*, another word not used by LXX. He gives no further description of their form or significance, and remarkably says nothing about the golden table for the Bread of the Presence.[22] That *bômos* here refers to the altar of incense, not to the table, is shown by the beginning of the next paragraph: on both the lampstand and the altar a light burns. He only remarks that the latter are of gold, giving their weight, probably in total: Exod. 25:39 says that the lampstand weighed one talent, and Exod. 30:3–4 that the altar of incense was encrusted with gold.

199   The fire on the golden altar and the light on the lampstand are inextinguishable, *anaposbestos*: this is an exceptionally rare word, not attested in classical Greek and unknown to LXX. It suggests that these 'eternal lights' are a particularly striking feature of the Temple Service: they are never extinguished, such that the worship of the Temple is perpetual. Indeed, the never-ceasing aspect of the Service is emphasized here: 'night and day' these lights burn, 'night and day' the priests carry out the rites. All this surely refers to the daily Service of the Temple, known as the Tamid (Hebrew *tâmîd*, 'continual, perpetual') since the Bible stipulates that certain elements in it are 'perpetual'. This word is used of the light continually burning on the lampstand (Exod. 27:20; Lev. 24:2–4); of the daily 'continual' offering of incense (Exod. 30:7–8), and of the daily offering of two lambs, one in the morning, the other in the evening, 'perpetually' (Exod. 28:39–42; Num. 28:3–8). Hecataeus does not refer to the lambs; but the incense and the lamps are a standard part of the ritual.

On the other hand, Exod. 27:21; Lev. 24:3 may seem to qualify the 'perpetual' burning of the lamp by ordering it to be tended from evening to morning. Philo would later take this to mean that the lamp burned only at night (*De Spec. Leg.* I. 296). But Josephus states clearly that three lamps burned by day, all seven by night (*Ant.* III. 199), while the Rabbis understood that at least one lamp burned continually throughout the day, the seven being kindled from it at evening (*m. Tamid* 3:9; 6:1; see also *Sifra 'Emor* Parasha 13:7 stating that the western light always burns, a point emphasized by *Sifre Num.* 59).

The lack of a statue (*agalma*) in the Jewish Temple would have been common knowledge: Diodorus (XL. 3:4) has Hecataeus point out that Moses made no divine images.[23] By votive offering (*anathêma*) we should understand an image or statue which often graced pagan shrines as a thank offering to the gods from their devotees. The grove (*alsôdês*) is explicitly condemned in the prophetic books (LXX IV Reigns 16:4; Jer. 3:6, 13; 17:8), and along with trees near the altar is forbidden by Deut. 16:21. This ban on groves and trees is a feature of the Hebrew Bible, and any pagan researching Jewish customs even superficially is likely to have encountered it. Indeed, it is possible that the lengthy and somewhat laborious explanation which Philo offers (*De Spec. Leg.* I. 74–75) for the lack of grove and vegetation in the enclosed precinct (*en tôi peribolôi*) of the Temple actually arose from questions posed to him by (non-Jewish?) readers of Hecataeus.

The priests kept watch throughout the night in the Temple, and slept on site (*m. Tamid.* 1:1; see also Ps. 134:1). Hecataeus says that they performed purificatory rites, *hagneias tinas hagneuontes*. The verb *hagneuô* is not found in LXX, and the words may be taken in a very general sense to mean that the priests 'make a point of strictly observing their religious duties', a remark strikingly confirmed and illustrated by Aristeas 92–99. On the other hand, the noun *hagneia* more commonly means 'purity, purification', such that the words refer to the state of purity and the rites which create and sustain it. From early Second Temple times, the Chronicler is witness that the preservation of the Temple's purity, and its restoration when defilement had occurred, was a matter of prime concern for the priests (1 Chr. 23:28; 2 Chr. 29:15, 16, 18). So important were the laws of purity that, according to *m. Sanh.* 9:6, a priest ministering in a state of impurity would be executed outside the Temple court by young priests. Purity may also govern the last piece of information which Hecataeus provides. The priests' absolute (*to parapan*) abstinence from wine in the Temple is asserted here in the same stark words as the absolute (*to parapan*) absence of images: the biblical law is found in Lev. 10:8–11, where it is glossed by a note on the priests' need for sobriety[24] so that they may distinguish between what is consecrated and unconsecrated, and between the impure and the pure.[25]

SUMMARY

Assuming that these fragments of Hecataeus are genuine, we have in our possession a brief but remarkably informative vignette of the way the Temple Service was perceived around 300 BC. If they are not from the pen of Hecataeus, they still testify to an understanding of the Temple and its Service deriving from (probably) the Hasmonean period, drawn up possibly by a Jew with non-Jews in mind. After a description of externals, the precinct with its gates and the square altar of burnt offering, the account concentrates on the Holy Place with its incense altar and lampstand: it does not appear at any point dependent on LXX. The language of paragraph 199 is very strong, even a language of extremes. Thus the light of altar and lamp is 'inextinguishable', burning 'night and day'; 'night and day' the priests serve; there is 'absolutely', 'not at all', any image or grove or plant; the priests drink 'absolutely' no wine. Whoever informed Hecataeus of Temple practice, therefore, seems to have laid particularly heavy emphasis on certain recurring aspects of the ritual. For this informant, what is significant about Jewish Temple ritual is, first, *its perpetual nature*: it is the notion of continuous and continuing worship of God that leaps to the eye. This continual worship is priestly, and is intimately bound up with *purity*, to be guarded so carefully that wine may never at all be drunk. The absolute lack of an image or representation would be known to all; but here it is juxtaposed with a light which never goes out. The unspecified 'rites of purification' which are perpetually carried out in this place, then, have to do with light which never goes out. This is a matter which will recur to occupy us later, not least when we consider the writings of Philo.

2

ARISTEAS

This work was written ostensibly by a Gentile courtier of Ptolemy II Philadelphus (285–246 BC), named Aristeas, to his brother Philocrates. It purports to tell how the Law of Moses was translated into Greek for King Ptolemy's renowned library by seventy-two Jewish scholars. These had been specially selected for the purpose and sent to Alexandria by the high priest, who is named Eleazar. This essential thread of the narrative is greatly embellished, the author losing no opportunity to discourse on the glories of the Jewish nation, its laws, superior wisdom, moral philosophy, and tradition. His account of the Temple and its Service, featuring an appearance of Eleazar wearing the high priestly vestments, is found in chapters 83–99, and what follows is concerned only with that passage.[1]

The author himself, it is generally acknowledged, must have been an Egyptian Jew, probably from Alexandria.[2] Establishing the date of his writing, however, is no simple matter, and is the subject of keen debate. Since Josephus used the work in writing *Ant.* XII. 12–118, it must have been composed before the end of the first century AD. This much is agreed; but thereafter students of the work sharply diverge in their opinions. Jellicoe summarizes four quite different proposed datings for the letter.[3] One group of scholars dates the work early, between 250 and 200 BC. A second group argues for a date of writing around 150–100 BC, while a third minority group suggests the first century BC as the most likely time of composition. Finally, there are a few scholars who argue that the composite nature of the work suggests that its final compilation, on the basis of older materials, took place as late as the first century AD.

It is difficult to decide which, if any, of these datings is preferable: the majority of students side with the second group, opting

26

for the first half of the second centry BC. Although strong arguments can be brought for a date at the very end of the third or the start of the second century BC, they do not settle the matter; and even those who favour the period 150–100 BC encounter such problems that the revisers of Schürer's *History of the Jewish People* remark that the author can 'only be dated with certainty to some time in the second century BC'.[4] The arguments for and against a particular dating are too lengthy and complex even to be summarized here, and readers are referred to rehearsals of the various scholarly stances set forth elsewhere.[5] As a working hypothesis for our present discussion, however, it seems most prudent to adhere to the 'majority view', generously interpreted by the revisers of Schürer's *History*, recognizing the while that it is not proven and that other, later dates may have points in their favour.

TRANSLATION OF ARISTEAS 83–99

83 For when we arrived at the places we saw the city lying in the middle of the whole of Judaea, on a mountain of considerable height.

84 On the summit was built the Temple, having a pre-eminent position. And there were three enclosed precincts over seventy cubits in size, the width and the length being in proportion to the house as regards its structure. Everything was constructed on a grand scale and expense entirely surpassing anything else.

85 It was plain that the expenditure of money on the doorway and on the fastenings surrounding it by the doorposts and on the solidity of the lintels had been lavish.

86 The shape of the curtain was in every way similar to that of the doorway. In particular, the material of the curtain acquired continual movement because of the draught of air, such that the draught worked from the bottom of the curtain through the folds to make a billowing effect up to the top. This action made a pleasing sight which it was difficult to drag oneself away from.

87 Now the construction of the altar was made commensurate with the place and with the sacrifices which were

utterly consumed in the fire; and that of the ascent to it was of the same kind. For the sake of decency, the place had an ascending gradient for the ministering priests, who were clothed in linen tunics reaching to their ankles.

88 Now the House faces the east with its back towards the west. And the whole floor is paved with stone and has slopes to the appropriate places, to allow for the flushing of water which occurs so as to cleanse the blood from the sacrifices. For many tens of thousands of beasts are brought for sacrifice on the days of the festivals.

89 And there is an endless supply of water, as if indeed a strongly flowing natural spring were issuing forth from within [the Temple]; and in addition there exist marvellous and indescribable reservoirs underground – as they showed me – for five stades around the foundation of the Temple; and each of them has numberless channels such that the streams join up together with each other from different sides.

90 And all these down to the bottom were leaded, and over the walls of these a vast quantity of plaster had been spread: everything had been done effectively. There were also very many openings at the base (of the altar) which were invisible to all except to those who have the duty of carrying out the Service, so that all the blood of the sacrifices, which is collected in huge amounts, is cleansed by the downward momentum and slope.

91 Now I myself inquired, and I shall explain the construction of the reservoirs as I was assured of it. For they led me more than four stades outside the city, and ordered me to bend down at a certain place and to listen to the sound made by the meeting of the waters so that the size of the reservoirs became clear to me, as I have explained.

92 The Service of the priests is in every respect unsurpassed in the physical strength (required of them) and in its orderly and silent arrangement. For they all labour spontaneously, even though the exertion is great, and each one takes care of an appointed task. And they minister without a break, some offering the wood, some the oil, some the fine flour, some the incense, others the sacrificial portions of

flesh, using their strength in different degrees for the different tasks.

93 For with both hands they take up the legs of the calf, each of which for the most part are more than two talents' weight, and in a wonderful manner throw them with each hand to the correct height (for the altar) and do not miss in their aim. Likewise the portions of the lambs and of the goats are also wonderful in weight and fatness. For those whose duty it is always choose those which are without blemish and which excel in fatness. The religious Service described earlier is thus discharged.

94 For pause (in the Service) there is a place appointed where those who are relieved from duty sit down. When this happens, those who have rested rise up at the ready, since no one gives orders about matters of the Service.

95 And a complete silence reigns, with the result that one might suppose that there was not a single person present in the place, even though there are around 700 ministering priests present and a great number of men bringing up the sacrifices; but everything is discharged with awe and in a manner worthy of the great Godhead.

96 It was a great astonishment for us when we saw Eleazar in the Service, both as regards the form of his robe and his splendour which consisted in the dress which he wore, a tunic and the precious stones upon it. For there were golden bells upon his ankle-length robe which gave out a particular sound of musical tone: on both sides of these were pomegranates with variegated flowers which possessed a marvellous colour.

97 He was girded with a girdle of excellent magnificence which was woven in most beautiful colours. On his breast he wore the oracle, as it is called, in which are set twelve stones differing from each other in kind, inlaid in gold and bearing the names of the leaders of the tribes according to their original order, each one shining forth with its own proper colour in a way which cannot be explained.

98 And on his head he had the so-called turban, and above this the inimitable mitre, the consecrated royal diadem with the Name of God in holy letters set in relief on a golden

plate in the midst of his forehead, gloriously completed. He had been adjudged worthy of these things in the public Services.

99   The overall appearance of these things created awe and confusion, so as to make one think that he has come close to another man from outside the world. And I am certain that everyone who comes near to the sight of the things described above will come to astonishment and indescribable wonder, and will be stirred in mind by the holy quality which pertains to each detail.

NOTE ON THE TEXT

The Greek text from which the above translation has been made is that edited by A. Pelletier, *Lettre d'Aristée à Philocrate*, Sources Chrétiennes 89 (Cerf: Paris, 1962).

COMMENTARY

83   Jerusalem is in the middle of the country, just as the Temple is almost in the midst of the city according to Hecataeus. Perhaps development of the notion that Jerusalem is the 'navel of the earth' and its Temple the centre of that navel, clearly articulated in Jubilees 8:19, is responsible for emphasis on the central location of the city.[6]

84–85   The elevated aspect of the Temple recalls statements, which perhaps had acquired an almost proverbial quality by late second Temple times, familiar from the Psalms (especially Pss. 48:2–3; 78:69). Such a lofty site for the building is entirely appropriate for the One who is worshipped therein as Most High, according to ben Sira and Jubilees. Aristeas, however, does not use this title for God. The 'enclosed precincts' are *periboloi*, the word found in Hecataeus, Philo, and Josephus describing the stone edifice surrounding the court with its altar of burnt offering and the complex of sacred buildings.[7] The grandeur of the buildings and their component parts, described here and in the next paragraph (85), seems clearly intended as a kind of pro-Jewish propaganda. This magnificence contrasts somewhat with descriptions of the rather unimpressive buildings dedicated in the days of Jehoshua ben Jehozadak: these were unfavourably compared with Solomon's original building (Hag. 2:3; Zech. 4:10; Tobit 14:5; Josephus *Ant.* XI. 81). It is possible that the structure had been improved and embellished by the time Aristeas wrote: does his description reflect the work of the high priest Simon known from ben Sira 50:1–2; or had earlier Zadokites improved the modest edifice of Jehoshua and Zerubbabel?

86　The earliest post-biblical description of the curtain at the entrance to the court of the priests says little of its significance. It is called *katapetasma*, a word used most often in LXX to speak of the veil which divided the Holy of Holies from the sanctuary (e.g., Exod. 26:31–37; 37:3; Lev. 16:2), but which could also signify, as here, the curtain at the entrance of the Tent of Meeting (LXX of Exod. 37:5, 16; Num. 3:26). Aristeas seems to focus on the arresting appearance of the curtain's movements: as in the previous paragraphs, he wishes his readers to be fully aware of the impressive external appearance of the Temple.

87　The altar of burnt offering (*thusiastērion*) is very sketchily described, in contrast with the notice in Hecataeus (198). The author seems more interested in the ramp which led up to it. Exod. 20:26 forbids anyone to ascend to the altar by steps lest they display their nakedness, a concern addressed also in Exod. 28:42–43. Certainly Herod's Temple had a sloping ramp leading to the altar (Josephus, *War* V. 225). Aristeas is witness to its existence in much earlier times; and reference to it is frequent in the Mishnah (e.g., *Midd.* 3:3–4, where it is said to have been 32 cubits long and 16 wide; *Tamid* 1:4; *Yoma* 2:1–2). For the linen vestments of the priests, see LXX of Exod. 36:35.

88　The orientation of the Temple is not specified in Scripture, but features in Josephus, *Ant.* VIII. 64 (Solomon's Temple); cf. *m. Midd.* 2:4. Aristeas devotes much time to the water supply, which cleanses the blood of the numerous sacrifices. Once more, the emphasis for the moment seems to be placed on the large numbers of the sacrificial victims.

89–91　Similarly, the supply of water is superabundant. Perhaps this water had its source in the spring Gihon. Aristeas exhaustively describes its progress through and collection in underground reservoirs, referred to also perhaps in Greek ben Sira 50:3.[8] These are placed around the foundations (*katabolē*) of the Temple. It is possible that the great interest displayed in these underground chambers (89, 91) may reflect a religious meaning attached to them. Were they symbolic of the abysses, in which the foundations of the world were fixed, the Temple forming an essential link between them, the earth, and heaven? The Greek version of ben Sira 50:15 may obliquely allude to these things, and it is noteworthy that concern with the descent of the sacrificial blood to the area beneath the Temple floor is highlighted by Aristeas in sections 88 and 90. Specifically, Aristeas 89 speaks of the *katabolē* of the Temple. The word occurs only once in LXX, at 2 Macc. 2:29, but in the Hellenistic Greek of the New Testament it is quite common, and is used to speak of the foundations of the cosmos (e.g., Matt. 13:35; 25:34; Luke 11:50; John 17:24; Eph. 1:4). The notion that the Temple and its Service guarantee the stability of the cosmos, which we have already encountered in other writings of the Second Temple period, necessarily involves thinking about the foundations of the universe.[9] While Aristeas says nothing definite about the meaning of the reservoirs, and seemingly alludes only to their practical significance, his lengthy treatment of them gives pause for thought. This is especially the case since later writings regard the foundations of the Temple and altar as in some way linked to the foundations on which the earth stands above the abysses.[10]

92   The term translated as 'Service' here and in 90, 94, 96, 98 is *leitourgia*, a word found often in LXX to describe Temple duties carried out by priests and Levites (e.g., Num. 18:4, 6; 1 Chr. 9:13, 19). Aristeas continues to concentrate on the magnitude of matters connected with the Service: the extent of the labour, the strength required of the priests, and the orderly disposition of it all. He emphasizes the latter with his reference to silence (see also 95), implying that no one gave verbal orders to those carrying out the numerous tasks: this is actually stated plainly at 94. It is not entirely clear whether these allusions to silence contradict the information given in *m. Tamid* 1:2–4; 3:2; 5:1–2, where we read of verbal instructions passed between the priests. Furthermore, *m. Tamid* 3:8 indicates that the Service could be a remarkably noisy business![11] Aristeas may be understood to mean that only the preparation of the sacrificial elements, and their placing on the altars of incense and burnt offering, was carried out in silence, while parts of the ritual which preceded and followed these things may have included instructions. If such is the purport of Aristeas, then he coincides with the information given by *m. Tamid* and ben Sira, neither of

whom suggests spoken words or orders accompanying the actual immolation of the offerings. On this understanding of the writer, we should conclude that Aristeas simply omits description of the preliminaries to the sacrifices, the sounding of the trumpets, and the songs of the Levites which followed them.[12]

93 The strength, precision, and accuracy of the priests, and the magnitude of their task, still claim Aristeas' attention. The victims named as calf, lamb, and goat indicate that Aristeas is speaking of sacrifice in general, and not of the Tamid or some particular ritual. They are without blemish: this requirement for sacrificial animals, not detailed at every turn in the Hebrew Bible, is none the less specified as a general demand of the Torah according to Philo, *De Spec. Leg.* I. 166. It is often specified by the Aramaic targums in their renderings of verses which speak of the victims (e.g., TN of Lev. 1:3, 10; 3:1, 6; 4:3, 23), and sometimes even added to Hebrew verses which do not explicitly refer to it (e.g., marginal note of TN to Exod. 29:38, and LXX of that verse).

95 This second reference to the complete silence of the proceedings seems to contradict common sense, and strongly implies that *the whole Service* takes place without any sound, because of the great awe and reverence attending the rite. If this implication is accepted, then the evidence of the Mishnah cited above is flatly contradicted. Equally the Chronicler's note that sacrifice was accompanied by the Levites' psalms and the sound of trumpets (2 Chr. 29:27), which most likely reflects the actual ritual practice of early Second Temple times, is cast aside; and Aristeas stands alone as witness to a wordless, soundless liturgy. Even so, the writer repeats his stress on the immensity of the business in hand: 700 priests and crowds of sacrificers make not a sound! A possible explanation for this fantastic statement is found at the end of the paragraph: Aristeas evidently believes that complete silence is the only appropriate manner of approach to 'the great Godhead' in the Temple ritual. Despite the business and noise which would necessarily have accompanied the sacrifices, Aristeas places before his readers 'a complete silence' as the essence of the ritual. There is no avoiding the question of his grounds for making such a statement.

Aristeas has most likely derived the notion of silence from the Bible and from Jewish tradition of his own day. Thus in Hab. 2:20 we read: 'But the Lord is in His holy Temple: be silent before Him, all the earth.' In similar vein, Zech. 2:17 (English versions 2:13) commands: 'Be silent before the Lord, all flesh: for He is aroused from His holy dwelling place.' Verses like these could only strengthen the belief, found in certain Qumran scrolls and targums, that the proper attitude of the highest heavenly beings in the face of the Divine Presence is a *silent* worship of God in their uttering the prescribed formulae of blessing. Thus 4Q405.11–13, speaking of the mysterious heavenly creatures who surround the throne of God, records:

> The spirits of the living God [or: divine beings] walk to and fro continually with the glory of the chariots of wonder. And there is a sound of *silence* of blessing in the tumult of their walking. And they praise the Holy One as they return on their journey. When they exalt, they exalt marvellously, and when they tabernacle [*wbšwkn*] they stand. The sound of ringing gladness *becomes silent, and a silence* of the blessing of God is in all the camps of God, and the sound of praises.[13]

While the exact date of this document is uncertain, its editor is prepared to put forward the working hypothesis that it is a product of the Jews of Qumran, in which case it must have originated before 70 AD.[14] The targum of 1 Kings 19:11–12, another witness whose date is uncertain, tells of Elijah's experience at Horeb. This also indicates that the Divine Presence is found, not among the camps of angels of the wind breaking the mountain and shattering rocks, nor among the angels of earthquake and fire; but with 'the sound of those who utter praise silently'.[15] Silent blessing is the prerogative of the highest heavenly creatures: the Jerusalem Temple, likewise, is wrapped in silence. In the earthly Temple, Aristeas suggests, this profound silence on the part of the worshippers is of one piece with the sense of awe (*phobos*) engendered by the rite, a notion which he will take up again in 99.

96–98 The description of the high priest's appearance may be compared with those found in ben Sira, Philo, and Josephus. Aristeas is clear that the vestments, along with the precious stones which adorn them, constitute the high priest's 'splendour' (or 'glory', *doxē*), a view which he shares with Greek ben Sira 45:7; 50:11. Unlike the latter, however, Aristeas draws attention to the bells and pomegranates of the full-length robe, whose significance Philo will later expound at length (*De Spec. Leg.* I. 93; *De Vit. Mos.* II. 119–120; *De Mig.* 103–105). The breastplate, with its stones bearing the names of the tribes in order (cf. Josephus, *War* V. 233–234; *Ant.* III. 166–169), he explains somewhat obliquely as an 'oracle' (*logion*: LXX normally speak of it as *logeion*, e.g., Exod. 28:15, 22, 29; 36:15, 22). Its shining forth, which Aristeas implies is quasi-miraculous, might be taken by non-Jews as a simple statement of a special intensity of unique natural brilliance, heightened by sacred use. In this sense, the 'oracle' breastplate would be simply a further example of the unsurpassed scale of magnificence of everything associated with the Temple. For Jewish readers, however, Aristeas may hint at the mode of operation of the 'oracle': its stones shone forth, predicting future events (see Josephus, *Ant.* III. 214–218). As ever, it is difficult to determine whether Aristeas' description of these things is merely 'on the surface', or conceals knowledge of their deeper meanings.

Turning to the high priest's head-dress, however, Aristeas is apparently less reticent, but somewhat confusing in his use of technical terms. In LXX, *kidaris*, here rendered 'turban', may represent either the cap worn by ordinary priests (the *migbâ'âh*, Exod. 29:9), or the more ornate head-gear peculiar to the high priest (the *miznepet*, Exod. 28:4): *mitra*, on the other hand, rendered here as 'mitre', stands in LXX Pentateuch for Hebrew *miznepet*. The head-dress, whatever Aristeas may consider its form, carries the golden plate (*petalon*) inscribed with the Divine Name YHWH.[16] It is called *basileion*, a 'royal diadem'. Again, it is not clear whether Aristeas implies that the wearing of this golden plate conveys some kind of royal authority to the high priest. He may indeed do so, if the following paragraph 99 refers to Eleazar; and in that case, his ascription of royal attributes to the high priest would recall what ben Sira has to say about Simon the Zadokite.[17] But he may also seek to indicate that the God of Israel is properly a king with the corresponding authority, the Temple Service bearing witness to this.

99 One effect of all this is the creation of awe (*phobos*) in the beholder: this same word has been used in 95 to speak of the awe attending the silent execution of the sacred ceremonies worthy of the Godhead. The other is the production of confusion (*tarachê*), a word which may refer to a state of mental disorientation brought about by startling circumstances. It is such 'as to make one think that he has come close to another man from outside the world': so runs our translation of the Greek *hôste nomizein eis heteron elêluthenai ektos tou kosmou*. In this, we agree with Andrews, understanding the

words to refer to Eleazar.[18] If this translation is adopted, then the high priest appears as a being with an aura of the supernatural attaching to him; and the royal aspects of his diadem already described would combine with the notice here to suggest that Aristeas ascribed a kingly dignity to the high priest. The latter may even have the character of an angel: he comes forth in the 'complete silence' of a service full of 'awe' fit for the Godhead: may he be an earthly counterpart to one of those 'who utter praise silently'? Sadly, the words of Aristeas do not permit an answer.

They are also ambiguous. The whole spectacle was one of which 'a man would think he had come out of this world into another one'. So Shutt translates the Greek: Pelletier renders 'one might believe he were in another world', and Thackeray speaks of the viewer coming 'into another sphere outside the world'.[19] While these renderings do not necessarily exclude reference to the high priest, they none the less direct attention to the Temple and its Service as a whole. And what follows does the same: whoever has sight of the *things* spoken of already (*tôn proeirémenôn*) will experience astonishment (*ekplêxis*, the emotion stirred by the sight of Eleazar's appearance according to 96) and indescribable wonder (*thaumasmos*, a word recalling the marvellous [*thaumasiôn*] reservoirs of 89 and the marvellous way [*thaumasiôs*] the priests place the sacrificial portions on the altar according to 93). The Service creates true astonishment and marvel in the beholder, not least because it is holy.

SUMMARY

Much of what Aristeas reports is intended to portray Judaism in the most favourable light to his pagan Greek readers. Jews worship the one true God; and the highest expression of this worship is concentrated in the one incomparable Temple, whose buildings and furnishings are of an almost unutterable grandeur, beauty, and magnificence. Everything connected with this building and the worship conducted within it is described in the superlative degree. Vast numbers of sacrifices are offered; unfailing water supplies ensure the absolute purity of the rites; hundreds of strong and able-bodied priests minister; the officiants exhibit perfect discipline, needing no commands; the appearance of the high priest in awesome majesty elicits wonder and amazement; and so forth. Much of this may, like his laudatory descriptions of the land of Israel, owe a good deal to the style adopted by Greek writers of the classical and later periods to describe their travels in far-flung, exotic lands.[20]

Beneath the surface descriptions, however, there are hints that Aristeas has a deeper knowledge of his subject. In dwelling at length on the subterranean reservoirs of the Temple and on details of the high priest's vestments, he may intend to indicate that these things have a particular significance for those who know the Temple. But he does not elaborate; and the reader is left wondering precisely what purpose he has in mind. On two matters, however, Aristeas leaves no room for doubt. First, the liturgy is a model of discipline and order: second, the whole ritual takes place in silence. Other texts yet to be examined, notably the poem of ben Sira 50, are familiar with the Temple service as an expression of order, particularly the order of the created universe. But no other writer asserts that the Service was offered in silence.

An attempt has been made here to provide an explanation of this apparently unique description of a silent liturgy. It is drawn from the Bible and later tradition, and suggests that Aristeas regarded the Temple Service, whatever else it might signify, as above all else a kind of display, an exhibition, a revealing on earth, of the heavenly world. For all his emphasis is on *what is seen* (99). He insists that nothing is heard. And yet, as if to heighten the mystery, he lets slip a tell-tale remark that the golden bells attached to the high priest's robe 'gave out a particular sound of musical tone' (96). The bells, if we take in an absolutely literal sense what he has said about silence elsewhere, must have been the only sound heard in the entire course of the liturgy. That sound would inevitably direct the worshipper's attention to its source, the high priest in his vestments, crowned with the Divine Name Itself. For Aristeas, the Service might be a vision of heaven evoking wonder, awe, and an inevitable loss for words in silence.

3

THE WISDOM OF JESUS BEN
SIRA IN HEBREW

This book affords one of the most valuable disquisitions on the
Temple Service as it was carried out in Second Temple times. The
author has given over almost the whole of chapter 50 to an elaborate and detailed description of the high priest Simon II, surrounded by his colleagues, officiating at a rite of sacrifice. This
description is set forth in language for the most part derived from
the Hebrew Bible. Individual words and phrases drawn from the
Scriptures are employed to create a subtle and nuanced poem of
great solemnity, as ben Sira grandly concludes his work with a
portrait of Simon the high priest performing his sacred duties,
arrayed in the glorious vestments proper to his office. By analysing
ben Sira's poem in detail, it is possible to acquire an understanding
of the inner meaning of the Temple Service as the writer
perceived it.

It would be difficult to exaggerate the significance for our subject of ben Sira's writing. Three particular reasons permit such a
statement; and the first of these concerns the date at which ben
Sira composed his work. It is almost universally agreed that ben
Sira wrote his Wisdom book in the first quarter of the second
century BC, before 175 BC. The poem in chapter 50 appears to
assume the death of Simon II, which occurred *c.*196 BC; the author
probably wrote his book, therefore, sometime between 190 and
175 BC. Such is the measure of agreement among scholars on this
matter that it is unnecessary to rehearse here evidence for the
dating, which can conveniently be found elsewhere.[1] Given this
date, we may be confident that ben Sira represents Jewish society as
it was before the Hellenistic crisis, which erupted in the reign of
Antiochus IV Epiphanes (175–164 BC).

The high priest Simon II and his successor Onias III (*c.*196–174

BC), in whose reign ben Sira probably wrote, belonged to the illustrious House of Zadok. This priestly dynasty had provided all the high priests of Jerusalem during the period of the Second Temple, from the time of its restoration and dedication in 515 BC (Ezra 6:13–22) when Jehoshua ben Jehozadak was high priest (Ezra 5:2), down to ben Sira's own day. The Zadokites claimed descent from the priest Zadok, who had been one of King David's priests at the time when he had wished to build a Temple (2 Sam. 8:17). This same Zadok had anointed as king Solomon (1 Kings 1:39), who built the First Temple in which Zadok ministered (1 Kings 4:2). His descendants were praised for their fidelity to the God of Israel and His Torah by the prophet Ezekiel: they had remained loyal when other priests and Israelites had gone after idols (Ezek. 44:15; 48:11). Accordingly, Ezekiel allotted to them alone the privilege of coming near to God to minister to Him (Ezek. 40:46).

Such distinguished ancestry, the antiquity of the house, and the central role of Jehoshua ben Jehozadak in the building of the Second Temple, inevitably gave the Zadokites of ben Sira's day a pre-eminence in Jewish society and affairs which was bound to find some sort of formal expression. The probability is overwhelming that the House of Zadok through the centuries evolved a particular understanding of its part in God's dispensation for Israel; of a sense of its own eternal worth as the chosen high priestly dynasty; and of the profound significance of the Temple Service for which it was ultimately responsible before God. It is evident from chapter 50 of his work that ben Sira held Simon II in the deepest awe and respect. His portrait of the man, as we shall see presently, is so painted as to convey a quite distinct theological impression of this high priest as he offers the appointed sacrifice. Naturally, we cannot be certain that ben Sira presents us with an appraisal of the Zadokites and the Temple Service which coincides with the priests' own understanding of these things; but he is more than favourably disposed towards them, and is unlikely to have presented them in a light which the Zadokites would have found unflattering. In fine, ben Sira discloses something of the inner world of the Zadokites, and of what it meant to one of their most ardent supporters.[2] Indeed, without ben Sira's book, we should be almost completely in the dark about these things.

The second reason for ben Sira's importance consists in the respect in which his work was held. It was widely read by Jews: fragments of its Hebrew text have been found at Qumran and

Masada, and it is quoted, sometimes with approval, by Rabbinic authorities.[3] The dissemination of ben Sira's work suggests that his stance towards the Zadokite priesthood embodied in the text may have commanded respect long after the Zadokites had ceased to rule as high priests. Among the Jews of Qumran, indeed, adherence to Zadokite teaching was a matter of some concern to the sectaries; and the Jewish Temple at Leontopolis, which survived until 73 AD, was presumably presided over by direct descendants of Simon II's family.[4] The Zadokite ideal, therefore, remained; and ben Sira's book constituted a continual reminder to pious Jews of the way things had been before the terrible events of the Hellenistic crisis.

Finally, ben Sira's work assumed even greater importance when it was translated into Greek by his grandson, and eventually became part of the Greek version of the Hebrew Scriptures commonly known as the Septuagint. The work was thus assured an even larger readership. In his prologue to the translation, ben Sira's grandson remarks that he went to Egypt in the thirty-eighth year of (Ptolemy) Euergetes, found a copy of his grandfather's work, and determined to translate it. It is generally agreed that the Ptolemy Euergetes named by the grandson is Ptolemy VII, and that the thirty-eighth year refers to his regnal year, which would be 132 BC. The Greek translation would therefore have been published sometime after that date.[5]

When ben Sira's grandson came to engage in his translation, the political and religious establishment in Jerusalem was very different from what had been familiar to his grandfather. The Zadokite dynasty no longer held the high priesthood, which had been assumed by Jonathan Maccabee in 153 BC and had since become hereditary in his family. Further, the country as a whole had now become politically independent, exercising some influence in the region roundabout. The Hasmonean high priest and political ruler, John Hyrcanus I (135/4–104 BC), in whose reign ben Sira's grandson almost certainly wrote, was held in the very highest regard by some elements (at least) in the Jewish community. Thus he was credited with the gifts of rulership, high priesthood, and prophecy (Josephus *War* I. 68; *Ant.* XIII. 282–283; 299–300), and considered an ideal monarch.[6] In such circumstances, it is not surprising that ben Sira's grandson may have thought to modify his grandfather's work.

Such, indeed, are the differences between the Hebrew text of ben Sira 50 and its Greek version that a separate translation of the latter is given here, with its own commentary. The differences themselves may arise from a number of considerations, as set out in the commentary; but it should be remembered that ben Sira's grandson, resident in Egypt, could not have been ignorant of the Jewish settlement and Temple at Leontopolis in the nome of Heliopolis. Its possible relevance to the circumstances of ben Sira's grandson is indicated by Josephus (*Ant*. XIII. 284–287), who records that those Jews were active in the complex political and military situation which arose in Egypt at the end of John Hyrcanus' reign.⁻ Their support for Queen Cleopatra in war against her son-in-law Ptolemy VIII Soter (II) may have indirectly influenced ben Sira's grandson, whose translation of those parts of his grandfather's work relating to the priesthood betrays traces of support for the Hasmonean settlement of his own day, rather than a yearning for the days of the Zadokites.

With these considerations in mind, the Hebrew text of ben Sira 50 may be examined. The translation set out here begins with 49:15, for reasons made plain in the following commentary. Not the least of these is the fact that the eulogy of Simon II concludes ben Sira's extended poem 'The Praise of the Fathers of the World', the title which stands at its head in the Hebrew text of 44:1. It is attached to the body of this poem by a catchword, and by other verbal similarities noted in the commentary. In particular, the description of Aaron the first high priest after the giving of the Torah, and of his granson Phinehas (45:6–26) are closely related to the description of Simon in chapter 50. Such is the importance of those verses that they are also translated, with a commentary, in the following pages.

HEBREW BEN SIRA 49:15–50:26
(TRANSLATION)

49:15 Was there born a man like Joseph?
And his body also was visited.

49:16 And Shem and Seth and Enosh were visited,
And above every living thing is the beauty of Adam.

50:1 Greatest of his brothers and the beauty of his people
Was Simeon the son of Johanan the priest;
In whose generation the house was visited
And in whose days the Temple was strengthened.

50:2   In whose days the wall was built,
        The corners of the dwelling in the king's Temple.

50:3   In whose generation the water-pool was dug,
        The reservoir in its immensity like the sea.

50:4   Who took care for his people to preserve them from robbery,
        And strengthened his city against the adversary.

50:5   How honourable was he as he gazed forth from the tent,
        And when he went forth from the house of the curtain;

50:6   Like a star of light from among clouds,
        And like the full moon in the days of festival;

50:7   And like the sun shining resplendently on the king's Temple,
        And like the rainbow which appears in the cloud;

50:8   Like blossom on branches in the days of festival,
        And like a lily by streams of waters.
        He was like a shoot of Lebanon on summer days,

50:9   And like the fire of incense upon the offering;
        Like golden vessels [? a pattern . . .]
        Which is overlaid upon beauteous stones;

50:10   Like a green olive tree full of berries,
        And like an oil tree laden with branches;

50:11   When he covered himself with the garments of glory
        And clothed himself in garments of beauty.
        When he went up to the altar there was majesty:
        He made honourable the court of the sanctuary.

50:12   When he received the portions from the hand of his brothers,
        And he himself stood up over the arranged pieces,
        Around him was the crown of his sons,
        Like shoots of cedar trees in Lebanon.
        And like willows of the brook surrounded him

50:13   All the sons of Aaron in their glory
        With the fire-offerings of the Lord in their hands
        Before the whole congregation of Israel;

50:14   Until he finished ministering at the altar
        And set in order the arranged pieces of the Most High.

50:16   Then the sons of Aaron the priests sounded forth
        On trumpets of turned metal-work:
        So they sounded and made heard the glorious noise
        To make invocation before the Most High.

50:17   All flesh together hastened quickly
        And fell on their faces to the ground
        To prostrate themselves before the Most High,

Before the Holy One of Israel.

50:18 And the singers gave their voice,
And at the sound they set in order His lamp.

50:19 And all the people of the land gave a ringing shout of joy
In prayer before the Merciful One;
Until he had finished ministering at the altar
And had completed his statutory duties.

50:20 Then he went down and lifted up his han[ds]
Over the whole congregation of Israel:
And the blessing of the Lord was on his lips,
And in the Name of the Lord he was glorified.

50:21 Then they fell down again a second time
[. . .] from before him.

50:22 Now bless the God of Israel, who performs wondrous
deeds on the earth;
Who makes man grow up from the womb,
And has made him according to his will.

50:23 May He give you wisdom of heart, and may he be among
you in peace:

50:24 May He confirm with Simeon His love,
And raise up for him the covenant of Phinehas
Which shall not be cut off for him or for his descendants
Like the days of heaven.

50:25 Two nations my soul loathes,
And the third is no people:

50:26 The people who dwell in Se'ir and the Philistines,
And the lawless nation which lodges in Shechem.

NOTES ON THE TEXT

The Hebrew text translated is from *The Book of Ben Sira: Text, Concordance and an Analysis of the Vocabulary*, foreword by Z. Ben-Hayyim (Academy of the Hebrew Language and the Shrine of the Book: Jerusalem, 1973) [all in Hebrew]. For recent assessment of textual work on ben Sira, with bibliography, see M. Gilbert, 'The Book of Ben Sira: Implications for Jewish and Christian Traditions', in Sh. Talmon (ed.), *Jewish Civilization in the Hellenistic-Roman World* (JSOT Press: Sheffield, 1991), pp. 81–91.

49:15; 50:1 The Ms reading 'was visited' (Hebrew *npqd*) is retained for reasons given in the commentary. At 50:1, P. W. Skehan and A. A. di Lella, *The Wisdom of Ben Sira, Anchor Bible* 39 (Double-day: New York, 1987), p. 548, propose reading *nibdaq*, 'was reno-vated', with the Greek. They appear to believe that ben Sira uses the root *bdq* at 34:10 in a slightly different sense; but this last verse has root *dbq*, 'to stick'. Perhaps they are referring to 2 Chr. 34:10, where root *bdq* is found meaning 'repair'.

50:3 Hebrew has 'the pool in them, *bm*, in its vastness'. For *bm* read *kym*, 'like the sea', following Greek; cf. B. G. Wright, *No Small Difference. Sirach's Relationship to its Hebrew Parent Text* (Scholars Press: Atlanta, 1989), p. 305, n. 218.

50:6 We omit the words 'from among' incorrectly repeated in Hebrew after 'full moon'.

50:8 Emending the meaningless Hebrew *knzp 'npy* with Wright, op. cit., p. 309, to *knz b'npy*, 'like a blossom on branches'. Possibly, however, the text originally read *k'np 'z 'bwt*, 'like a bough of the leafy tree', a reference to the ceremonies of the Feast of Sukkoth: see Lev. 23:40 and the commentary below.

COMMENTARY

Verse 1. The description of Simon as the 'beauty', *tip'eret*, of his people establishes more than a formal link with the preceding chapter (49:16), where the 'beauty', *tip'eret*, of Adam is named.[8] As will be made plain in the commentary on verses 6–10, Simon officiating at the sacrifice is about to be presented as one who exercises a God-given authority; and in this he shares a fundamental characteristic of the first man Adam as ben Sira understands him. Telling of God's creation of Adam (17:1–8), ben Sira speaks of the authority over created things which was granted to him; his cre-ation in the divine image; and his dominion over the beasts. With these gifts he is given knowledge of understanding (17:7). Without warning, however, ben Sira's discussion of Adam moves imper-ceptibly to a consideration of Israel: this man is to praise God's Name, and has been given knowledge and a law of life as an in-heritance (17:10–11), an expression which recalls Lev. 18:5 with its assurance of life for Israel if the nation observe the commands of the Torah. That Israel is now in ben Sira's view is confirmed by what follows, for he tells how God made an everlasting covenant with them and shewed them His statutes, and how their eyes saw

His glory and their ears heard His voice (17:12–13). These words recall Israel's experiences at Sinai recorded in Exod. 19:17–20; Deut. 5:2–3; and Ps. 147:19. Ben Sira seems to imply that the privileges granted to the first man, and thus to all humankind, are also peculiarly summed up in Israel whose representative is Simon in his function as sacrificing high priest. His understanding of Wisdom herself is very similar: she is granted to all nations (1:9–10), yet pitches her tent in Israel, is established in Zion, and has her authority in Jerusalem (24:8, 10–11).

In so expounding Adam's place in the universe, ben Sira succeeds in presenting him as an Israelite patriarch.[9] Such is also indicated by Adam's appearance in the company of Joseph, Shem, Seth, and Enosh in 49:15–16; but it is the high priest Simon who now pre-eminently is linked to Adam, through ben Sira's use of the word *tip'eret*, 'beauty', to speak of them both. This word elsewhere in ben Sira's book can be used to describe clothing, as in Exod. 28:2, 40 where it describes priestly vestments. Thus in verse 11 of this chapter Simon's high priestly vestments are called *bigdê tip'eret*, 'garments of beauty'; Aaron in these same vestments, according to 45:8, was clothed with *k^elîl tip'eret*, 'perfection of beauty'; and the one who cleaves to Wisdom will crown himself with her as with *^ateret tip'eret*, 'a crown of beauty' (6:31). Perhaps ben Sira implies that Adam's *tip'eret* is analagous to Simon's high priestly robes: if so, he may suggest here what later writers state openly, that the high priest's vestments are the garments of the first man.

The tradition that Adam's garments were the high priestly robes, handed down through successive generations until they reached Aaron, is well known from Rabbinic writings: *jer. Meg.* 1:11; *Gen. Rab.* 20:12; 97:6; *Num. Rab.* 4:8; *Tanḥuma B. Toledot* 67 and *Bereshith* 9; *Aggadath Bereshith* 42; FTP of Gen. 48:22; PJ of Gen 27:15; *Tanḥuma Toledot* 12; and *Midrash Abkir* on Gen. 3:21 all testify to it, as does Jerome in *Quaestiones Hebraicae in Genesim* on Gen. 27:15. It also occurs in Syriac sources, a fact which very likely indicates its antiquity.[10] None of these writings in their present form, however, dates from ben Sira's times; and they cannot be used to demonstrate that the tradition was known to him. Those Qumran texts (e.g., 1QS 4:23; CD 3:20; 1QH 17:15) which speak of *k^ebôd 'âdâm*, 'the glory of Adam', are certainly of pre-Christian vintage. But they evidently do not refer to Adam's *tip'eret*; nor do they require knowledge of the tradition that Adam's garments were high priestly vestments for their interpretation.[11] None the less, the Qumran allusions to Adam's glory show the high regard in which this group, strongly influenced as it was by priestly ideals, held the first man. They also suggest another possible approach to the 'beauty of Adam'.

The Qumran group ascribed great authority to the Book of Jubilees (see, for example, CD 16:2–3; 10:8–11), which was almost certainly produced around the year 160 BC. This work insists that it is transmitting teaching which is of high antiquity (e.g., Jubilees 1:5–6; 10:13–14; 21:10; 32:21–22), and the final date of its composition indicates that the traditional material it contains will have been more or less contemporary with ben Sira.[12] Jubilees is excellently disposed towards Adam, and in 3:27 presents him as the first priest:

> And on that day when Adam went out from the garden of Eden, he offered a sweet-smelling sacrifice – frankincense, galbanum, stacte, and spices – in the morning with the rising of the sun from the day he covered his shame.

This morning incense offering of the Tamid, for such is the sacrifice, is made in accordance with Exod. 30:1–8; and Jubilees records that it was first offered on the day when Adam wore garments. Given that Jubilees elsewhere delights in showing how the patriarchs followed the prescriptions of the Law before it was given at Sinai, the implication may be that Adam wore priestly garb to burn the incense. In this regard, it may be significant that when Jacob appoints Levi as priest, Jubilees merely notes that he put the garments of the priesthood on him (32:3). We are not told the source of these garments: they appear ready to hand, and thereby Jubilees encourages speculation on their origins.

The evidence of Jubilees allows the possibility that Adam's and Simon's *tip'eret* consists in the priestly vestments. It also demonstrates how and why ben Sira could so easily juxtapose Adam and Simon the high priest, the latter as it were doing duty for the former in ben Sira's lifetime. Further, Jubilees speaks of Adam as specially blessed by God in the same way as were Enoch, Noah, and Shem (19:27). Abraham also prays (19:25) that in Jacob, whose name will later be called Israel, his name and the name of his fathers Shem, Noah, Enoch, Mahalalel, Enosh, Seth, and Adam be blessed. For ben Sira, as we shall see presently, Simon represents the people Israel: he is the last-named in ben Sira's poem praising the ancestors of Israel, who in a sense find their 'modern' realization and culmination in him as the *tip'eret* of his people.[13] And immediately prior to the praise of Simon, ben Sira has lauded Enoch (49:14), then Shem, Seth, Enosh, and Adam (49:16); Noah has appeared in 44:17–18.

Three other occurrences of *tip'eret* in ben Sira associate the word with the fear of the Lord (9:16; 10:22) and perfection (34:10). The first of these qualities is famous as the beginning of wisdom (Ps. 111:10; Prov. 9:10), the second, Hebrew *tâmîm*, is often associated with righteous conduct according to the commandments (e.g., Ps. 15:2). These usages turn our attention again to Wisdom, which ben Sira himself famously identifies with the Torah in 24:23.

As proof of Simon's illustrious character, ben Sira notes first that the house (Temple) was visited (*npqdh*) in his days. This expression places the Temple in the same continuum as Joseph's bones and the patriarchs Shem, Seth, and Enosh, who were also visited (49:15–16). The verb used indicates the involvement of God's special favour: Joseph made his brothers swear an oath to carry his bones from Egypt to the land of Israel, because God would surely visit them (Gen. 50:25): the terms of the oath, with reference to God's visitation, were duly carried out by Moses (Exod. 13:19). Ben Sira uses the verb *pqd* to speak of God's activity in other settings (e.g., 16:18; 32:21; 46:14). The visitation of the Temple in Simon's days, then, is a special mark of direct divine favour; and the note that the Temple was also strengthened leads to consideration of the high priest as a builder.

Verses 2–4. It is striking that ben Sira sets at the head of his praises, before all else, Simon's activity as a builder of the Temple (verses 1–3) and the city of Jerusalem (verse 4). In this matter, he was no doubt motivated by reminiscence of what he had said a few verses earlier (49:11–13) about Zerubbabel, Jehoshua ben Jehozadak the ancestor of Simon, and Nehemiah. Of Zerubbabel and Jehoshua he had written: 'And they raised up the Temple of holiness,/Which is prepared for everlasting glory' (49:12). The full significance of these words is appreciated when set alongside a rather different estimation of the Second Temple built by Zerubbabel and Jehoshua. This is articulated in the Book of Tobit, a work which either antedates ben Sira's poem, or is roughly contemporary with it:[14]

God will have mercy on them (Israel), and bring them again into their land, where they shall build a Temple, but not like to the first, until the time of that age be fulfilled: and afterwards they shall return from all places of their captivity, and build up Jerusalem *gloriously*, and the house of God shall be built in it *for ever* with a *glorious* building, as the prophets have spoken thereof.

(Tobit 14:5)

The author of this programme envisages Israel's return from Babylon as a partial return of Jewish exiles, and the Temple which they build under Zerubbabel and Jehoshua as correspondingly temporary: it is explicitly differentiated from Solomon's original. Only with the return of all exiles will Jerusalem be built in glory, and the Temple as an eternal and glorious House in accordance with prophecy. It would seem that ben Sira disagrees vehemently with such a lukewarm evaluation of the Second Temple. For him, the work of Zerubabbel and Simon's Zadokite ancestor Jehoshua is precisely the Temple prepared for eternal glory. There is no trace in ben Sira's writing of an idea that the Temple he knew might be merely temporary, awaiting the future appearance of the genuine article. Did he also believe, again in stark disagreement with the author of Tobit, that the building of the Second Temple had fulfilled the words of the prophets?

That he may indeed have done so is suggested by his account of Nehemiah's work (49:13), which follows immediately the description of Zerubbabel and Jehoshua. The former 'raised up our waste places/And healed our ruins, and set up doors and bars'. Nehemiah's work is here described in words drawn directly from Biblical prophecy. Nehemiah was the one who raised up our waste places, Hebrew *hmqym 't hrbtynw*. In Isa. 44:26, God says of Jerusalem that He will raise her waste places, *whrbwtyh 'qwmm* (see also Isa. 51:3; 58:12; 61:4). The word *hrbh*, 'waste place', is not found in the Hebrew text of Nehemiah's book. Nehemiah is also said to have healed our ruins, *hrystynw*: the word *hrsh, hryswt* is found only twice in the Hebrew Bible, at Isa. 49:19 and Amos 9:11, both prophetic verses which speak of the restoration of Jerusalem. All this implies that Nehemiah has fulfilled Biblical prophecy in his rebuilding of Jerusalem; and the Temple in its midst would doubtless, in ben Sira's mind, hold a status appropriate to a city conforming to prophetic concerns.

According to ben Sira, Simon shares yet another activity with Nehemiah in building the corners (*pnwt*) of the Temple: Nehemiah took care over these architectural features (Neh. 3:24, 31–32) also.

It is likely ben Sira refers specially to this detail to stress Simon's pre-eminience as a builder of real, physical structures: the word *pnwt* may be used in the Bible to speak of persons of power and influence (see, e.g., Judg. 20:2; 1 Sam. 14:38; Isa. 19:13), and its singular form was used by Qumran writers in a symbolic sense (1QS 8:7ff.) to describe high-ranking members of their society. Simon, by contrast, built real, architectural corners, like his ancestor Jehoshua.[15] They seem to be features of the Temple wall which were particularly noticeable. The Temple itself is the house of God, who is here called king, a title used again at verse 7 in respect of His dwelling in the Temple. The royal attributes of the God of Israel are thus recalled, just as in verse 7 the royal aspects of His high priest will be brought into clearer association with the Temple of God who is king.

The 'water-pool' is Hebrew *miqwâh*, 'reservoir', the word used in Isa. 22:11 to speak of one of King Hezekiah's construction works in the city of David. Whereas Isaiah censured Hezekiah for digging this pool, ben Sira praises Simon for this enterprise, which he regards as meeting with divine approval: indeed, he even approves Hezekiah's original work, alluding to it in 48:17. Simon thus follows royal, as well as priestly precedents. The reservoir may be additional to those Temple reservoirs spoken of in Aristeas 89, or a completely separate work intended for the inhabitants of the city. His strengthening of the city against the adversary again associates him with Nehemiah, who according to Neh. 3 repaired and made strong the city walls with his voluntary helpers, including priests.

Verses 5–11. These verses describe the appearance of Simon, vested in the high priestly robes, as he comes forth from the sanctuary to take his part in the sacrificial service conducted at the altar of burnt offering. At his appearance he is described as 'honourable', which translates Hebrew *nhdr*, and on his ascent to the altar he is said to make honourable (*wyhdr*) the sanctuary court. The choice of the verbal root *hdr*, 'to honour, adorn', to qualify Simon's appearance in splendid array may be significant. The verb is not common in Hebrew ben Sira. It is used to speak of Joshua and his valour at 46:2. But it also qualifies the glory of the rainbow (43:11), the firmament of heaven (43:1), and the glory of the stars (43:9): all these celestial wonders ben Sira will use later as points of comparison with Simon's appearance (50:6, 7, 24). It would seem that the high priest is here described as related to things of great beauty above the terrestrial sphere, and as if he had in some manner made these things present in the Temple. The scene recalls in many respects the words of Aristeas 99.

In speaking of the Tent, ben Sira refers to the Holy Place in standard Biblical language: the Temple building is understood as a permanent form of the original Israelite sanctuary, which had been a tent (see, e.g., Exod. 25:1–9 and chapters following). The House of the curtain, *byt hprkt*, almost certainly refers to the Holy Place, separated from the most sacred innermost shrine of the Holy of Holies by a finely wrought curtain. It has been suggested, however, that ben Sira here describes Simon's exit from the Holy of Holies itself, which is called *byt lprkt* at Exod. 26:33; Lev. 16:15; and possibly at Num. 18:7. If indeed the priest is leaving the Holy of Holies, then what follows in this poem almost certainly describes the ceremonies of Yom Kippur; for the high priest never entered the Holy of Holies, but on that day alone (Lev. 16:2, 29–34).[16]

There are solid reasons, however, for dismissing the theory that ben Sira is describing Yom Kippur. First, not one of the distinctive rituals of that day as set forth in Lev. 16 and *m. Yoma* is found in our chapter, which furthermore is redolent of triumphant celebration far removed from the affliction and fasting demanded on Yom Kippur (Lev. 16:23; 23:26–32). Second, ben Sira does not use the biblical phrase *byt lprkt* to designate the place where Simon has been, but another expression (*byt hprkt*) which differs from it and is not found in the Bible.[17] And while it is true that *prkt* may designate the veil separating the Holy of Holies from the Holy Place (the veil separating the Holy Place from the court of the priests being called *msk* at Exod. 36:37), it may also be used, as it probably is used in Num. 18:7, to refer to the curtain dividing the Holy Place from the court.[18] Third, the striking similarities between the Tamid ceremonies as described in the Mishnah, and the order of ritual presupposed by ben Sira, strongly support the view that Simon is here depicted as taking part in the daily sacrificial Service.[19] Finally, Simon's splendour is appropriate for one robed in the full complement of high priestly vestments, as verse 11 makes plain; but if he were emerging from the Holy of Holies on the Day of Atonement he would have been wearing a white linen robe of great simplicity (Lev. 16:4; *m. Yoma* 3:6; *Lev. Rab.* 16:3; PJ of Lev. 16:4), which would hardly merit the lavish comparisons which ben Sira goes on to make.

The splendour is now expounded through comparison of Simon

with the heavenly bodies, trees and flowers which themselves hold particular meaning for ben Sira and the Bible, on which he draws for most of the points of comparison. In verses 6–7 Simon is likened to a star of light and the moon, then to the sun: these luminaries are together invited in Ps. 148:3 to praise the Name of the Lord, because He commanded and they were created, and because He has made them stand (*wayya"mîdêm*) for ever and ever. According to this Psalm, they specifically witness to the stability of the created order; and as we shall see presently, the Temple Service has a good deal to do with this matter.

The comparison of individuals with a star, the sun, and the moon is far from common in the Bible. It occurs, however, in poetry devoted to the Davidic king. According to Ps. 89:38, God promises that David will be established like the moon: the preceding verse states that his throne will be like the sun. David's own words in 2 Sam. 23:4 compare the ideal Israelite ruler with the light of the morning when the sun rises; and the famous star which is to arise out of Jacob (Num. 24:17) is probably a royal figure, given the general tenor of the oracle which predicts its rise.[20] These verses betray a sense of Simon's quasi-royal presence and authority, a sense which is resoundingly endorsed in verse 24. There, ben Sira prays that the covenant made with Phinehas be assured for Simon 'like the days of heaven'. This phrase is used in the Bible not of the priesthood, but of the permanence of David's royal throne assured by divine covenant (Ps. 89:30, 35), and of righteous ones in Israel (Deut. 11:21). That ben Sira has David's *covenant* in mind is evident from 45:15, where he attributes to the high priest Aaron an everlasting covenant enduring for 'all the days of heaven'.[21] He does not use this phrase in his treatment of David, Solomon, or the other kings of David's house; and we may reasonably conclude that ben Sira has in some measure transferred to Simon and the Zadokite dynasty royal attributes which were once characteristic of the House of David. As previously noted, there is no external proof that the Zadokites had promoted or acquiesced in such transferral; but the possibility exists that ben Sira's poem represents something of their own self-understanding.

Covenant is once more the essential element in the comparison of Simon with the bow seen in the cloud (verse 7), which is intended to recall the rainbow as the sign of God's covenant with Noah in Gen. 9:13–17. That covenant guaranteed the stability of the created order after the eruption of chaos at the Flood: Simon is compared with its visible sign, a sign of God's remembering His creation (Gen. 9:15) and of His mercy. Ben Sira here again implies that the Temple Service itself as carried out by Simon has a part to play in the stability of creation, the high priest himself representing the assurance that God will never again destroy the world by a flood.[22] The comparisons which follow in verses 8–10 bear out this perception, for they all display Simon's affinities with Wisdom, who is herself the fundamental principle of order and unity underlying and sustaining the whole of creation.[23]

The Hebrew text of ben Sira 24 which eulogizes Wisdom is not extant; but from the Greek version we can sufficiently discern how the author co-relates Simon with Wisdom through applying to them both the same points of comparison. The links between Simon and Wisdom appear much more strongly in the Greek translations of chapter 50 and 24, and will be discussed below; but the Hebrew of chapter 50 will form the basis of investigation for the present. There Simon is likened to the lily and shoot of Lebanon (verse 8); to the incense (verse 9); and to the olive tree and oil tree (verse 10). Wisdom, too, is compared with the cedar of Lebanon (24:13, see also 50:12 for Simon's sons as cedars); the incense (24:15, where its ingredients are also listed); and the olive (24:14). Both Simon and Wisdom are compared with blooms on branches (50:8; 24:16, 17). Vested for sacrifice, Simon embodies also something of that Wisdom which ben Sira identifies with the Torah (24:23), the divine order undergirding all created things.[24]

While together many of these points of comparison link Simon with Wisdom, individually they have other tales to tell, so highly wrought is ben Sira's poem. In verse 8, the textual notes indicate that we have followed Wright's emendation of the Hebrew to read 'like blossom on branches' in the days of the festival. The festival is probably a reference to the Feast of Sukkoth, whose distinctive ceremonies ben Sira alludes to in verse 12. There, Simon's sons surround him *k'rby nḥl*, 'like willows of the brook', one of the species laid down for Sukkoth by Lev. 23:40. Regarding this, it may be significant that Jubilees located at Sukkoth both God's promise to Abraham that Israel should become a kingdom of priests and a holy nation (Jubilees 16:17–18), and Jacob's investiture of Levi as priest (Jubilees 32:3–4).

The language relating to the lily, shoot (*prḥ*) of Lebanon, and olive in verses 8 and 10 is also strongly reminiscent of the final prophecy of Hosea about Israel, who is compared with these things (Hos. 14:6–7). Hosea here speaks of the status of an Israel who has finally returned to her God, accepting that He is the one with whom the orphan finds mercy (Hos. 14:4): note that ben Sira alludes to God as the Merciful One in verse 19. Thus ben Sira seems to attribute to Simon the same qualities as the Israel of Hosea's prophecy, who is the completely obedient servant of God and rightful recipient of the divine blessings.

Verse 9 introduces the comparions with incense which was offered in relation to the *minhah*, the cereal offering (Lev. 2:1, 15). The incense forms the memorial portion, *'azkârâh*, of the cereal offering, and is sacrificed to the Lord in the fire of the altar (Lev. 2:2, 9, 16). The notion that Simon may be like a memorial or reminder to the Lord reflects what ben Sira says about Aaron's vestments in 45:9, and is consonant with other aspects of the Temple Service whose purpose is to serve as a reminder to God, like the blowing of the trumpets (verse 16). The cereal offering will certainly include the Bread of the Presence, which had its own special incense as an *'azkârâh* and was invested with the highest degree of sanctity.

Finally, the mention of the olive and the oil tree in verse 10 may have further ramifications, in that the two trees are compared with Simon as he stands in the Temple. Ps. 52:10 presents the author of that psalm as one who is 'like a green olive tree in the house of God'; and the writer tellingly counts himself among the *zaddîqîm*, the 'righteous' who are named in verse 8 of the poem. As for the oil tree, this was used in the time of Ezra and Nehemiah to celebrate the Feast of Sukkoth (Neh. 8:15). It was also employed in the construction of Solomon's Temple to make the two cherubim in the Holy of Holies, and the doors of this innermost shrine (1 Kings 6:23, 31–33). Here we witness an association of Simon the Zadokite with the *zaddîqîm* and the Temple building which ben Sira will explore further in verse 12.

Verse 11 makes it clear that Simon is robed in his high priestly vestments, called here 'garments of glory' and 'garments of beauty', *tip'eret*. The latter expression has been discussed in the commentary on verse 1; but the words 'garments of glory' are here added to define it further. This last expression is found in 6:31, where it refers to Wisdom put on by the diligent pupil; and it is analogous to a 'crown of beauty', *tip'eret*. The phrase 'garments of beauty' also reinforces the fact that the highest degree of ritual purity attaches to Simon and the Temple Service, since Isaiah calls on Jerusalem to assume the garments of beauty (*bigdê tip'artêk*) only when the prophet assures her that the uncircumcised and the unclean will no longer enter into her (Isa. 52:1).

The second half of verse 11 records Simon's ascent to the altar of burnt offering to begin his part in the ritual which ben Sira will describe. We are told nothing of any part he may have played earlier in the Service: according to *m. Tamid* 6:3, he had the right to offer the incense on the golden altar in the Holy Place. This rite immediately preceded the throwing of the sacrificial portions on to the great altar of burnt offering, and occasions the tractate's first reference to the high priest. The special form of address to the high priest is recorded, and his own prostration in the Holy Place.

Ben Sira seems concerned only with the duties of the high priest as they were actually seen by the other priests, that is, those which were performed publicly outside the Holy Place in the court of the priests. But according to *m. Tamid* 7:1–2, the high priest seems to have pronounced the priestly blessing after his departure from the Holy Place and before offering the sacrifice: of this, ben Sira says nothing. Rather, he speaks of the priestly blessing being given at the very end of the proceedings (verse 20), an event not recorded in the Mishnah. These apparent discrepancies in the rite may be explained in a number of ways. For example, it is possible that the ritual was modified for some reason between the time of ben Sira and the Mishnah; but we have no evidence for such modification. It is more likely that the Mishnah is silent about the final blessing recorded in ben Sira's poem because the author–compiler of *Tamid* 7:3, which describes the sacrifice and accompanying wine libation, regarded the ritual as concluding with the blowing of the trumpets and the prostration. What ben Sira records as coming after these things, the shout of the people, their prayer, the second priestly blessing and the second prostration of the people (verses 19–20) may have been regarded by the Mishnah as not integral to the rite, being more popular than priestly in nature. Certainly ben Sira's description of this blessing envisages it as taking place in the presence of the people, the non-priests (verse 20); hence the Mishnah passed over it, and the people's part, in silence. Ben Sira, on the other hand, may have omitted mention of the priestly blessing *before* Simon's ascent to the altar on the grounds that it was properly part of the priestly incense-rite, and not integral to the public ceremonies which concern him.

Indeed it is precisely the public and visible elements of the

Service which interest ben Sira, as verse 13 also indicates. Hence the stress on Simon's appearance from the Holy Place, and his ascent to the altar. The latter is described in terms of majesty, Hebrew *hôd*: an equally valid rendering of the Hebrew would yield 'when he went up to the altar of majesty'. However the words are translated, ben Sira viewed *hôd* as something which could be predicated as belonging to God (see 10:4; 36:19; 42:25), and which He could communicate to the priesthood. Thus God set *hôd* upon Aaron (45:7), and this attribute is clearly connected with his vestments (45:7–8, 12). One can easily envisage the 'majesty' as Simon went up to the altar consisting in his stately progress in the high priestly robes. Alternatively, the altar itself may be called majestic, since it partakes in some measure of God's own majesty.

Verses 12–14. The high priest had the right to officiate at the sacrifice whenever he chose, according to *m. Yoma* 1:2; *Tamid* 7:3; but Josephus, *War* V. 230, suggests that he did so mostly on Sabbaths and new moons and the great festivals. What follows is almost certainly a description of the Tamid, which (by definition) was offered twice every day, since in almost all respect, Simon's actions follow those laid down years later for the high priest by the Mishnah. He receives the portions (*n'tâḥîm*) of the sacrificial lamb from the hands of his fellow priests: *m. Tamid* 7:3 tells how he would ascend to the altar assisted by the Segan (deputy high priest) on his right hand. One priest would offer him the lamb's head and hind leg, on which he laid his hands before throwing them on to the altar. Then another priest would present the two front legs, and others the remaining parts of the lamb. On all these without exception he would lay his hands; but if so disposed he would let the other priests cast them into the altar fire. This done, he went in solemn procession around the altar.

Simon is thus surrounded by his colleagues, and everything is done in order: he stood over the 'arranged pieces', *m'rkwt*, a word which emphasizes the ordered nature of the proceedings. It is especially used of the ordered 'arrangement' of the lamps in the Holy Place (Exod. 39:37), and of the Bread of the Presence (Lev. 24:6–7; 1 Chr. 9:32; 23:29; 2 Chr. 13:11; 29:18), where exactitude and precision in their disposition is of central importance. The emphasis on order is renewed in verse 14, where we are told that Simon set in order (root *sdr*) the 'arrangements', *m'rkwt*, of the Most High. Here we encounter *sdr* in verbal form of Qal Infinitive

Construct. In biblical Hebrew *sdr* is not found in verbal form: the root appears as the nouns *sêder*, 'order' (Job 10:22), and *s'dêrâh*, 'rank' at (for example) 2 Kings 11:8. In Rabbinic Hebrew, however, the verb *sdr* is very commonly used as a technical term for the proper ritual order of actions in the Temple Service, and to describe the order of prayers in the synagogue liturgy. It also occurs in legal settings, referring to the due order of statutes and judgements in case-law. The Temple Service is a grand display of order, since God Himself has commanded its rules in Torah, and the exact realization of these rules is essential for the correct carrying out of His will. This will be emphasized later in verse 19, where ben Sira is careful to state that Simon had completed all which was required of him by the Law. The high priest's circumambulation of the altar described by the Mishnah is not explicitly alluded to by ben Sira; although it is possible that finishing the ministry of the altar (verse 14) included it.

The phrase 'the crown of his sons' (verse 12) recalls Prov. 17:6, which appropriately remarks that 'the crown of the aged are children's children, and the beauty (*tip'eret*) of children are their fathers'. Simon's sons are described in language borrowed from Ps. 92:12–14. They are like 'shoots of cedar trees in Lebanon', *kštyly 'rzym blbnwn*: speaking of the *zaddîq*, 'the righteous', the Psalm says that he will increase *k'rz blbnwn*, 'like a cedar in Lebanon'; and that those planted *štwlym* in the House of the Lord will blossom in its courts. Once more we have an oblique reference to the 'righteous', the *zaddîqîm* fixed in the Temple, like the Zadokites. The 'willows of the brook', which recall the Feast of Sukkoth (Lev. 23:40), have already been noted.[25]

Verse 15, which spoke of the wine libation, is missing from the extant Hebrew text: it was almost certainly omitted by scribal error, as Skehan and di Lella suggest.[26] It was the next item in the ritual set out by *m. Tamid* 7:3, and it is disucussed below in the commentary on the Greek version of ben Sira.

Verses 16–18. According to *m. Tamid* 7:3, when the high priest was about to pour the libation of wine, a preliminary trumpet-blast was sounded, after which the trumpeters came and stood either side of the cymbalist ben Arza. Whenever the high priest stooped to pour the wine at the corners of the altar, the Segan, standing at the corners of the altar, would wave a towel as a signal to ben Arza to sound the cymbals: then the Levites would burst into song. On each occasion when there was a break in the singing, the trumpets would sound again, and the people prostrate themselves. What ben Sira describes is, in general, consonant with the Mishnaic procedures, although he says nothing of the preliminary trumpet sound, the duty of the deputy high priest, or the cymbal-player. The trumpets are of turned metalwork, exactly as prescribed in Num. 10:2, and they are sounded to make invocation (*lhzkyr*) before God. Num. 10:9 states that with the blowing of trumpets Israel will be remembered before God; in addition, we may note the form *lhzkyr* in the headings of two psalms (38; 70), and its use in 1 Chr. 16:4 of the Levites who invoke (*lhzkyr*), thank, and praise God in the singing of psalms. The notion of the ritual as calling on God to remember Israel was present in verse 9, with its implied reference to the *'azkârâh*; and it is also possible that ben Sira's remark that the Temple was 'visited' in Simon's days is intended to express God's remembrance of Israel through the Temple Service.[27]

The prostrations which now occur were a particular feature of the Service in the Temple (see 2 Chr. 20:18; 29:28–29), the house of God's earthly residence and the dwelling-place of His Name. It is appropriate that the Divine Presence should be acknowledged with human obeisance, the worshippers kneeling and touching the ground with their foreheads. But here the prostrations are associated with the title Most High, Hebrew *'elyôn*, which ben Sira has applied to God already in this poem at verses 14 and 16, and uses as a divine title some nineteen times outside chapter 50. In the Bible, this title often refers to God as resident in Jerusalem, to whom the Temple Service is addressed. Especially is this the case in Pss. 9:3–12; 46:5; 78:17; in Ps. 47:3 the title is found in a setting which speaks of trumpets blown to proclaim His universal kingship (note ben Sira's use of the title King at 50:2, 7). Significantly, 'Most High' is the God served by Melchizedeq, King of Salem, who is priest of God Most High (Gen. 14:18–20, 22). Salem was early identified as Zion–Jerusalem (see Ps. 76:2–3). The prophet Isaiah had proclaimed that *zedeq* (righteousness) once dwelt in Jerusalem (Isa. 1:21), and announced that Jerusalem, purged and purified by God, will be called *'ir hazzedeq*, the city of righteousness (1:26). That Isaiah's words are likely to be in ben Sira's mind is confirmed by the divine title which he links with Most High, namely the Holy One of Israel, which is well known as Isaiah's favourite description of God.[28] Jerusalem, city of *zedek*, once ruled by *Melchizedeq* priest of God Most High, is now ruled by a descendant of *Zâdôq*, Simon the Zadokite high priest. The title God Most High serves to mark continuity with a remote past, and to indicate the legitimacy (the 'rightness' or 'righteousness', Hebrew *zedeq*) of its Zadokite priests and the Service which they offer. The association of this title with Melchizedeq also links the Temple Service and the Zadokite priesthood to the pre-Mosaic period, to the time of Abraham: the antiquity of priesthood and Temple Service already implied in the description of Simon as *tip'eret* of his people is again subtly re-asserted.

The first half of verse 18 speaks clearly of the singers, who belonged to the order of Levites. Their importance in the Service of the Second Temple is apparent already in the writings of the Chronicler,[29] who ascribes their organization as a corps of singers to King David (1 Chr. 15:16–22; 16:4; 23:1; 5; 25:1–31). The Chronicler's description of the first sacrifice offered in Solomon's Temple refers to the offering, the priests standing according to their offices, and the Levites 'with the instruments of the Lord's song which David the King had made to give thanks to the Lord ... and the priests sounded on trumpets before them, while all Israel stood' (2 Chr. 7:4–6).

The clearest indication of the significance attached to the Levites' singing is given by 2 Chr. 29:20–30, which tells of Hezekiah's first sacrifice in the Temple which he had cleansed and restored. The order of the ritual is very similar to that of ben Sira 50. First, the victims are killed, and the burnt offering made (29:21–24). Next, the Levites are positioned with David's instruments, while the priests hold trumpets (29:25–26). Then, when the offering begins, 'the song of the Lord' also started, along with the trumpets (29:27). All the congregation prostrated, the singers sang, and the trumpeters sounded 'until the whole burnt offering was completed' (29:28; cf. ben Sira 50:17–19). When the offering was completed, the king and the people bowed and prostrated a second time, and the king made the Levites sing psalms; and they prostrated yet again (29:29–30; cf. ben Sira 50:21 for the second prostration). The Chronicler thus shows how the Levitical song and the offering ascend to God at the same time: the song is timed to coincide with the offering as it burns on the altar.[30] What neither the Chronicler nor ben Sira says openly is that the sacrifice and the song must take place on earth at the same time as some heavenly adoration is offered to God. None the less, the Chronicler insists that the disposition of the priests and Levites, as much as the Temple buildings and furniture, derive from a 'pattern' (*tabnît*) which David gave to Solomon (1 Chr. 28:11–13), David himself having received this *tabnît* in writing from the hand of the Lord (1 Chr. 28:19).[31] The arrangements, therefore, represent an earthly replica of a blueprint which comes direct from heaven.

In his remarks about David, ben Sira especially notes that he set singers before the altar to make melody and to offer praise, shouting for joy each morning (47:9–10). No details are given of what they sang, although later tradition enshrined in the Mishnah (*m. Tamid* 7:4) records that the Levites sang particular psalms at the Tamid each day. Thus Ps. 24 was allotted for Sunday; Ps. 48 for Monday; Ps. 82 for Tuesday; Ps. 94 for Wednesday; Ps. 81 for Thursday; Ps. 93 for Friday, and Ps. 92 for the Sabbath.

The second half of verse 18 in Hebrew is literally translated, and appears confused: Skehan and di Lella prefer to read with the Greek.[32] Certainly the latter follows more naturally mention of the Levites' song; but the Hebrew is not without sense, and may be a reference to the preparation of the seven-branched lampstand (the Menorah) in the Holy Place. The Hebrew for 'they set in order His lamp' is *h'rykw nrw*, which is very close to language used of the Menorah in Exod. 39:37 and Lev. 24:4; the lamps were replenished and trimmed daily, as part of the Tamid ritual. But *m. Tamid* 3:6, 9 indicates that the Menorah was prepared early in the proceedings, while the lamb was being prepared for slaughter and before its portions were offered. If the Hebrew represents what ben Sira wrote, he has either reported the details of the ritual out of order, or the half-verse itself is misplaced in the present text; but it must be admitted that the Hebrew may be corrupt, and that the Greek version should be preferred.

Verses 19–21. The people gave a ringing shout of joy (*yrnw*), as often in the Temple (see Ps. 100:2). This is associated with the people's prayer (*tpllh*), which immediately precedes the final priestly blessing and general prostration. This practice of the Second Temple is reflected also in the Chronicler's description of a sacrifice offered by Hezekiah at Pesaḥ, which concluded with the priests blessing the people, and the note that their prayer (*tplltm*) came up to heaven (2 Chr. 30:27). This prayer at the end of the formal, liturgical action was later taken up in synagogue worship, where intercessions (*taḥanun*) are said after the 'Amidah on weekdays in imitation of Temple practice of the sort recorded here.[33] God is here called the Merciful One (*rḥwm*) as often in the Bible (Exod. 34:6; Deut. 4:31; Pss. 111:4; 112:4; 145:8; 2 Chr. 30:9). The final act of the Service is thus a plea for God's *mercy* on Israel, which ben Sira elsewhere (36:17–18) formally requests for Israel and Jerusalem:

> Have mercy (*rḥm*) upon the people called by Thy Name,
> Israel whom Thou didst surname 'firstborn'.
> Have mercy (*rḥm*) on Thy holy city,
> Jerusalem the habitation of Thy dwelling.

These two petitions occur in a prayer (36:1–17) which contains material stongly reminiscent of Benedictions in the present synagogue liturgy. The possibility exists that they represent part of a more or less formal liturgical prayer which had already evolved in ben Sira's days.[34] It may even have played its part in the Temple Service; for tradition certainly has it that individual prayers of the synagogue service had been uttered in the Temple while it still stood.[35] Whatever the case, these prayers for mercy would appropriately be addressed to God as the Merciful One (*rḥwm*); and we may tentatively suggest that the themes which they articulate may well echo the sentiments of many of the worshippers on the Temple mount.

All this went on until Simon had finished the ministry of the altar, and had completed the obligations. The Hebrew *wmšpṭyw hgy' 'lyw* is rendered by Skehan and di Lella as 'by presenting to God the sacrifice due', which undoubtedly captures one particular sense of the words.[36] But *mšpṭ* has also the meaning of rule, statute, duty laid down by law; and ben Sira may intend to convey the idea that the people prayed until Simon had discharged all his obligations connected with the Tamid. In other words, the high priest did not evade his duties, but solemnly fulfilled them all.

Simon's descent from the altar is singled out by ben Sira in verse 20. It corresponds to his going up to it recorded in verse 11; *m. Tamid* 7:3, however, does not refer to it. This, and the fact that 2 Chr. 30:27 couples the final prayer of the people with the priestly blessing, suggests that the Mishnah breaks off its account of the Tamid with the completion of the high priest's duties at the altar, and does not concern itself with what happened thereafter. What follows is a ritual very much involving the people; and we may reasonably assume that there were often occasions when worshipping crowds were very numerous. Then, perhaps, one group of worshippers would wait until another had finished its prayer before entering the Temple court; in such cases, it is entirely likely that the priestly blessing was uttered more than once, over different groups of suppliants. The blessing itself is well known, and its text is set out in Num. 6:24–26. It is specifically intended as a means of putting God's Name upon Israel (so Num. 6:27). In giving this blessing, says ben Sira, Simon 'was glorified', *htp'r*. This verb derives from root *p'r*, which also provides the noun *tip'eret*, 'beauty': it would seem that Simon is particularly regarded as the *tip'eret* of his people (verse 1) when he utters the Divine Name in blessing Israel.

The utterance of YHWH's Name over Israel claims that people as His own (cf. Deut. 32:8–9). Isaiah, whose prophecies have been noted already as having influenced ben Sira's description of Simon and the sacrifice, prophesied that one day all of Israel would be righteous, *zaddiqîm*, the shoot of God's planting and the work of his hands *l'hitpâ'êr*, that He be glorified (Isa. 60:21). A little later he declared that God would give to the mourners on Zion a garland (*p''êr*) instead of ashes (*'êper*), and that they would be called 'trees of righteousness', *'êlê hazzedeq*, the planting of the Lord *l'hitpâ'êr*, that he be glorified (Isa. 61:3). These prophecies associate the root *p'r* very closely with the root *zdq*, from which derive *zedeq* and *Zâdôq*; and they speak also of God's planting and of trees. It will be recalled how, in verse 12, ben Sira had compared Simon's sons with cedar trees, imagery deriving from Ps. 92:12–14, where we hear of the *zaddîq*, and those planted in the house of the Lord. In all this, ben Sira implies that Simon and his *Zadokite* family are the true representatives of biblical types; and that the *tip'eret* of Israel is fully realized in them as they offer sacrifice, 'planted' in the house of their God. With the blessing, the people prostrate a second time; and the description of the liturgy comes to an end.

Verses 22–25. Although not part of the description of the Service, these verses are included here for the sake of completeness, and because they tell us more of ben Sira's attitude to the Zadokites. Verse 24 prays that God raise up for Simon the covenant of Phinehas, who turned away God's wrath from Israel through his zeal. This zeal led him to execute an apostate Israelite who, along with other apostates conniving with foreigners, had brought plague as divine punishment on Israel. Through Phinehas's action the plague was brought to an end; and God rewarded him with a covenant of peace, and for his descendants a covenant of everlasting priesthood, because of his zeal and since he had atoned for Israel (Num. 25:1–13). His deed is praised in Ps. 106:30–31, where he is said to have 'stood and executed judgement; . . . and it was attributed to him as justice (*ẓdqh*) for every generation to eternity'.

Of these biblical data, ben Sira in 45:23–24 (Hebrew) singles out the zeal of Phinehas for the God of all, and makes some additions to the bliblical information. Phinehas stood in the breach of his people (cf. Ps. 106:29), as his heart had freely offered; and he made atonement for Israel. Therefore God established for him a statute, a convenant of peace to support the sanctuary, which should be for him and his descendants, the high priesthood for ever. It will be noted that the non-biblical material which ben Sira introduces here refers to the voluntary offering of Phinehas' heart and the aim of the covenant of peace 'to support (*lklkl*) the sanctuary': these lead to the promise of perpetual *high* priesthood.

It is clear that ben Sira has hopes that Simon's high priesthood should directly correspond with that of Phinehas. As a consequence, we may conclude that Simon was regarded by ben Sira as zealous for the Torah (cf. the description of his immediate succesor Onias III in 2 Macc. 4:2), and willing to take necessary action to punish apostates and foreign enemies of the Jews. The voluntary character of Phinehas' zealous act in ages past is conveyed by the root *ndb* (45:23), and carries certain implications. This root is used to speak of voluntary contributions to the fabric of the tabernacle and Temple (Exod. 25:2; 35:21, 29; 1 Chr. 29:5, 6, 9) and of individuals who offer themselves in holy war (2 Chr. 17:16). Its Greek equivalent is *hekousiazesthai*, which is found in 1 Macc. 2:42 as a description of the Ḥasidim, mighty military men who *volunteered* themselves for the Torah.[37] Presumably the notes that Phinehas had the duty of supporting the sanctuary and was granted high priesthood derive from tradition. Certainly later generations believed that Phinehas had defended the true sanctuary against the idolatrous and illegitimate shrine set up (according to Judg. 17) by Micah; his stance is recorded at length by *LAB* XLVII:1–12. TN of Num. 25:11 speaks of Phinehas as high priest.

Simon succeeds to these things as strengthener of the Temple (50:1–3) and as a priest who opposes those hostile to Israel, and Edomites who live in Se'ir, the Philistines, and the Samaritans with their rival Temple (like Micah's sanctuary) at Shechem (verse 26). These last are scathingly described as *gwy nbl*, translated above as 'lawless nation'. The expression occurs at Deut. 32:21 in parallel with the phrase 'a non-people'; and the setting of these two expressions in the poem of Deut. 32 makes it clear that religious apostasy and rebellion against divine authority is in the author's mind. The adjective *nbl* has the particular sense of what is opposed to Torah (cf. Deut. 32:6), and the general sense of 'foolish, disgraceful, lacking in sense'. The Shechemites are thus described as fools, lacking wisdom which is Torah, and illegitimate as a people, tarnished with rebellion against God's Law, apostates. The language is very hostile, and suggests that the Samaritans were sharply opposed to the Zadokite house and the Jerusalem Temple at the time when ben Sira was writing. Ben Sira's invocation of the covenant with Phinehas, the implacable opponent of apostates, takes on enhanced meaning in the light of these observations.

Finally, it is ben Sira's prayer that the covenant with Phinehas may be applied to Simon 'like the days of heaven', a phrase used by the Psalmist, and already noted, to speak of God's covenant with David. And since David's covenant is in some way related to that of Phinehas in ben Sira's mind, it is now appropriate to pass in review the latter's poem about Aaron and Phinehas.

HEBREW BEN SIRA 45:6–22

45:6   And He raised up an holy one, Aaron of the tribe of Levi;
45:7   And He set him for an everlasting statute
       And put majesty upon him, and he ministered to Him in His glory;
       And He girded him with strength of a wild ox
       And clothed him with bells.
45:8   And He clothed him with perfection of beauty,
       And beautified him with glory and strength;
       The breeches, tunic, and mantle.
45:9   And He surrounded him with bells,
       And pomegranates as a sound round about,
       To make a sweet sound as he took his steps:
       To make the sound of him heard in the Most Holy place
       As a memorial for the sons of his people.
45:10 (He clothed him with) garments of holiness of gold, blue,
       And purple, the work of cunning craftsmanship,
       The breastplate of judgement, ephod, and girdle,
45:11 And scarlet thread, the work of the weaver.
       Precious stones were upon the breastplate

Engraved as a seal in set[tings]:
Every precious stone as a memorial in engraved writing
According to the number of the tr[ibes of Is]rael.

45:12 The crown of pure gold, the mantle and turban
And 'flower' [. . .] holiness.
Majesty, glory, and praise of strength,
Desir[able . . . be[auty].

45:13 [. . .]
[. . . for]ever . . . stranger.
[He confirmed] . . . for his sons . . .
And likewise his sons [for] their [gener]ations.

45:14 His [off]ering shall be burned entire,
Even each day, continually, twice,

45:15 Moses [fi]lled his hand and anointed him with the holy oil;
And it became for him an everlasting covenant,
And for his descendants, like the days of heaven:
To minister and to act as priest to Him,
And to bless His people in His Name.

45:16 And He chose him out of all the living
To bring near whole-offering and fat portions
And to offer in sacrifice a sweet-smelling savour and a
    memorial portion,
And to make atonement on behalf of the sons of Israel.

45:17 And He gave to him His commandments
And gave him authority in decree and statute
That he might teach His people the decree
And the sons of Israel the statute.

45:18 But strangers burned with anger against him
And in the desert were envious of him,
The men of Dathan and Abiram
And the congregation of Qorah in the fierceness of their
    anger.

45:19 And the Lord saw it, and was enraged
And brought them to an end in the fury of His anger,
And brought a sign for them,
In that He devoured them with the flame of His fire.

45:20 [. . .] to Aaron his glory
And gave to him his inheritance
[. . . holy] He gave bread to him
[. . .] his portion.

45:21 The fire-offerings of the Lord they shall eat,

Even a gift for himself and for his descendants.
45:22 Bu[t] ... he shall have no inheritance,
And in their midst he shall not divide the inheritance.
The fire-offerings of the Lo[rd] ...
45:23 And Phinehas the son of Eleazar also
In strength ...
In his zeal for the God of all;
And he stood in the breach of his people,
Whose heart freely volunteered him
That he should make atonement for the sons of Israel.
45:24 Therefore for him also He established a decree,
A covenant of peace, to support the sanctuary,
Which should be for him and for his descendants
As the high priesthood for ever.
45:25 So also His covenent with David
The son of Jesse of the tribe of Judah
Was the inheritance of (one) man in respect of his glory.
The inheritance of Aaron is for all his descendants.

NOTES ON THE TEXT

The translation renders the Hebrew, which in places is fragmentary. For suggested reconstructions of damaged portions of text, and emendations of perceived textual difficulties, see Skehan and di Lella, op. cit., pp. 509–510.

45:7 The subject of the verse is God, except in the sentence 'and he ministered to him in his glory', where it is Aaron himself. Either this is an aside, an observation as it were in parenthesis; or the text is corrupt. Skehan and di Lella, op. cit., p. 509 follow the Greek for this sentence; but the simple and straightforward reading of that version may be a simplification of the rather angular train of thought found in the Hebrew.

'With strength [lit. horns] of a wild ox' represents Hebrew *btw'pwt r'm*, a phrase used in Num. 23:22; 24:8 with reference to God. A gloss in the margin of the Ms reads *tw'r*, presumably instead of *r'm*, which would give 'strength of beauty'. This may have been what ben Sira wrote, 'strength of a wild ox' representing a conscious scribal alteration of his words to conform with Num. 23:22; 24:8, as Skehan and di Lella (ibid.) and others suggest. But Wright, op. cit., pp. 171–173, offers qualified support for the originality of 'strength of a wild ox'; and to his arguments should be added the observations in our commentary.

COMMENTARY

The following notes concentrate on details which may help to elucidate further the poem about Simon the high priest. As first high priest, Aaron naturally occupies a special place in any understanding of the priesthood's significance. We shall here focus on four particular topics: Aaron's divine appointment and its implications for the people Israel; the high priestly vestments as expressive of Aaron's *tip'eret*; the 'memorial' aspects of Aaron's office; and the material about Phinehas and David.

Aaron's appointment

In 50:12 Simon's sons are depicted as shoots, young saplings of cedar trees in Lebanon, imagery which was noted as deriving from Ps. 92:12–14 with its references to the *ẓaddiq* in the Temple. This psalm, which according to *m. Tamid* 7:4 was sung by the Levites at the Tamid on Sabbaths, speaks of the machinations of the wicked and the Lord's enemies. These God will destroy (verses 7–10); the Psalmist, by contrast, will enjoy God's favour:

> But my horn Thou shalt exalt (*wattârem*) like (that of) a wild ox
> (*kir''êm*);
> I am anointed with fresh oil . . .

> The righteous (*ẓaddîq*) shall blossom like a palm tree;
> Like a cedar in Lebanon he shall increase;
> Those planted in the house of the Lord
> Shall blossom in the courts of our God.
>
> (verses 11, 13–14)

Aaron's appointment, according to ben Sira (45:6–7), began when God exalted (*wyrm*) him; and He girded him with the strength of the wild ox (*r''êm*). The Bible nowhere speaks of God's having exalted Aaron; nor does it apply to him the image of a wild ox. The language which ben Sira uses, however, is strongly redolent of this psalm: that the psalter was in the author's mind at this point is confirmed by his calling Aaron 'an holy one', a designation which depends on Ps. 106:16. It is these thoughts of the psalter which probably induced ben Sira to go futher in his thinking about the *r‘'êm*, the wild ox, and to connect with Aaron the 'strength of a wild ox' spoken of in Num. 23:22; 24:8.

These last verses speak of God as possessing the strength of a wild ox. According to tradition represented by the Aramaic Targums Neofiti, FTV, and FTP, this means that 'to Him belong might, praise, and exaltation': PJ adds 'strength' to these qualities. Although it cannot be demonstrated that these explanations date to the time of ben Sira, the biblical phrase itself is metaphorical, and is presumably intended to convey something of God's might and exaltation. In addition, *r‘'êm* is easily associated in pronunciation with forms of *rûm*, 'to be high'; and exegetes could have exploited this fact at any time.[38] To Aaron, therefore, ben Sira ascribes a phrase used in the Bible metaphorically of the God who had powerfully brought Israel out of Egypt: through Ps. 92:11–14, with its references to exaltation and the wild ox, it was possible for ben Sira to link the phrase in Numbers to the *ẓaddîq* also.

Along with this quite extraordinary and non-biblical exaltation of Aaron goes his consecration by Moses (see Lev. 8), which ben Sira speaks of in equally extraordinary terms as constituting 'an everlasting covenant ... like the days of heaven' (45:15). Nowhere in Scripture is Aaron said to have been granted an everlasting covenant: the notion is either derived from tradition, or is ben Sira's own.[39] It is evidently meant to refer eventually to Simon the Zadokite, since in 50:24 ben Sira will pray that the covenant with Phinehas be established with Simon 'like the days of heaven'. This last expression serves, as we have seen, to link the high priesthood to biblical ideas about the Davidic covenant and the righteous in Israel.[40] Political and religious authority is thus firmly in the high priest's hands by covenant. God has *chosen* him to offer sacrifice and make atonement (45:16), and has granted him rulership (*wymšylhw*) in matters of Torah (45:17). There is an everlasting quality about all this (45:7, 15) which necessarily grants to the high priest (both Aaron and Simon) the qualities of *hôd*, 'majesty', and *kâbôd*, 'glory' (45:7, 12; 50:11).

The high priest's vestments and *tip'eret*

The qualities of *hôd* and *kâbôd* are most evident as the high priest ministers in his sacred vestments: this is apparent when Simon goes up to the altar (50:11) and when Aaron is fully vested (45:8, 12).

The Bible says that these garments are for glory and for beauty, *l'kâbôd ûl'tip'eret* (Exod. 28:2, 40); and ben Sira makes it clear that one aspect of Aaron's 'beauty' is his being vested in these garments. They constitute the perfection of beauty (45:8), and are lovingly listed by name. Significantly, description of Aaron in the vestments leads directly to explicit mention of the Tamid (45:14). This may confirm the view that Simon also is offering the Tamid, since in Chapter 50 the progression of thought, from vested priest to sacrifice, is the same as in this account of Aaron. Ben Sira does not attribute symbolic significance to the vestments as some later writers do; but the fact that he lists each robe separately and by name is an indication of the importance he attaches to them. And although 45:13 is fragmentary, enough survives to indicate that they are the rightful emblems of the high priest alone: perhaps some polemic against the rival Temple and priesthood at Shechem is in view. One particular feature of these robes, however, is singled out and emphasized: twice we are told that items making up the garments constitute a 'memorial', an idea which seems to be of particular interest to ben Sira.

Memorial

The importance which ben Sira attributes to the activities of the high priest as effecting a 'memorial', or reminder before God of Israel His people, is evident from three allusions in this chapter (verses 9, 11, 16). In speaking of Simon, ben Sira has already drawn attention to both to *'azkârâh* and the trumpets as a reminder, in 50:9 and 16 respectively. In 45:9 he refers to the bells which, alternating with pomegranates, fringed the vestment known as *me'îl hâ'êpôd*, 'the robe of the ephod' (see Exod. 28:33–34; 39:25–26) and are to make his sound heard in the Most Holy Place. So much agrees with the Bible (Exod. 28:35). But ben Sira adds that this sound is a memorial for Israel, an opinion which is found not at all in the Bible. A little later (45:11) he notes that the precious stones in the breastplate constitute a memorial of Israel *bktb ḥrwt*, 'in engraved writing'. Exod. 28:12, 29 makes clear that the names of the tribes of Israel engraved on precious stones worn by the high priest make up a 'memorial'. The first of these verses refers to the names of the tribes of Israel engraved on the two large emeralds, six on each stone, which the high priest wore on either shoulder. The second verse speaks of the twelve stones set in the breastplate (*ḥōšen*), each inscribed with one tribal name. Even so, ben Sira embellishes his account of the precious stones by fixing the 'memorial' in writing which is *ḥrwt*, 'engraved': this word occurs nowhere else in his book, and is found only once in the Bible, at Exod. 32:16. There, it describes the manner of the writing engraved on the two stone tablets recording the Ten Commandments, writing which was 'the work of God' and 'the writing of God'. Finally, in 45:16 he lists the *'azkārâh* as one of the sacrificial actions characteristic of the high priest's duties.

At the very least, ben Sira by these means suggests that the Temple Service and the high priest in his vestments have as one of their fundamental purposes the business of bringing Israel to God's attention. But he hints at much more. His use of language reserved for God's personal writing of the Ten Commandments to speak of the 'memorial' inscribed on the precious stones also implies that God Himself has ordered the 'memorial' in a quite direct and powerful way. Later generations, indeed, were to ascribe the writing on the precious stones of the ephod to a miraculous creature, the Shamir (*b. Giṭṭ.* 68a), which was specially created by God on the eve of the first Sabbath (*b. Pes.* 54ab; *Sifre Deut.* 355; *Mekh. de R. Ishmael Vayassa'* 6:53–60; PJ of Num. 22:28; *PRE* 19:1). This Shamir also cut the stones for Solomon's Temple. It appears without any explanation of its nature in the earliest Rabbinic writings, at *m. Soṭ.* 9:12 and *Abot* 5:6, where it seems already traditional. It is not possible firmly to date the tradition of the Shamir earlier than the Mishnah; but its very existence indicates that the Rabbis accepted the supernatural origin of the engravings on the precious stones of the high priest.

None the less, belief that the stones and the writing on them were of supernatural origin is more ancient than the Mishnah. *LAB* XXVI:4, 8–15, which dates from the first century AD and includes much material of pre-Christian date, tells of the supernatural origin of stones related to those in the breastplate,[41] and expressly states that the writing was engraved by an angel (*LAB* XXVI:8): the stones were destined to be before God 'as a memorial for the house of Israel' (*LAB* XXVI:12). Philo's evidence without doubt takes us into pre-Christian times. He remarks (*Quis Heres* 176) that the pariarchal names on the two emeralds of the high priest's robe were 'inscribed as divine letters, memorials of divine natures'.[42] These divine natures are, in one sense, the patriarchs themselves; but in *QE* II. 109 Philo indicates that the emeralds also represent the two hemispheres, each housing six signs of the Zodiac. A little later (*QE* II. 114) he asks why the twelve stones of the breastplate are named after the patriarchs: he replies that the stones represent the twelve creatures of the Zodiac and symbolize the patriarchs, whose name He (God) engraved in them. He wished to make them stars and to allot one constellation to each patriarch, such that each patriarch became a constellation, a heavenly body moving about in the aether. Here we find a well developed body of speculation about the supernatural qualities of these stones, to which ben Sira may be an early witness.

The latter's choice of the words *bktb ḥrwt*, intimately linked as they are with God's own writing of the Ten Commandments, most likely means that ben Sira was aware of the supernatural aspects of the precious stones and their memorial. In any event, the precious stones were closely bound up with the Urim and Thummim (Exod. 28:30; Lev. 8:8), the famous priestly oracle (Num. 27:21) which directly communicated God's decisions to Israel. Although the original form of Urim and Thummim is a matter of some interest, it need not concern us here.[43] In Second Temple times, however, it was commonly believed to be located in the region of the high priest's breastplate, Hebrew *ḥôšen*, which LXX regularly translated as 'oracle', *logeion*. Urim and Thummim themselves were rendered as *dēlôsis* and *alētheia*, 'showing forth' and 'truth', at Exod. 28:30; Lev. 8:8, and their ability to give divine messages was thereby connected with the precious stones on the breastplate. Hence it was entirely appropriate for ben Sira to apply to these stones a Scriptural expression otherwise reserved for God's writing on the tables of the commandments.[44]

The covenants

In 45:23–25 ben Sira relates God's covenants with Phinehas and David to what he has previously said about Aaron. Although his remarks about Phinehas have already been discussed (above, commentary on 50:22–25), it should also be noted that ben Sira encourages his readers to see in the figure of Phinehas a very model of what a high priest should be. The covenant granted to Phinehas, which ben Sira prayed might be established for Simon also (50:24), leads the author directly to ponder the covenant with David. In 45:25 the two covenants are compared and contrasted, the sense seeming to be as follows. On the one hand, the priestly covenant

God granted to Phinehas has certain qualities in common with that granted to David. Thus the high priest Simon is described in terms normally reserved for the Davidic monarch (see comments on 50:6–7): and he performs the duties of a priestly monarch in the Temple of the *king* (50:2, 7). He is directly compared with Adam (50:1), who was given kingly authority over the creatures (Gen. 1:26–28; ben Sira 17:2 Greek). Finally, his qualities as a ruler are praised (50:4; cf. Aaron in 45:17).

On the other hand, the royal authority was passed to only one of David's sons: only one, therefore, succeeded to the terms of the covenant at any given time. In Aaron's case, however, all his sons were to be priests: that is their inheritance, in the terms of the covenant.[45] None the less, the high priesthood is a particular office restricted to one individual; and in so far as this is the case, the covenant with Phinehas which governs it may legitimately be compared with the Davidic privileges. Thus ben Sira draws the high priesthood as near as he may to the promises made to David; and the Zadokites, at any rate on his understanding of their office, take on a quasi-Davidic aura. The Temple Service over which they preside is the theatre in which their true character is publicly demonstrated.

SUMMARY

Ben Sira describes the Tamid as carried out by the Zadokite high priest Simon. Careful analysis of his language reveals his understanding of that rite, which is the fundamental sacrifice of the whole Temple Service. In it, the high priest represents the people Israel, of whom he is the *tip'eret*, the 'beauty': this description links him to the patriarch Adam, such that Simon offering sacrifice sums up the whole human race as he carries out his priestly duties before God. He is depicted in words ben Sira uses elsewhere to describe Wisdom, the principle of order which sustains and undergirds the created universe: the Tamid ritual displays this Wisdom, and symbolizes thereby the stability of the universe which it recalls. Thus Simon is described in language derived from God's covenants, especially from his covenant with Noah guaranteeing the future stability of the world. The covenants with David and Phinehas are prominent in ben Sira's poem: offering the Tamid, Simon reflects royal privileges, which themselves have affinity with the Temple of God, the divine king's palace. Comparison of Simon with celestial objects as he offers the sacrifice further strengthens the super-terrestrial character of the rite, and serves to underline the involvement of both earth and heaven in this event. As the Tamid is offered, ben Sira's words seem to envisage a union of earthly and heavenly worlds in the person of the high priest.

The sacrificial service, with the high priest in full vestments officiating, stands as a 'memorial' before God of His people Israel. This is heavily emphasized, particularly in ben Sira's description of Aaron, the ancestor of all high priests. The 'memorial' is one appointed by God Himself in a most intimate way, the high priest as he offers the Tamid bearing the names of the twelve tribes, inscribed on precious stones in a manner reminiscent of the Ten Commandments, carved on stone by God Himself. Throughout the ritual it is presupposed that he is *zaddiq*, 'righteous', a characteristic which ben Sira, in various nuanced and subtle ways, predicates of both Aaron and Simon. The play on words derived from the root *zdq* is associated with the language of Ps. 92, speaking of the *zaddiq* planted in the Lord's house.[46] The *Zadokite* house is thus intimately bound to the Temple, on the one hand through the sacrifice described in chapter 50, and on the other through the work of Simon as a builder and conserver of the sanctuary. As the latter, Simon continues the work of his Zadokite ancestors; and the Temple is 'visited' with divine blessing. In fine, the Tamid offered by Simon is a glorious manifestation of Zadokite privileges: it offers proof of Wisdom's residence in Zion (ben Sira 24:10–11) ensuring a universe stable and ordered in accordance with the will of God. Its significance, therefore, extends far beyond Israel to the whole human race, whose ancestor Adam is even now mysteriously bound to Zadok's successor Simon.

4

THE WISDOM OF JESUS BEN SIRA IN GREEK

GREEK BEN SIRA 49:15–50:26 (TRANSLATION)

49:15 Nor was there born a man like Joseph,
Leader of his brothers, support of the people,
And his bones were visited.

49:16 Shem and Seth were glorified among men,
And above every living thing in the creation is Adam.

50:1 Simon, son of Onias, was the high priest
Who in life patched up the house
And in his days made firm the Temple;

50:2 And by him was laid the foundation of the height of the
court,
The high underwork of the enclosed precinct of the
Temple.

50:3 In his days was hewn out the reservoir for the waters,
A cistern like the circumference of the sea.

50:4 Who took thought for (preventing) his people from falling,
And strengthened the city against siege.

50:5 How was he glorified when the people gathered round him,
In his coming out of the house of the veil!

50:6 He was like a morning star in the midst of a cloud,
Like a full moon on festival days,

50:7 Like the sun shining on the Temple of the Most High,
Like a (rain)-bow giving light in clouds of glory;

50:8 Like a flower of roses on new-moon days,
Like a lily by springs of water,
Like a shoot of Lebanon on summer days;

50:9 Like fire and incense upon the censer,
Like a vessel of gold all beaten out,

73

Ornamented with every kind of precious stone;

50:10   Like an olive tree blooming with fruits,
And like a cypress exalted in the clouds,

50:11   When he put on the robe of glory,
And put upon himself the perfection of boasting;
When he went up to the holy altar,
He made glorious the enclosed precinct of the holy place.

50:12   And when he received portions from the hands of the
priests,
And he himself was standing by the hearth of the altar,
Around him was the crown of his brothers
Like a shoot of cedars in Lebanon,
And they surrounded him like trunks of palm trees,

50:13   Even all the sons of Aaron in their glory,
And the offering of the Lord was in their hands
Before the whole congregation of Israel.

50:14   And completing the service at the altars,
To adorn the offering of the Most High, the Almighty,

50:15   He stretched out his hand to the libation cup
And poured out of the blood of the grape:
At the foundations of the altar he poured out
A sweet-smelling savour to the Most High, the King of all.

50:16   Then the sons of Aaron gave a shout;
They sounded forth on trumpets of beaten work:
They made a great sound to be heard
As a memorial before the Most High.

50:17   Then all the people hastened together
And fell to their faces, to the ground
To bow in homage to their Lord
To the Almighty, God Most High.

50:18   The singers then praised with their voices,
Sweet was the melody made with the greatest sound.

50:19   And the people besought the Lord Most High
In prayer before the Merciful One,
Until the order of the Lord was completed
And they had perfectly finished His Service.

50:20   Then he came down and lifted up his hands
Over all the congregation of the sons of Israel,
To give the blessing of the Lord with his lips
And to be glorified in His Name.

50:21   Then a second time they bowed in homage

To receive the blessing from the Most High.

50:22 And now bless the God of all,
Who does great things on every side,
Who exalts our days from the womb
And deals with us according to His mercy.

50:23 May He give you joyfulness of heart
And may there be peace in our days,
In Israel, for the days everlasting,

50:24 To entrust his mercy with us:
And may He deliver us in our days!

50:25 With two nations my soul is offended,
And the third is no nation:

50:26 Those who dwell on the mount of Samaria, and the
Philistines,
And the stupid people who inhabitant Shechem.

NOTES ON THE TEXT

The Greek text translated is from the edition of J. Ziegler, *Sapientia Iesu Filii Sirach*, Septuaginta XII/2 (Vandenhoeck & Ruprecht: Göttingen, 1965). In 50:1, some witnesses read 'sketched in outline' for 'patched up', and 'people' for 'Temple', correspondingly weakening Simon's association with building activity. In 50:2, many witnesses read some form of the word 'double', which features as *diplēs* in the edition of A. Rahlfs, *Septuaginta*, vol. 2 (Württembergische Bibelanstalt: Stuttgart, 1935), to yield '. . . the foundation of the height of the double wall'. In 50:3, some witnesses read *hupodochia* for *apodocheion*, 'reservoir': the former is similar to the *hupodocheion*, 'reservoir', spoken of in Aristeas 89.

COMMENTARY

Before we inspect individual verses, it is worth noting that ben Sira's grandson makes a particular use of divine names in his translation, which effectively highlights the universal significance of the ritual he describes. He retains the title Most High, translated as *hupsistos*, where it occurs in the Hebrew (50:14, 16, 17). But quite remarkably he introduces this title in three verses (50:7, 19, 21) where it has no Hebrew *Vorlage*. He also has it in 50:15, where the Hebrew is not extant. The term retains the meaning it had in the Hebrew (see above, commentary on Hebrew 50:16–18); but by the time this Greek translation was made it had become closely associated with the Hasmonean dynasty. In a decree of Augustus quoted by Josephus (*Ant.* XVI. 163), John Hyrcanus II in the days of his power was called High Priest of God Most High, *archiereus theou hupsistou*: see also *Testament of Moses* 6:1; *b. Rosh Ha-Shanah* 18b. Indeed, the epithet *hupsistos* was often applied by pagan Greeks to Zeus, to indicate his headship of the pantheon and his universal dominion. The increased use of this term by ben Sira's grandson may therefore testify to his acceptance of the Hasmonean settlement: the dynasty was keen to establish its legitimacy, and seems to have done so by emphasizing its high priesthood as that of God Most High, of *'él 'elyôn*, the title of the God of Jerusalem served by Melchizedeq in the time of Abraham. The title served another purpose, however, as its application by pagans to Zeus indicates. It describes a God with supreme and universal authority, and was used by Jews to demonstrate the universal authority of the God of Israel, especially over against idols. This use is evident in Jubilees (see particularly Jubilees 20:9; 21:22, 23; 22:19), concerned as that work is to differentiate Israel's unique monotheism from pagan polytheism and immorality.

The universal significance of the sacrifice offered by Simon is further emphasized at 50:15, where the wine libation is offered to the Most High, further named 'the King of all'. This last is Greek *pambasileus*, a word unique in LXX but entirely faithful to Hebrew ben Sira's claims for the God of Israel over pagan idolatry: the God whom Phinehas champions in his zeal by executing apostates is named *'lwh[y] kl*, 'the God of all', in the Hebrew text of 45:23. This title occurs in Jubilees (22:10, 27; 30:19; 31:13, 32), well known for its staunch defence of Jewish traditions over against Gentile innovation. Again, this reference to God as king in the Greek of 50:15 makes clear the *universal* scope of God's royal authority. He is king of all, not simply of Israel; and possibly for this reason the Greek translator speaks simply of 'the Temple' in verse 2 (Hebrew has: 'the king's Temple'), and of 'the Temple of the Most High' in verse 7, where Hebrew has the same expression as in verse 2. Note also how the Hebrew 'the Lord, the God of Israel' at 50:22 is translated into Greek as 'God of all'. Probably for similar reasons the title 'Holy One of Israel', found in the Hebrew at 50:17, is replaced in the Greek with 'the Lord the Almighty'. The Greek adds 'Almighty', Greek *pantokratôr*, also at verse 14. In LXX this word most often renders Hebrew *ṣᵉbā'ôt*, 'hosts', in the divine title 'Lord of Hosts', which (*inter alia*) declares the God of Israel's supremacy over all other heavenly creatures. For ben Sira's grandson, then, the Jewish high priest as he offers the daily sacrifice is engaged in an action affecting the whole world; and we shall see presently how he uses the Greek language to show the Temple Service as the focus of the world's order and stability.

Verse 1. It will be seen at once that the Greek version says nothing of Simon as the 'beauty' of his people. Simon is not linked to Adam by means of that word; and in 49:16 Enosh is no longer named. The rich and powerful imagery of the Hebrew, which joined Simon to primeval times and gave him a universal status as priest, has been abandoned. There is not the slightest hint in this verse that his vestments might have significance for his office: given the Greek translation alone, we should not have any inkling of their importance until 50:11. Distinctly lacklustre is the description of his work on the Temple. The latter was 'patched up', not 'visited', and any notion of divine favour attaching to Simon's repairs is thereby quietly eliminated. The House of Zadok no longer ruled in Jerusalem when ben Sira's grandson translated his grandfather's poem; and his translation of 50:1 no doubt reflects the changed circumstances. Such may account for his specification of Simon as high priest, a public title which the Hasmoneans used on their coins.[1]

Verses 2–4. The wall and corners of the Temple spoken of in the Hebrew become foundations and underworks, the significance of the corners now being lost. Instead, ben Sira's grandson uses words expressive of the massive structure of the Temple which caught the eye of an observer such as Hecataeus of Abdera (preserved in Josephus, *Contra Apionem* I. 198), who also remarked on the enclosed precinct (*peribolos*) and its size. If we follow the reading adopted by Rahlfs in verse 2 (see textual notes above), we have a reference to the height of the 'double wall' (*hupsos diplês*), which recalls the double gates (*diplas pulas*) remarked upon by Hecataeus in the same quotation. The description is purely external and architectural, lacking the subtlety of the Hebrew. The reservoir, Greek *apodocheion*, no longer hints at the work of King Hezekiah: the word is not used in LXX of Isa. 22:11, but is similar to the massive *hupodocheion* (also 'reservoir') spoken of by Aristeas (89). The latter also enthuses (Aristeas 84) over the massive external structures of the Temple and of the three enclosed precincts (*periboloi*); and one is left with the impression that ben Sira's grandson is speaking of the Temple more in the manner of an interested outsider than as someone who fully appreciated the sense of his grandfather's poem. Never the less, his remark that the foundation of the wall was laid (*ethemeliôthé*) by Simon may hint at an interest in 'foundations' which is of more than architectural significance: see further comments on the foundations of the altar in verse 15.

Verses 5–12. Most of the comments on the original Hebrew text still apply to these verses, although the following changes of emphasis should be particularly noted. First, the public aspects of the Service are emphasized, the people gathering around Simon as he leaves the Holy Place (verse 5). Second, the points of comparison linking Simon and Wisdom are very firmly drawn: in addition to those found in the Hebrew text, the Greek compares both characters with roses (50:8 and 24:14) and the cypress (50:10 and 24:13). His brother-priests are compared with palm trees (50:12), as is Wisdom in 24:14. In short, the Greek translation preserves and even strengthens Simon's embodiment of Wisdom, resident on Zion. Overtones of the Feast of Sukkoth, represented in Hebrew by reference to the 'willows on the brook' in 50:12, are retained, but through another species used at the Feast: we hear instead of 'palms' as prescribed in Lev. 23:40. This establishes a further link with Wisdom as described in chapter 24.

Third, in verse 9 of the Greek Simon is compared with the offering of incense in general, not the '*azkârâh*. This again corroborates his association with Wisdom, because incense is compared with Wisdom at 24:15, and with students of Wisdom at 39:14. It also strengthens his links with Sukkoth. In the first of these two verses, ben Sira compares Wisdom with seven ingredients which made up the incense: these turn out to be virtually the same seven aromatics offered by Abraham when the first feast of Sukkoth was celebrated on earth, according to Jubilees 16:24. The incense is offered in the Temple at the very place where God promises to meet with Moses (Exod. 30:6, 36). Fourth, the Greek words 'perfection of boasting' or 'perfection of exultation' (Greek *sunteleian kauchêmatos*) used to describe Simon's vestments in verse 11 somewhat blunt the force of the original Hebrew, 'garments of beauty, *tip'eret*'. But the translator has already used them at 45:8 to describe Aaron's vestments, so that there is no mistaking what is meant in this chapter.

Verses 12–14. Although at first blush the Greek seems to lack the stress on order expressed in Hebrew through the words 'arranged pieces' (50:12, 14) and 'set in order' (50:14), there are grounds for believing that ben Sira's grandson has rather underlined this aspect of the poem. It is true that in verse 12 the 'hearth of the altar'[2] stand for the Hebrew 'arranged pieces'; but in verse 14 Hebrew 'set in order' is translated as *kosmēsai*, which we have rendered as 'to adorn'. This Greek word requires explanation. It means at root 'to order, arrange, dispose, govern, rule, embellish, adorn': its cognate noun is *kosmos*, which has the sense of 'order, good behaviour, decoration, ruler', but is also very commonly used to mean 'world, universe'. It is noteworthy that LXX used *kosmos* at Prov. 20:29 to render Hebrew *tip'eret*, 'beauty', which has loomed large in earlier discussions.

In 50:19, the Hebrew tells how Simon finished ministering at the altar and completed his duties: in Greek, this is expressed by saying that 'the order, *kosmos*, of the Lord was completed'. On one level, the Greek translator speaks of the order and the adornment of the rite; on another, we are invited to see the implication that the *kosmos*, the universe, is somehow 'completed', Greek *suntelesthêi* (50:19) in the Tamid. This last word is a form of the verb *sunteleô*, which often has the sense of 'perform a sacred rite': its cognate noun is used in verse 14 in our rendering 'completing the service at the altars', where the Greek has *sunteleian leitourgôn epi bômôn*. Like the original author, the translator relates the Tamid to the stability and order of the universe, the sacrifice in the Temple serving to establish to perfection God's order for the world. But Greek readers of this translation of ben Sira's work who were also familiar with the LXX would no doubt recall the latter's translation of Gen. 2:1. The Hebrew of this reads: 'And the heavens and the earth were finished, and all their host.' LXX has: 'And the heaven and earth were completed, *sunetelesthêsan*, and all their *kosmos*, adornment (or world).'

Given this, we may understand that ben Sira's grandson looked on the Tamid as the final adornment of the world created by the universal and almighty king. Was this adornment of a heavenly sort? LXX used *kosmos* to render Hebrew *ẓb'*, 'host' elsewhere (e.g., Deut. 4:19; 17:3; Isa. 24:21; 40:26), where 'host' indicates the heavenly beings. Did ben Sira's grandson view the Tamid as linking earth and heaven in such a way that the earthly Tamid in some manner participated in a heavenly reality? It is difficult to know; for

LXX could also use *kosmos* to render Hebrew *"dî*, 'ornaments' (e.g., Exod. 33:5, 6; Jer. 2:32; 4:30; Ezek. 7:20; 16:11), and ben Sira's grandson certainly uses the word in this sense (6:30; 21:21; 22:17). But at 43:9 the word may have the sense of 'world', referring to the beauty of the moon and stars. Similarly, the grandson uses the verb *kosmein* to mean 'to adorn': see especially 38:28, of a smith perfecting a vessel, and 50:9 of Simon's attire. But he also uses it to refer to God's *ordering* of His created works at 16:27; and 42:21, where we read:

> The great works of His Wisdom he set in order *ekosmēsen*:
> He is One before the ages and to the ages.
> They are neither added to nor diminished,
> And He has no need of any counsellor.

The high priest, as we have seen, embodies Wisdom as he offers the Tamid: ben Sira's grandson has expressed this more clearly than his grandfather by comparing Wisdom and the high priest with exactly similar items in the course of verses 6–12. It is entirely likely, therefore, that the high priest's completion of the order, *kosmos*, of the daily sacrifice, referred to in 50:19, belongs to the same sort of continuum as God's ordering of the works of creation. Further evidence that the worship of the Temple and the order of creation are closely inter-connected is afforded by 47:9–10, where David is said to have arranged the Temple singers and set the times in order (*ekosmēsen*) to perfection (*mechri sunteleias*), while they sang praises to God's Holy Name. The latter was inscribed on the golden plate which the high priest wore above his forehead: this, and its appurtenances, ben Sira's grandson speaks of in 45:12 as 'the beautiful (*kosmounena*) desires of the eyes'. Both the universe and the sacrifice can be called *kosmos*; and what is implied through the careful use of biblical words and phrases in ben Sira's original poem is seemingly expressed more openly in Greek by his grandson.

Verse 15. The wine offered in libation is described as 'the blood of the grape', the same expression being used at 39:26 where it is listed as one of the chief necessities for the life of man. The phrase is derived from the Bible (cf. Gen. 49:11; Deut. 32:14). This wine is regarded as a sacrifice in its own right: ben Sira calls it 'a sweet-smelling savour' (cf. Exod. 29:18, 25, 41), and its redness is explicitly related to blood (cf. also I. Macc. 6:34). Most significantly, we hear that it was poured at the foundations, *themelia*, of the altar, an expression otherwise not found in the LXX. According to the Mishnah, the wine and water libation at Sukkoth were poured into bowls with outlets (*m. Sukk.* 4:9), from which they ran down into the *shîtîn*. These were the 'foundations', pits where the wine libations offered throughout the year collected (*t. Sukk.* 3:15); and tradition taught that they had existed from the six days of creation (*b. Sukk.* 49a; *jer. Sukk.* 54d). The Mishnah also tells how there was access to the *shîtîn* from the pavement by the altar, so that they could be cleaned (*m. Midd.* 3:3).

In its present form, the Rabbinic tradition set out above dates from a time much later than ben Sira's grandson. Yet keen interest in the subterranean areas of the Temple is already to the fore in Aristeas, where they are discussed in detail; and it is precisely focused on the disposal of the sacrificial blood (Aristeas 88–91). Aristeas has no direct comment on the likely meaning of these things.

Verses 16–18. The Greek makes explicit with the noun *mnêmosunon*, 'memorial', the sense of the Hebrew verbal form *lhzkyr*: the same noun is used in the description of Aaron in 45:9, 11, and 16. In verse 17 describing the people's bowing down, the word translated 'together' is *koinêi*, doing duty for Hebrew *yhdyw*. It may be rendered also as 'publicly, in concert, in common'. The prostration of the people may thus be interpreted as their public act of worship as opposed to some private homage on the part of themselves as individuals. Such is the force of *koinêi* in 2 Macc. 4:5 and 9:26, where it represents public as distinct from private action. The translator, however, may wish to convey the notion that the people acted 'in concert', performing their public duty without prompting like the priests described in Aristeas 92. The only other occurrence of the word in Greek ben Sira is at 18:1, where we are told that He who lives for ever created everything *koinêi*, 'together, in common'.

Verses 19–21. For comments on verse 19, see the remarks above on verses 12–14. The Hebrew of verse 21 is fragmentary; but the Greek translation specifies that the Lord is the Most High. The Greek translation of these verses is not far removed from the original Hebrew.

Verses 22–26. Here we find the clearest indications that ben Sira's grandson altered his grandfather's work to take account of changed political and religious conditions in Jerusalem. All references to Simon, the covenant of Phinehas, and the promise to Simon's descendants 'like the days of heaven' are removed from verse 24, and replaced with a plea for God's mercy and deliverance in His own time. As the Greek text stands at present, there is no necessary relationship remaining between these verses and the rest of the poem. Verse 21, it might be argued, completes the description of the Temple Service, and verse 22 begins a quite new, general series of concluding blessings and curses. Phinehas was regarded by the Hasmoneans, ruling in Jerusalem when the grandson translated ben Sira's work, as their glorious ancestor and exemplar (1 Macc. 2:23–26, 54); consequently, the grandson has eliminated any links between Phinehas and the now dispossessed Zadokites, and allows himself to express obliquely his loyalty to the new masters in Judaea.

This last concern is apparent also in the grandson's treatment of ben Sira's words about Aaron and Phinehas (45:6–24). In the Greek version, Phinehas is said 'to have the leadership of the holy ones and of his people' rather than 'to support the sanctuary' (45:24). Aaron, the first high priest, is subtly presented as a leader. In an addition to the Hebrew 45:6, the grandson describes Aaron as being like Moses, whom God glorified in the sight of kings (45:3), and whose great power and direct communion with God are set forth in detail (45:1–5). Aaron was given by God an everlasting covenant: both Hebrew and Greek say as much at 45:15, but the grandson introduces the point again at 45:7. The notion is not biblical, and indicates the increased prestige of the high priesthood in ben Sira's times.[3] The grandson clearly feels it appropriate to reinforce the point in the light of the Hasmonean ascendancy. He also explains the 'majesty' which God gave to Aaron (Hebrew of 45:7) as 'the priesthood of the people', once more emphasizing that the high priest has an official standing which is divinely guaranteed. And it is entirely in keeping with his enhanced description of the high priest as leader of the nation that ben Sira's grandson alters his grandfather's invective against the three nations (50:26) to refer to those living on the mountain of *Samaria* rather than Se'ir. They were, in all probability, those whom the Hasmonean high priest John Hyrcanus I attacked and conquered, and who most likely supported the rival temple at Shechem (Josephus, *Ant.* XIII. 275–283). For ben Sira's grandson, it would appear that the Hasmonean settlement had divine approval: not for him a longing for an ideal Zadokite past.

A full commentary on the Greek version of ben Sira 45:6–24 will not be necessary: the reader is referred to comment on the Hebrew text already given. None the less, 45:12–13 in Hebrew is very fragmentary and damaged, and the Greek translation offers material for comment. This is especially so in the case of those verses which describe the high priest's head-dress and his sole right to the vestments:

45:12 A golden crown upon the mitre,
      An engraving of a seal of holiness;
      The glory of honour, work of might,
      The desires of the eyes, beautiful adornments.
45:13 Before him, such things did not exist;
      No person of another race ever put them on,
      But his sons only,
      And his descendants for ever.

Verse 12 describes the mitre with the golden plate on which the Divine Name was inscribed (see Exod. 28:36–37; Lev. 8:9) as a glory of honour: these words represent the Hebrew *hwd kbwd*, 'majesty of glory'. From this text we may now deduce that a principal element in Simon's 'majesty' (*hôd*), which features so prominently in his performing the Tamid, consists in his wearing the Divine Name above his forehead (see above, verses 5–11). This same privilege is here called 'beautiful adornments', Greek *kosmoumena hôraia*. It is possible that the adjective 'beautiful' should be read with the following verse, to yield '. . . the desires of the eyes, adornments. Before him, such beautiful things did not exist' (Ziegler, p. 337). The fragmentary Hebrew text has remains of a word recognizable as 'beautiful' at the end of verse 12; but it has nothing extant which corresponds to *kosmoumena*, translated here as 'adornments'. The Greek term is of some interest, given the observations above on *kosmos* and *kosmein*; and there was a tradition, already well established when the grandson wrote, that God had actually created the world by means of His Name (see Jubilees 36:7).

Verse 13 may suggest that the high priest's vestments did not exist before the time of Aaron. The Hebrew of the verse is so badly preserved that we cannot tell what ben Sira wrote; consequently, there is no means of determining whether his grandson has fairly represented his words. If the Greek is rendered as above, and is held to reflect what ben Sira wrote, then the comments on *tip'eret* linking the word to the garments of Adam as priestly vestments (above, on 50:1 Hebrew) must be modified. It might even be argued that ben Sira (or his grandson) had engaged in polemic with traditions about the primeval origin of the vestments. The Greek, however, is rendered by Skehan and di Lella (p. 507) as 'Before him no one was adorned with these, nor may they ever be worn by any . . . .' Their translation captures a sense of the Greek which implies that the garments may have existed, but had not been assumed by any person. On this understanding, Aaron's position is once again heightened, and the priestly covenant accorded to him as a national leader is corroborated.

5

THE BOOK OF JUBILEES

Jubilees offers one of the most distinctive and influential under-standings of the Temple Service known from Second Temple times. In its present form, the work was most probably completed around 160 BC. Although it was used and regarded as authoritative by the Qumran covenanters (see CD 16:2–4), internal evidence suggests that it did not necessarily originate with that group.[1] After an introduction in which God addresses Moses directly, Jubilees is set forth as revelation given to Moses on Mount Sinai, delivered in a speech uttered in the first person by one of the angels of the Presence (2:1). Among the principal purposes of the book is the setting forth and inculcation of a peculiar solar calendar, for which Jubilees argues consistently and with some force.[2] The calendar has a profound effect on the worship of the Temple as envisaged by Jubilees, since the timing of almost every ritual act and festival day is tied, through this calendar, to some particular event or nexus of events in Israel's patriarchal past. Furthermore, the calendar ex-presses a heavenly order of things to which the earthly Temple Service is expected to conform, such that there should be complete harmony between the world above and the world below. The impli-cations of this are far-reaching, and Jubilees loses no opportunity to address them.

Jubilees shows signs of being a strongly didactic work (e.g., 1:5–18; 6:38; 13:25–26), and tends to expound quite openly aspects of the Temple Service which ben Sira had spoken of obliquely through allusive biblical language. Indeed, the two writings show a remarkably similar appreciation of the fundamental meaning of the Temple Service, and particular details of it, despite their different aims and presentations of the evidence. For example, as in ben Sira's poem, the title 'Most High' is applied by Jubilees to God as he is worshipped in the Temple Service.[3] Thus Abraham addressed his offering on the altar between Bethel and Ai to God Most High (13:16), and kept the festival of Sukkoth in His honour (16:17). Fourth-year fruit is holy, acceptable to God Most High (7:36). Of greatest import is Levi's dream that he is ordained as the priest of God Most High (32:1); earlier, Abraham was promised that Isaac 'should become the portion of the Most High', and that his seed 'should become a kingdom and priests and a holy nation' (16:18). So Rebecca prays in her blessing of Jacob:

> And may thy name and thy seed endure to all the ages,
> And may the Most High God be their God,
> And may the God of righteousness dwell with them,
> And by them may His sanctuary be built unto all the ages.
>
> (25:21)

Here the Most High is also God of *righteousness*: the parallelism of the poetry makes this clear.[4] Presumably 'righteousness' here represents an original Hebrew *ẓedeq*. Israel is the 'plant of righteousness' (1:16; 16:26; 21:24; 36:6; cf. 7:34): again, the original Hebrew probably had *ẓedeq* for 'righteousness', a word whose significance for Hebrew ben Sira was examined earlier.[5] Jacob's seed is to build a sanctuary for the Most High, a building designated by God at the very beginning of the book as 'My sanctuary, which I have hallowed for Myself . . . that I should set My Name upon it . . .' (1:10). God's Name dwells in the sanctuary (32:10; 49:21; cf. 49:19, 20), and is so bound up with it that defilement of the Temple can be spoken of in the same breath as profanation of God's holy Name (30:15; cf. very closely 23:21). And that Name is regarded by Jubilees as the author of the whole creation:

> And now I shall make you swear a great oath – for there is no oath which is greater than it by the Name glorious and honoured and great and splendid and wonderful and mighty, which created the heavens and the earth and all things together – that ye will fear Him and worship Him.
>
> (36:7)

This very Name dwells in the Temple whose Service, as will presently be seen, has a good deal to do with the continuing stability and order of the creation. Once more, we are reminded of ben Sira's concerns elucidated earlier. Jubilees explicitly asserts that the Most High is the creator (12:19; 22:6; 25:11); the Most High is also, as befits One whose Name dwells in the Temple, frequently invoked as a source of blessing (21:25; 22:13, 19, 27; 25:3; 36:16); see also Greek ben Sira 50:20–21.

The whole nation descended from Jacob–Israel is destined by God to be 'a kingdom and priests and a holy nation' (16:18; 33:20), an idea deriving ultimately from Exod. 19:5–6, but understood by the author of Jubilees in a very particular sense. By definition, all holiness derives from God; and one's closeness to God determines one's degree of holiness. In the heavenly realm, Jubilees names as the two orders of angels closest to God the angels of the Presence (of God) and the angels of sanctification, and these two classes of angels alone keep Sabbath with God in heaven (2:18). On earth, Israel alone out of all the nations is instructed to keep Sabbath (2:19, 31). Furthermore, the covenant between God and Israel is constituted by the rite of circumcision, which is binding on all male Jews for ever (15:24–26). They share this privilege with the angels of the Presence and the angels of sanctification, who were created circumcised (15:27–28). Thus there is to be a complete correspondence between Israel on earth and the two highest orders of angels in heaven as touching these sacred matters.

This principle of 'as in heaven, so on earth' is clearly enunciated in the case of the priesthood. The angel of the Presence who dictates Jubilees to Moses states unambiguously:

And the seed of Levi was chosen for the priesthood, and to be Levites, that they might minister before the Lord, as we [namely, the highest order of angels], continually . . . .

(30:14)

Later, Jacob blesses Levi and his descendants:

And may the Lord give to thee and to thy seed greatness and great glory, and cause thee and thy seed, from among all flesh, to approach Him to serve in His sanctuary as the angels of the Presence and as the holy ones. (Even) as they, will the seed of thy sons be for glory and greatness and holiness, and may He make them great unto all the ages.

(31:14)

The Service offered by the priests on earth, therefore, corresponds with that offered by the highest orders of angels in heaven. According to 30:14 this service is to be offered 'continually', an almost certain reference to the Tamid of which, as will presently become clear, Jubilees has a highly developed understanding. The life of the Jews is intimately bound up with the heavenly world. This notion is not restricted to Jubilees: PJ of Num. 15:40 indicates that Jews are like the angels who serve before the Lord, when they carry out the commandments summed up in the law of *ṣiṣith*, the fringes of garments. But for Jubilees, in no area of Jewish life is this clearer than in the Service of the sanctuary and the duties of the priests. And this Service, we are assured, traces its beginnings to the earliest days of mankind. Jubilees offers its interpretation of elements of the Service through linking them with individual patriarchs, and it will be convenient to follow that scheme.

FROM ADAM TO NOAH

According to Jubilees, aspects of the Temple Service and the order of the festivals were known from the time of Adam and his descendants, and were carefully carried out before the days of Moses. Noah's sacrifice (Gen. 8:20–22) is held to mark a crucial stage in the history of the Service; before Noah, however, certain fundamental principles had already been established. Pre-eminent among these is the keeping of the Sabbath: this is declared binding on Israel, since both the day itself and Israel are separated, blessed, and sanctified by God from the beginning (2:19–20). Consequently, the Sabbath stands virtually at the head of the book: its laws are set before all others, and are repeated with some emphasis at the start (2:17–33) and at the finish (50:6–13). The ritual prescribed for the Sabbath is the only work permitted on that day:

> For great is the honour which the Lord has given to Israel that they should eat and drink and be satisfied on this festival day, and rest thereon from all labour ... save burning frankincense and bringing oblations and sacrifices before the Lord for days and for Sabbaths. This work alone shall be done on the Sabbath-days in the sanctuary of the Lord your God; that they may atone with sacrifice continually from day to day for a memorial well-pleasing before the Lord, and that He may receive them always from day to day as thou hast been commanded.
>
> (50:10–11)

The Sabbath sacrifices are here regarded as having the same significance as the Tamid. They are to be offered to ensure that the

Tamid does happen daily, 'continually'; and, like the Tamid to be discussed in the next section, their main function is atonement. They thus deal with sin, and take on the character of a 'memorial' in consequence: they call Israel to mind before God, and Israel's sacrifices are thus divinely approved and accepted.

What has been said, however, implies the existence of a sanctuary. Jubilees states at the outset that

> the Lord has four places on the earth, the Garden of Eden, and the Mount of the East, and this mountain on which thou (Moses) art this day, Mount Sinai, and Mount Zion (which) will be sanctified in the new creation for a sanctification of the earth; through it will the earth be sanctified from all (its) guilt and its uncleanness throughout the generations of the world.
>
> (4:26)

The Garden of Eden is to be the first home of Adam and Eve. They were created, however, outside it; and God brought Adam into it on the fortieth day after his creation. Eve was brought in on the eightieth day (3:9). In this way, Jubilees traces back to the first human couple the laws of Lev. 12:2–8, which require of a woman a period of forty days purification if she bear a son, eighty days if she bear a daughter, before she may enter the Temple.[6] This indicates that a sanctuary was an integral part of creation itself from the outset: indeed, the Garden of Eden was specially created on the third day (2:7). More specifically, Jubilees states that Eden is holier than all the rest of the earth (3:12). According to 8:19, Noah

> knew that the Garden of Eden is the holy of holies, and the dwelling of the Lord, and Mount Sinai the centre of the desert, and Mount Zion – the centre of the navel[7] of the earth: these three were created as holy places facing each other.

It would appear, then, that Adam and Eve were brought into the Holy of Holies prior to their disobedience: their expulsion from Eden thus signifies their removal from the place where God's Presence on the earth is most immediate for Israel. The high priest's entry into the Holy of Holies on Yom Kippur might, then, in some manner typologically correspond to the first man's return to Eden, for a season, to be reconciled with his Maker face to face. Even so, this notion is only implied: Jubilees does not say as much, either in the verse quoted above, or when discussing Yom Kippur (36:12–19). The close ties which this book establishes between Eden and Zion's Temple, however, cannot fail to recall ben Sira's poem. There, the high priest appears now as a latter-day Adam, now as an embodiment of Wisdom, herself a minister in the holy tabernacle and resident on Zion (ben Sira 24:10–11), abundant like the rivers Pishon, Tigris, Euphrates, and Gihon (24:25–27) which issue from the Garden of Eden (Gen. 2:11, 13, 14).

Both ben Sira and Jubilees, in their different ways, bring Adam into direct association with the Temple understood as Eden. According to Jubilees, the first ritual act of worship was offered by Adam immediately after his expulsion from the garden.

> And He made for them coats of skin, and clothed them, and sent them forth from the Garden of Eden. And on that day on which Adam went forth from the Garden, he offered as a sweet savour an offering, frankincense, galbanum, and stacte, and spices in the morning with the rising of the sun from the day when he covered his shame.
>
> (3:26–27)

The note that Adam made his offering after God had clothed him has already been discussed: Jubilees possibly held that God had made for Adam priestly vestments.[8] He offers the first morning Tamid incense offering; and the language of the text suggests that he did so each day thereafter. This is the first act of sacrifice recorded in Jubilees, and as such it may hold a particular meaning for the writer. Adam is thereby constituted the first priest in a succession which will lead to Levi, and then to Aaron and his sons. He is thus an Israelite patriarch, blessed by God, whose blessing can, and should, pass over to the Israel of the future (see Jub. 19:23–25 and 22:11–12). As part of the Tamid the incense offering may, in the author's opinion, have atoning value: his statements about the Tamid in 6:14 are clear that the rite as a whole is a means of seeking forgiveness from God. Consonant with this, the later writer of the Apocalypse of Adam and Eve recorded Adam's plea that God allow him to take aromatics from Eden, so that he would have something to offer to God outside Paradise, that God might hear him (29:2–4).

Equally, however, Adam is the father of the whole human race; and his priestly offering, *ipso facto*, takes on the character of a representative act on behalf of all who will descend from him.

Jubilees also insists that Israel's ancestor Jacob is analagous to Adam. This fact is strikingly emphasized: just as Adam is the twenty-second work of God's creation, so is Jacob–Israel the twenty-second 'head of mankind' counting from Adam (2:23).[9] Over a century later, Philo would assert that the Temple Service offered by the Jews was a liturgy undertaken for all people; and he would elaborate on the symbolism of the Temple, its furniture, and the vestments of the high priest as representing the whole created order in an united act of thanksgiving to the creator.[10] In presenting Adam as a priest, therefore, Jubilees does more than point to his personal piety;[11] it makes a claim for the Jewish people in relation to the rest of the universe, a relation which is explicitly proclaimed as priestly.

According to the Bible, however, the first sacrifice was offered by Cain and Abel (Gen. 4:3–5), Cain presenting fruit of the ground, Abel the first-born of flocks and their fat. Jubilees passes over all this in silence, radically reducing the episode to God's reaction to the offerings, and Cain's murder of Abel: 'And in the first (year) of the third jubilee, Cain slew Abel because (God) accepted the sacrifice of Abel, and did not accept the sacrifice of Cain' (4:2). Unlike many other post-biblical writings which treat of Cain and Abel, this account lacks all details of what the two offered, and fails to explain how Cain knew that his sacrifice was rejected. No rationale for the divine reaction to the sacrifices is even suggested. Instead, the episode is recalled in the most terse manner possible to introduce the law of the killer recorded in Deut. 27:34, which Jubilees describes as being written on the heavenly tablets (4:5–6). It is possible, though unlikely, that Jubilees has deliberately reduced the scope of this incident because the biblical account involved the offering of animals: these, according to Jubilees 6:6, were not permitted for human consumption before Noah's Flood. Whatever the reason, however, Jubilees effectively underlines the incense offering of Adam as the first sacrificial act by quickly passing over the Cain and Abel story, and by relating another non-biblical incense sacrifice offered by Enoch:

And he burnt the incense of the sanctuary, (even) sweet spices, acceptable before the Lord on the Mount. For the Lord has four places on the earth, the garden of Eden ....

(4:25–26)

From Enoch later generations also received rules about the Temple Service. Noah instructs his children:

> For three years the fruit of everything that is eaten will not be gathered; and in the fourth year its fruit will be accounted holy [and they will offer the first-fruits], acceptable before the Most High God, who created heaven and earth and all things. Let them offer in abundance the first of the wine and oil (as) first-fruits on the altar of the Lord, who receives it, and what is left let the servants of the house of the Lord eat before the altar which receives (it).
>
> (7:36)

Abraham, too, transmits as from Enoch fundamental rules for sacrifice:

> And if thou dost slay a victim as an acceptable peace offering, slay ye it, and pour out its blood upon the altar, and all the fat of the offering offer on the altar with fine flour (and the meat offering) mingled with oil, with its drink offering – offer them all together on the altar of burnt offering; it is a sweet savour before the Lord. And thou wilt offer the fat of the sacrifice of thank offerings on the fire which is upon the altar, and the fat which is on the belly, and all the fat on the inwards and the two kidneys, and all the fat that is upon them, and upon the loins and liver thou shalt remove, together with the kidneys. And offer all these for a sweet savour acceptable before the Lord, with its meat offering and with its drink offering, for a sweet savour, the bread of the offering unto the Lord, and eat its meat on that day and on the second day, and let not the sun on the second day go down upon it till it is eaten, and let nothing be left over for the third day; for it is not acceptable [for it is not approved] and let it no longer be eaten, and all who eat thereof will bring sin upon themselves; for thus I have found it written in the books of my forefathers, and in the words of Enoch, and in the words of Noah.
>
> (21:7–10)

Not all of these rules may derive from Enoch, as indeed the last sentence makes plain; but enough is said here to indicate that Enoch was held responsible for transmitting laws about blood sacrifice. This makes it unlikely that Jubilees was reticent about Abel's offering in that it involved the sacrifice of animals. Given this, it is remarkable that incense alone of all the sacrificial materials is explicity singled out by Jubilees as having been offered before the Flood, by Adam and Enoch. It is defined in biblical language as a sweet savour, acceptable before the Lord; but as to its deeper meaning, nothing is stated or implied.

FROM NOAH TO ABRAHAM

The Bible itself indicates that the great Flood destroyed all living things apart from Noah and his immediate family (Gen. 7:21–23). Noah thus became the head of the entire human race, which descends from him. His first act after the Flood was the offering of sacrifice:

> And on the new moon of the third month he went forth from the ark, and built an altar on that mountain. And he made atonement for the earth, and took a kid and made atonement by its blood for all the guilt of the earth; for everything that had been on it had been destroyed, save those that were in the ark with Noah. And he placed the fat thereof on the altar, and he took an ox, and a goat, and a sheep and kids, and salt and a turtle-dove, and the young of a dove, and placed a burnt sacrifice on the altar, and poured thereon an offering mingled with oil, and sprinkled wine and strewed frankincense over everything, and caused a goodly savour to arise, acceptable before the Lord.
>
> (6:1–3)

Noah already appears to know that the blood of certain animals effects atonement for sin, even though this fundamental aspect of Jewish sacrifice (see Lev. 17:11) has not yet been enunciated. All the animals listed here the Torah classes as fit for sacrifice, and are offered with oil, wine, and incense: the note in Gen. 8:20 that Noah offered some of every clean beast and bird is thus expanded to conform to the rules of Jewish sacrifice.[12] The sacrifice atones for the earth: as Charles suggests, the pollution of the land by horrendous sin is entertained by Lev. 18:26–28; Num. 35:33–34, such that Noah's sacrifice acts as a cleansing agent.[13]

This sacrifice, however, effects much more than atonement for a defiled earth. It leads to the establishment of a covenant between God and Noah that there should never again be a flood to destroy the earth; and that the annual seasons and day and night should be stabilized for ever (6:4). God requires Noah and his descendants not to eat blood (6:7–8). Up to this point, Jubilees follows the biblical text (Gen. 8:21–9:7) fairly closely; but a highly significant addition to the biblical narrative is found in 6:10–14. According to this, Noah and his sons swore never to eat blood, and Noah made a covenant 'for ever throughout all the generations of the earth in this (namely, the third) month' (6:10). This insistence on the pro-hibition of consuming blood, already instanced (6:7, 8) will be repeated (6:12, 13; 7:29–33); and its rationale is given in 6:11–13, where the angel says to Moses:

> On this account He spake to thee that thou shouldst make a covenant with the children of Israel in this month upon the mountain with an oath, and that thou shouldst sprinkle blood upon them because of all the words of the covenant, which the Lord made with them for ever. And this testimony is written concerning you that you should observe it *continually*, so that you should not eat on any day any blood of beasts or birds or cattle during all the days of the earth ... . And do thou command the children of Israel to eat no blood, so that their names and their seed be before the Lord our God *continually*.

Noah's sacrifice, which initiates a covenant in the third month, is here brought into line with the covenant mediated by Moses in the third month (Exod. 19:1) at Sinai (Exod. 19–24). Jubilees binds to-gether these two covenants through reference to blood. This must never be eaten: it is reserved for covenant-making. Noah makes a covenant, which includes an undertaking never to eat it: Moses is to take it and sprinkle it on Israel (Exod. 24:5–8) to make the covenant on Mount Sinai. Indeed, what Moses does in sprinkling the blood is to re-establish the covenant made with Noah, which should rightly have been renewed each year on the Feast of Weeks (6:17).

> This whole festival was celebrated in heaven from the day of creation till the days of Noah ... and Noah and his sons observed it ... till the day of Noah's death, and from the day of Noah's death his sons did away with it, until the days of Abraham, *and they eat blood*. But Abraham observed it, and Isaac and Jacob and his children observed it up to thy days, and in thy days the children of Israel forgot it until ye cele-brated it anew upon this mountain.

(6:18–19)

Quite striking and remarkable is the way in which Jubilees links Noah's sacrifice, and thus the covenant ritual performed by Moses, to the Tamid, the 'continual' daily offering in the Temple. A hint of this coming link is given in the passage quoted above from 6:11–13, where the word *continually* is used twice, first of the command never to eat blood, second of the effect of obedience to it: Israel's name will be before the Lord *continually*. Then, with respect for the rule about blood, we read in 6:14 that

> for this law there is no limit of days, for it is for ever. They shall observe it throughout their generations, so that they may continue supplicating on your behalf with blood before the altar; *every day and at the time of morning and evening* they shall seek forgiveness on your behalf *perpetually* before the Lord that they may keep it and not be rooted out.

Here, the function of blood as a means of atonement (Lev. 17:11) is explicitly brought into play: blood is the agent not only in covenant-making, but also in supplication for forgiveness. When the morning and evening Tamid is sacrificed, therefore, the writer of Jubilees expects his readers to recall, first, Noah's sacrifice on leaving the ark and its biblical consequences; second, the covenant which Noah made not to eat blood; third, the covenant renewed with blood by Moses on Mount Sinai; fourth, the Feast of Weeks on which this covenant was ratified; and fifth, the forgiveness which the Tamid itself implores from God. And this immensely rich understanding of the Tamid leads at once to a consideration of the rainbow, which Jubilees now introduces as a sign of the covenant that there should never be another flood to destroy the earth: for this reason, the Feast of Weeks must be kept to renew the covenant each year (6:15–17).

Of the similarities between Jubilees and ben Sira's poem (chapter 50), which almost certainly describes the Tamid, we may note especially that ben Sira used language drawn from God's covenant with Noah as he likened the officiating high priest to the rainbow (50:7); and that covenant and stability of the universe feature prominently in his understanding of the Tamid. Both texts, in their different ways, point to the heavenly dimension of the rite.[14] On the other hand, ben Sira is silent about the blood of the sacrifice, and, perhaps in consequence, makes no mention of the ritual as effecting atonement or forgiveness. Jubilees, having forged a link between the Tamid and Noah's sacrifice which atoned for the earth, joins hands with later sources such as *b. Yoma* 62b, PJ Num. 28:4, and the *Yalqut* on that verse which make the morning Tamid an atonement for sins of the night, and the evening Tamid atonement for sins of the day. Furthermore, unlike ben Sira, whose language at times suggests that the Feast of Sukkoth has coloured his view of the Tamid, Jubilees clearly associates the daily offerings of the Temple with the Feast of Weeks, through the covenant ceremonies of Noah and Moses.

Jubilees emphasizes this feast because of its unique character. The Hebrew title *šb't* may be vocalized either as *šābu'ôt*, 'Weeks', indicating the calendrical significance of the day (see Lev. 23:15–21; Deut. 16:9–12); or as *š'bu'ôt*, 'oaths', identifying it as a feast of covenants: for the Bible depicts the various covenants as oaths which God *swore*, Deut. 29:12–15; Ps. 105:8–10. Its character as a feast of covenants has already been explained: later, we learn that on this feast-day God made His covenant with Abraham 'between the sacrificial portions' (Jubilees 14:9–29). During a later celebration of it, God revealed to Abraham the covenant of circumcision (15:1–14); and Isaac, the heir of all God's promises to Abraham, was born on it (16:13). Yet its calendrical significance is absolutely central to the programme of Jubilees. The commands to keep it on its own day, the fifteenth of the third month (6:17, 20, 22), as a feast of covenant renewal are *at once* followed by reference to the four new-moon days of the first, fourth, seventh, and tenth months ordained by Noah for future generations as memorials of the Flood and his part in it: these are placed

> on the heavenly tables; each had thirteen weeks . . . and all the days of the commandments will be two and fifty weeks of days, and (these will make) the entire year complete. Thus it is engraven and ordained on the heavenly tables.
>
> (6:22–31)

This heavenly cycle of feasts is to be reproduced on earth by Israel. It necessitates a regularly recurring year of 364 days determined solely by the sun, and divided into four equal parts of thirteen weeks, which begin each of Noah's memorials.[15] Noah himself adheres to this division of times, celebrating the first day of the first month as a wine festival whose sacrifices are described at 7:3–6. Any other calendar is false. Failure to observe this heavenly calendar will disturb and dislodge festivals and Sabbaths from their proper days (6:32–36), produce confusion of holy day with days abominable and unclean (6:37), and will end in the *eating of all kinds of blood* (6:38). Thus we are brought back to the subject of *blood*, and its two-fold purpose (as the writer conceives of it) as agent in covenant-making and in forgiveness, both of which are *continually* represented in the Tamid offering of the Temple.

Between the days of Noah and Abraham, Jubilees has little to say about worship. The latter is shown offering sacrifice in 13:8–9 and paying tithes during the episode of Melchizedeq (13:25–27). The covenant 'between the sacrificial portions' recorded in Gen. 15 is reported with embellishments at 14:9–20; these include its date in the middle of the third month at Shabu'ot (14:10); reference to the altar on which the victims' blood is poured (14:11); and the offering of the portions, the birds, with fruit offerings and drink offerings on the altar (14:19). The event is directly linked with Noah's covenant in 14:20:

And on that day we made a covenant with Abram, according as we had covenanted with Noah in this month; and Abram renewed the festival and ordinance for himself for ever.

Abraham again celebrated Shabu'ot as feast of first-fruits according to 15:1–2; this is a prelude to the covenant of circumcision (15:11–14). In this way, Abraham is also indissolubly linked to that festival.

According to 16:19–31, Abraham celebrated the Feast of Sukkoth, having been divinely assured that from Isaac's sons should come a 'holy seed', a people for the Lord's possession above all other nations, and 'a kingdom and priests and a holy nation' (16:17–18). The reference to priests here is significant. It has already been noted how ben Sira's description of Simon's offering the Tamid echoes the language of the Feast of Sukkoth,[16] a festival which seems particularly associated with the priesthood in Jubilees: this much is evident from Jacob's celebration of Sukkoth described in 32:1–29. Abraham built an altar and booths for the feast which he kept for seven days (16:19–21), and the details of the sacrifices are set out in 16:22–24. The latter do not correspond to the biblical requirements: but verse 22 describes the animal victims as sin offerings and thank offerings. These reveal nothing of Jubilees' appreciation of this feast; but 16:24 is a note of some importance:

And morning and evening he burnt fragrant substances, frankincense and galbanum, and stacte, and nard, and myrrh, and spice, and costum; all these seven he offered, crushed, mixed together in equal parts (and) pure.

Charles noted[17] that seven ingredients of the Temple incense, which is what is being described here (cf. Exod. 30:34), are listed by ben Sira in his praise of Wisdom at 24:25. There, ben Sira directly compares Wisdom with the incense; and we have already remarked upon his vivid comparison of the high priest Simon with both Wisdom and incense. Thus 16:24 seems yet another indication that Sukkoth is a feast peculiarly significant for the priesthood. This is indirectly confirmed by 16:26–27 telling how, after keeping the feast for seven days without any stranger or uncircumcised, Abraham blessed God, 'for He knew and perceived that from him would arise the plant of *righteousness* for the eternal generations, and from him a holy seed'. The language of 'righteousness' (probably Hebrew *zedeq*) again recalls ben Sira's (Hebrew and Greek) description of the high priest. It is noticeable that in most cases where the phrase 'plant of righteousness' recurs in Jubilees (1:16; 7:34; 21:24; 36:6), the setting is one of Temple Service. It thus seems reasonable to suggest that Jubilees and ben Sira may both have been influenced by a tradition which interpreted Sukkoth as the feast *par excellence* of the Jewish priesthood.[18]

On the Feast of Passover Abraham offered up Isaac. According to 17:15–16, on the twelfth day of the first month Mastema persuaded God to require Isaac's sacrifice: Abraham arrived at the place of sacrifice 'on the third day', that is, the 14th/15th of the first month, the Feast of Passover. This festival Abraham celebrated thereafter every year for seven days (18:18–19), corresponding to the seven days of Maẓẓoth, the Feast of Unleavened Bread (see Exod. 12:15; Lev. 23:6). Jubilees is the oldest known document to associate the offering of Isaac with Passover.[19] The fact that first-born sons are rescued from death by the blood sacrifice of a lamb is the most striking of many parellels between the two biblical narratives (Gen. 22:1–19; Exod. 12:1–13); and there is not the least doubt that Jubilees regarded the Passover as commemorating Isaac's sacrifice as well as the Exodus from Egypt: for Abraham

celebrated this festival every year, seven days with joy, and he called it the festival of the Lord according to the seven days during which he went and returned in peace. And accordingly has it been ordained and written on the heavenly tables regarding Israel and its seed that they should observe this festival seven days with the joy of festival.

(18:18–19)

That Abraham has a major role to play in establishing correct priestly practice is clear from 21:5–17, where he gives Isaac instructions about sacrifice transmitted by Enoch: these were noted above (see p. 92). Isaac is reminded that, if he obeys these, and other ethical commands which Abraham gives him, 'the plant of righteousness' will arise from him, and his name and Abraham's will never be forgotten under heaven (21:24).

FROM ISAAC TO JACOB

Isaac, like his righteous forefathers, kept Shabu'ot (22:1); apart from his offering at Passover, no major development in worship is associated with him. His son Jacob, however, begins a new phase in the ordered service of God. During a visit with his sons Judah and Levi to his father Isaac at Bethel he builds an altar on the first day of the seventh month, Rosh Ha-Shanah (31:3). Isaac blesses Judah and Levi: this is a prophetic act in which Levi is given precedence. Isaac takes him by his right hand, Judah by his left (31:12). He blesses Levi with these words:

> May the God of all, the very Lord of all the ages, bless thee and thy children throughout all the ages. And may the Lord ... cause thee and thy seed, from among all flesh, to approach Him to serve in His sanctuary as the angels of the presence and as the holy ones. (Even) as they, will the seed of thy sons be for glory and greatness and holiness, and may He make them great unto all the ages. And they will be princes and judges, and chiefs of all the seed of the sons of Jacob;
> They will speak the word of the Lord in righteousness,
> And they will judge all His judgements in righteousness.
> And they will declare my ways to Jacob
> And my paths to Israel.
> The blessing of the Lord will be given in their mouths
> To bless all the seed of the beloved ....
> Let His table be thine,
> And do thou and thy sons eat thereof;
> And may thy table be full unto all generations ....

And let all who hate thee fall down before thee,
And let all thy adversaries be rooted out and perish;
And blessed be he that blesses thee,
And cursed be every nation that curses thee.

(31:13–17)

The correspondence between the ministry of Levi and his sons on
earth and that of the highest orders of angels in heaven has already
been noted above, and is fundamental to Jubilees' thinking about
Temple Service and priesthood.[20] Although this particular notion is
not explicit in ben Sira's work, a careful comparison of the verses
just quoted with ben Sira 50 and 45 once again displays themes
common to both writings. Thus the political aspects of the priests
as 'princes and judges and chiefs' recalls ben Sira 50:6–7, 24–26;
45:10, 25; the emphasis on righteousness occurs in both writings, as
already noted; the declaration of God's judgements, ways, and
paths features in ben Sira 45:17; the blessing of God is in their
mouths, as in ben Sira 50:20; and their rights to eat of the Lord's
table are expressly declared by ben Sira 45:20–22. Jubilees, however,
predicates these things of Levi, the ancestor of all the priests,
rather than of Simon and Aaron the high priests as does ben Sira.[21]
It should also be noted that the formula 'blessed be he that blesses
thee . . .', applied in the Bible (Gen. 12:3; 27:29; Num. 24:9) to
Abraham, Jacob, and Israel as a nation, is now addressed to the
priesthood as a whole, who thus take over a profoundly representative function for the whole people. In much the same way, ben Sira
had presented Simon as Israel's representative in the Temple
Service.

On the night of the fourteenth day of the seventh month, the
eve of the Feast of Sukkoth, Levi dreamed that he had been ordained priest of God Most High (32:1). Jacob paid the tithes which
he had promised (32:2; cf. 31:29).

And in those days Rachel became pregnant with her son Benjamin. And Jacob counted his sons from him upwards and
Levi fell to the portion of the Lord, and his father clothed
him in the garments of the priesthood and filled his hands.

(32:3)

Levi, the ancestor of the priestly tribe, thus represents the 'tithe' of
Jacob's sons, now offered to God along with all the other tithes
which Jacob had vowed (32:4–5, 8, 10–15), Levi acting as priest 'in

preference to his ten brothers' (32:9). These tithes seem to dominate Jacob's celebration of Sukkoth, and may in part explain why the number of victims offered does not correspond exactly to the biblical laws of Lev. 23:34–44; Num. 29:12–40.

Yet there is another reason why Levi is consecrated priest at this particular time. It has already been said that Rachel was pregnant with Benjamin (32:3); thus Jacob has his full complement of twelve sons, and the prophetic blessing uttered by his mother Rebecca years before is now fulfilled. She had blessed Jacob, praying that God make his sons 'arise according to the number of the months of the year' (25:16), and that 'the God of righteousness dwell with them, and by them may His sanctuary be built unto all the ages' (25:21). The twelve months of the year, indeed the whole calendar, is for Jubilees a heavenly mystery and reality whose knowledge God has granted to Israel. The very number of the tribes serves to place the unique people of Israel on a level with the pre-ordained order of time itself. The sanctuary, where earth and heaven meet, and where Israel is to observe heavenly times, seasons, and festivals on earth, is appropriately introduced in this setting; this, no doubt, is why Jacob on the twenty-second day of the seventh month

> resolved to build that place, and to surround the court with a wall, and to sanctify it and make it holy for ever, for himself and his children after him.
>
> (32:16)

That night, God appeared to him and changed his name to Israel: the biblical story of his wrestling with a mysterious opponent is entirely omitted.[22] Instead, Jacob is promised a universal *royal* dominion:

> I shall increase thee and multiply thee exeedingly, and kings will come forth from thee, and they will judge everywhere the foot of the sons of men has trodden. And I shall give to thy seed all the earth which is under heaven, and they will judge all the nations according to their desires, and after that they will get possession of the whole earth and inherit it for ever.
>
> (32:18–19)

From heaven an angel then descended with seven tables which were given to Jacob, who learned from them all that would happen to him and his sons throughout the ages (32:21). He later wrote down all that he had seen on these tablets (32:36), having first been forbidden to build an eternal sanctuary in Bethel and to dwell there; 'for this is not the place'.[23] This aspect of the incident closely recalls the story of King David, who wished to build a Temple for God, but who was forbidden to proceed, being promised instead that God would build a house for him, which will consist of royal descendants (2 Sam. 7:1–17).

In fine, Jubilees here offers a quite striking interpretation of the story about how God changed Jacob's name to Israel (Gen. 35:6–15). This change of name occurs on the seventh day of Sukkoth, and follows directly the priestly consecration of Levi, the tenth son of the twelve sons of Israel (corresponding to the months of the year): Jacob–Israel is cast as a type of King David, forbidden to build a sanctuary, but promised royal dsecendants who shall exercise universal sway. In consequence of this, Jacob celebrated Sukkoth for an additional eighth day, itself written on the heavenly tables (32:27–29). In this way, Jubilees anchors the Jewish priesthood and kingship firmly 'in Israel', that is, in the person of Jacob–Israel who is the twenty-second 'head of mankind' and on whom rest all the blessings accorded to previous patriarchs.[24] The heavenly reality which this represents on earth is constantly emphasized with reference to the heavenly tables; and Sukkoth is set as an everlasting 'memorial' of these beginnings of Israel's formal status as 'a kingdom and priests and a holy nation'. Further, Jacob–Israel wrote down all that was destined to happen to his sons: later, we learn that he gave all his books and the books of his fathers to Levi, to preserve them and renew them for his children 'until this day' (45:16).

Yom Kippur is now the only great day not yet named by Jubilees. This finds its place in Jacob's mourning for his son Joseph, treacherously sold into Egypt by his brothers, who persuade Jacob by a ruse that he is dead.

> For this reason it is ordained for the children of Israel that they should afflict themselves on the tenth day of the seventh month – on the day that the news which made him weep for Joseph came to Jacob his father – that they should make atonement for themselves thereon with a young goat on the tenth of the seventh month, once a year, for their sins; for they had grieved the affection of their father regarding Joseph his son. And this day has been ordained that they should grieve thereon for their sins, and for all their trans-

gressions and for all their errors, so that they might cleanse themselves on that day once a year.

(34:18–19)

Considering the importance of Yom Kippur, it is extraordinary that Jubilees pays so little attention to it. The only ceremony noted is that of a young goat, which provides the link to Joseph's death: his brothers had killed a goat and dipped in its blood Joseph's garment, which they showed to Jacob as proof that Joseph was dead (Gen. 37:31–34). On Yom Kippur, two goats were presented, one for God as a sin offering, the other sent out to the desert 'to Azazel' (Lev. 16:7–10). Jubilees does not specify which of these it has in mind. There is no explicit reference to the day being ordained on the heavenly tables; and the superficial impression is given of a day which simply recalls Jacob's mourning. Yet perhaps behind this interpretation lies a principle not explicit in Jubilees, but made clear in later sources, that the blood of a goat should make atonement for the sin of Joseph's brothers, who killed a goat in their act of deception.

MOSES

Moses is naturally associated in particular with the Feast of Passover. Jubilees probably describes the ritual as it was actually performed around the mid-second century BC, although the programmatic character of the book suggests that caution is in order: Jubilees may well describe what ought to happen, rather than provide a strictly historical record.[25] First, an account of what was done on the night of the Exodus from Egypt is given. On the fourteenth day of the first month the Passover lamb was killed before evening, to be eaten by night on the evening of the fifteenth from sunset (49:1). The blood of the first-year lamb was daubed on the lintels of the houses, a sign that all the powers of Mastema should not enter to kill the first-born. While the Egyptian firstborn were being slaughtered,

> all Israel was eating the flesh of the paschal lamb, and drinking the wine, and was lauding and blessing, and giving thanks to the Lord God of their fathers, and was ready to go forth from under the yoke of Egypt, and from the evil bondage.

(49:6)

This is the first datable written reference to the use of wine at Passover, a custom well known from later sources as an obligatory element in the meal: even the poorest in Israel must be provided with not less than the customary four cups, according to *m. Pes.* 10:1. The 'lauding and blessing, and giving thanks', along with the wine, suggest a day of great joy (Jub. 49:2) in the tradition of the Chronicler's description of Hezekiah's Passover (2 Chr. 30:21, 25–26). The Mishah, too, requires all Jews celebrating Passover to see themselves as having come out of Egypt:

> Therefore are we under obligation to give thanks, to praise, to sing, to glorify, to exalt, to declare renowned, to bless, to elevate, to laud Him, who performed for our fathers and for us all these miracles.
>
> (*m. Pes.* 10:5)

The customary manner of proclaiming God's praise at Passover is the singing of Hallel (Ps. 113–118); but Jubilees has no explicit mention of it here. The Chronicler refers to general but continual praise by the priests and Levites during the Passover period (2 Chr. 30:21).

A command to observe it on its proper day follows, in a calendrical notice typical of Jubilees: the day of Passover is fixed, and the ordinance is engraved on the heavenly tables (49:7–8). Every man 'who is clean and close at hand' must offer the Passover on pain of extirpation (49:9). Jubilees has interpreted Num. 9:13, which implies exemption from the offering for those on a journey far off, to mean that those close at hand are under an obligation. No definition of the distance is attempted as it is in *m. Pes.* 9:1–2.

The ritual of Passover to be offered by later generations is now set forth. The fourteenth day of the first month is again specified,

> between the evenings, from the third part of the day to the third part of the night, for two portions of the day are given to the light, and a third part to the evening. This is that which the Lord commanded thee that thou shouldst observe it between the evenings. And it is not permissible to slay it during any period of the light, but during the period bordering on the evening, and let them eat it at the time of the evening until the third part of the night, and whatever is left over of

all its flesh from the third part of the night and onwards, let
them burn it with fire.

(49:10–12)

Scripture orders that Passover be offered *bên hâ'arbayim*, 'between
the evenings' (Exod. 12:6; Lev. 23:5; Num. 9:3, 5, 11), a phrase
patient of differing interpretations. Jubilees is quite precise in its
understanding: the victim must be slaughtered between two and six
o'clock of the afternoon; and the Paschal meal must finish before
two o'clock of the morning.[26] The time of the sacrifice agrees *more
or less* with Josephus, *War* VI. 423 (ninth to eleventh hour), Philo,
Quaestiones et Solutiones in Exodum I. 11 (not before the ninth hour),
and *m. Pes.* 5:1 (effectively around the ninth hour on weekdays, an
hour earlier if Passover fell on a Sabbath). The third part of the
day given to the evening, before which it is unlawful to slay the
victim, is not a precise definition of the exact time for slaughter,
suggesting only the period after two o'clock; the 'period bordering
on the evening', however, probably indicates a later time in this
section of the day than two o'clock. Jubilees also indicates that the
meal must finish by a certain time, which recalls the prescription of
m. Pes. 10:9, *Zeb.* 5:8 that the victim must be consumed before
midnight.

Biblical injunctions about the manner of the victim's cooking
are repeated in 49:13, along with the rubric that no bone of it be
broken: this last is specially emphasized, to indicate that no bone
of the Israelites shall be broken. Passover is thus intended to preserve the people in physical wholeness and entirety; and its correct
celebration ensures the safety of the people for the coming year.
Thus we read that the victim must be slaughtered on the festival
day itself (49:14 and 15), precisely because the rite has a particular
effect and meaning:

> it will come for a memorial well pleasing before the Lord, and
> no plague will come upon them to slay or to smite in that year
> in which they celebrate the passover in its season in every
> respect according to His command.

(49:15)

This verse clearly articulates the intended effects of Passover
properly observed in the writer's own day: the original Passover
celebrated in Egypt and described earlier had a particular apotro-
paic and saving effect then (49:2–6); for the generations to come,

Passover will be a good memorial of Israel before God, and ward off plague and disaster. Jubilees thus appears to distinguish between the mode of celebration of Passover in Egypt and that of future generations, as do *m. Pes.* 9:5; *Mekh. de R. Ishmael Pisḥa* 3:43–44; *b. Pes.* 96a; PJ of Exod. 12:3, 11. Future celebrations correctly offered will preserve Israel as a physical whole and will ward off demonic attacks; for the 'plague' which was unleashed during the first Passover was let loose by 'the powers of Mastema' (49:2).

One of the major differences between the 'Passover of Egypt' and the 'Passover of the generations' involved the ritual use of the victim's blood. In Egypt, Israel was ordered to smear some of the blood on the lintels and door-posts of their houses (Exod. 12:7, 22); in later generations this could not be done, for the custom had grown up, following the law of Deut. 16:5–7, of slaughtering and eating the victims at the central sanctuary and pouring out their blood at the altar. Jubilees orders this later custom, insisting

> they shall not eat it (the lamb) outside the sanctuary of the Lord, but before the sanctuary of the Lord . . . and every man who has come upon its day shall eat it in the sanctuary of the Lord from twenty years old and upward; for thus it is written and ordained that they should eat it in the sanctuary of the Lord.
>
> (49:16–17)

Furthermore,

> in the days when the house has been built in the name of the Lord in the land of their inheritance, they shall go there and slay the passover in the evening, at sunset, at the third part of the day. And they will offer its blood on the threshold of the altar, and shall place its fat on the fire which is upon the altar, and they shall eat its flesh roasted with fire in the court of the hosue which has been sanctified in the name of the Lord. And they may not celebrate the passover in their cities, nor in any place save before the tabernacle of the Lord, or before His house where His name hath dwelt; and they will not go astray from the Lord.
>
> (49:19–21)

These rulings make no mention of any special dress for the participants, which was a feature of the Passover of Egypt (Exod. 12:11); and they very largely reflect the state of affairs witnessed by

the Chronicler in his description of Hezekiah's and Josiah's Pass-
overs. He tells how the victims were slaughtered in the Temple,
their blood poured at the altar, and the fat burned on it (2 Chr.
30:15–16; 35:6, 11, 13–17). It is also clear from the Chronicler's
description that the worshippers consumed the lamb roasted (2
Chr. 35:13) within the Temple area. But the Chronicler says
nothing of the Passover as a feast which wards off physical danger
and demonic attack.

In Jubilees 49:22–23, rules for Maẓẓoth follow,

> that they should eat unleavened bread seven days, (and) that
> they should observe its festival, and that they bring an obla-
> tion every day during these seven days of joy before the Lord
> on the altar of your God. For ye celebrated this festival with
> haste when ye went forth from Egypt till ye entered into the
> wilderness of Shur; for on the shore of the sea ye com-
> pleted it.

Jubilees ends with the feast dearest to its heart: the Sabbath and the
Sabbatical years and jubilees form the climax of the book. The
prohibition of work on Sabbath is reiterated (50:7–9). The only
exceptions are

> the burning of frankincense and bringing oblations and sacri-
> fices before the Lord for days and for Sabbaths. This work
> alone shall be done on the Sabbath-days in the sanctuary of
> the Lord your God; that they may atone for Israel with sacri-
> fice continually from day to day for a memorial well-pleasing
> before the Lord, and that He may receive them always from
> day to day as thou hast been commanded.
>
> (50:10–11)

Thus Jubilees ends with mention of the first sacrifice ever recorded. For incense was offered by Adam (3:27); and the first *blood*
sacrifice which the book specifies was Noah's, itself the archetypical Tamid offering (6:14). It is the Tamid which is in the writer's
mind at the last, for Sabbath sacrifice is offered, despite the prohibition of work on that day, to ensure daily atonement and Israel's
memorial *continually* before the Lord. No greater tribute to the basic
necessity of the daily offerings in the Temple can be imagined.

107

6

THE WRITINGS OF PHILO OF ALEXANDRIA

Philo himself offers an account in *Legatio ad Gaium* of his partici-
pation in an embassy sent by the Jews of Alexandria to the
Emperor Caligula in 39–40 AD. At that time, he describes himself as an old man (*Leg.* 1). Possibly, therefore, he was born around
20 BC, or a little later. The date of his death is unknown: it may
have occurred around 50 AD.[1] He records at least one visit to the
Temple in Jerusalem when he offered prayers and sacrifices (*De
Providentia* Frag. 2.64), and it is not necessary to assume from
what he tells us that this was his only visit. He was thus, however
briefly, an eye-witness of some aspects of the Temple Service. His
distinctive interpretations of the Service and its details, however,
are deeply coloured by his particular philosophical-cum-allegorical
understanding of the Hebrew Bible and its laws.[2]

Philo places before us a wealth of material incorporating his
understanding of the Service. For present purposes, it will be best
to order this first by introducing some of Philo's fundamental ideas
about the general significance of the Temple and its rites: it will be
appropriate in this section to consider his explanation of the high
priest's vestments. His views of the Tamid and the individual rites
(incense offering, preparation of the Menorah, sacrifice of the
lamb) which make up the whole will then be considered. Next,
thought must be given to the Tamid offering of the Sabbath: this
will allow discussion of the table and Bread of the Presence, which
were attended to on that day. Finally, the Service peculiar to particular festivals will be noted.

NOTE ON THE TEXT

For the Greek text of Philo's works, and for all references to works of Philo surviving in Greek, we have used that in *Philo*, 10 vols, trans. F. H. Colson, G. H. Whitaker, and J. W. Earp, Loeb Classical Library (Heinemann: Harvard, 1962–1971). Translations are ours. We have also made use of *Philo Supplement I. Questions and Answers on Genesis*, and *Philo Supplement II. Questions and Answers on Exodus*, trans. R. Marcus, Loeb Classical Library (Heinemann: Harvard, 1961).

GENERAL PRINCIPLES

From *De Spec. Leg.* I, we glean perceptions of the Temple, its worship, and the high priest's role which Philo assumes as foundational for his treatment of individual acts of sacrifice and prayer. Most important is his conviction that the Temple in some manner represents the universe, the high priest a figure mediating between earth and heaven, and the public sacrifices of the Temple representing in a fashion the homage not only of Jews, but of the whole human race to God. The following passages will serve to illustrate these notions.

> The whole universe must be regarded as the highest and, in truth, the holy temple of God. As sanctuary it has the heaven, the most holy part of the substance of existing things; as votive offerings it has stars; as priests it has angels, ministers of His powers, unbodied souls, not mixtures of rational and irrational nature such as ours turn out to be, but having the irrational cut out, in all respects wholly intellectual, unmixed reasonings made like to the One. As for the temple made by hands – it was necessary that there be no driving back of the eagerness of men who pay their religious dues to piety, and who wish by sacrifices either to give thanks for the good things which happen, or to ask forgiveness and pardon for matters in which they have sinned.
>
> (*De Spec. Leg.* I. 66–67)

Concomitant with this, Philo declares that the priests of other nations offer sacrifices for their own people:[3]

> But the high priest of the Jews offers both prayers and thanksgiving not only for the whole race of men, but also for the parts of nature, earth, water, air, and fire, considering that

the universe (which is in fact the truth) is his native land, on whose behalf he is accustomed to propitiate the ruler with supplications and entreaties, beseeching him to make what he has created a partaker of his own fair and merciful nature.

(ibid. 97)

Further, as leader of the Jewish people, God gave to Moses kingship over that nation which is sanctified over all others to make prayers continually on behalf of the whole human race (*De Vit. Mos.* I. 149). The Temple Service possesses, therefore, a foundational significance for the whole universe. The latter itself is a Temple, especially in so far as its duty is to give thanks to God: as Philo remarks in *De Plantatione* 130, God's most characteristic activity is doing good, and the proper response of the creation to this activity is thanksgiving. Thanksgiving (*eucharistía*), as will become abundantly plain, is one of the most important functions of the Temple Service, a thanksgiving expressed by the universe itself, by the human race, and by individuals in particular acts of sacrifice and strivings after virtue.[4]

Since the high priest possesses the dominant role in the Service, he naturally requires a distinctive character, which Philo finds presumed by that law (Lev. 21:10–12) which prohibits the high priest from mourning:

For he (the high priest) is, indeed, otherwise assigned by lot to God, and has become commander (*taxiarchos*) of the sacred battle-array (*taxis*: literally, 'order, rank'); and he ought to be estranged from things relating to his origin, and not so lost to kind feelings for parents or children or brothers as to pass over or set aside any of the holy duties which were better performed absolutely straightaway. . . . For the law wishes him to be allotted a better nature than that of human sort, approaching near to the divine, bordering on both, if one must speak the truth; so that men may propitiate God through a certain mediator, and God, making use of an underservant, may extend and suppply favours to men.

(*De Spec. Leg.* I. 114, 116)

Thus the cosmos itself may be viewed as a Temple, and the earthly Temple in Jerusalem, presided over by the high priest, as a material representation of the universe constantly presenting to God thanksgiving due to Him through the prescribed Service of the high priest and his deputies. Yet the cosmos, which is the macro-cosm, finds its microcosm in human beings, who themselves may function as a Temple:

> For there are two temples of God, I believe: the one is this universe in which indeed the high priest is the first-born, the divine Logos; and the other is the rational soul, whose priest is the Man-in-Reality,[5] whose sensible copy is that one who offers the ancestral prayers and sacrifices. To him it has been committed to put on the aforementioned tunic which closely imitates the whole heaven, so that the cosmos too may jointly offer sacrifices with mankind, and that mankind might do the same with the cosmos.
>
> (*De Somniis* I. 215)

This passage makes it clear that the worship offered by the cosmos and by human beings is to be one harmonious whole: perfect *unity* between humanity on earth and the world of the heavens is prop-erly shown forth in the earthly Service of the Temple, the high priest himself being intermediary between the two realms, and symbolic of that rational element in human beings which is capable of offering pure worship to God.[6] In both these sanctuaries, the high priest is in truth the Logos, whom the earthly high priest symbolically represents.[7] Thus the high priest is no ordinary part of the holy congregation, but the soul's president and chief magis-trate. When alone, he is in fact many, representing a whole senate and people, the whole human race; and he stands mid-way between God and man, of lesser status than the former, but superior to the latter.[8] Although the mode of expression is different, Philo's sentiments recall in many respects ben Sira's understanding of the high priest both as representing the human race through his rela-tionship to Adam, and as in some sense embodying Wisdom, the principle which orders both the universe and the life or soul of the 'righteous', the *zaddiq*.[9] His indebtedness to earlier Jewish tradition is apparent also in *De Plantatione* 46–50, where he offers an exegesis of Exod. 15:17–18. These verses, uttered by Moses, speak of God's planting Israel on the mountain of His inheritance, the place of His dwelling, the sanctuary. Philo interprets them to mean that Israel should be planted in Eden, the spot from which Adam was banished; and he comments that Moses had understood that God, setting the seeds and roots of all things, is indeed the cause of the greatest of all plants, which is the universe. Thus the expression 'mountain of inheritance' in Moses' song properly refers to the universe; and just as the song goes on to speak of the mountain as a sanctuary, so the universe is God's sanctuary, an effulgence of holy things, a copy of the archetype. With this, we should compare the statements of Jubilees noted earlier, that Eden is one of the four places of the Lord on earth, specially created by God, holier than all the earth, and a sanctuary prepared at the beginning for Adam and Eve, now the Holy of Holies in Israel's Temple.[10]

Similarly, when he comes to consider the significance of the high priest's vestments, Philo reflects notions found in another Jewish source which is either slightly older than his time, or more or less contemporary with him.[11] In *Wisdom of Solomon* 18:20–25 we find a 'rewritten version' of the story of Qorah's rebellion and of the plague which followed (Num. 16:1–50), the latter assuaged by Aaron's timely appearance 'between the living and the dead' (Num. 16:48) to offer incense. Performing this act of atonement, Aaron is robed in his priestly garments:

> For upon his garment which reached down to his feet
>   was the whole universe;
> And the glories of the Fathers were upon the
>   engraving of the four rows of stones;
> And Thy majesty was upon the diadem of his head.

(*Wis.* 18:24)

Indeed, the items of attire which the author of *Wisdom* has singled out are among those specially noted earlier by Aristeas 96–98: for the writers of both documents they serve to create supernatural awe, confusion, and reverence. That the high priest's robe should depict the whole universe (*holos ho kosmos*), however, is especially striking: commenting on this passage, Winston notes its close similarity to Philo's exegesis of the high priest's robe (which we shall presently consider), and records the Stoic and Cynic affinities of the ideas set forth.[12] The possibility that Greek thought may have influenced the author of *Wisdom* and Philo can hardly be excluded; even so, it is worth recalling the cosmic significance of the high priest's attire and service as described by ben Sira. The latter seems to develop his portrait of the high priest and his garments through detailed exegesis of Biblical texts, cunningly selecting Scriptural images to allude to the high priest's unique role in the cosmic order.[13]

We begin with the full description of the vestments as given in

De Vit. Mos. II. 109–116; and the chapters following (117–135) which spell out the significance which Philo attributes to each separate garment. Philo slightly varies his interpretation of individual items in other writings: these will be noted as they occur. First, he speaks of the full-length violet tunic called in Hebrew *me'îl* (see Exod. 28:4, 31–35; 29:5; 39:22–26), rendered by LXX as *podêrês* (a robe reaching to the feet). The Hebrew text says that this was fringed with golden bells and pomegranates alternately; LXX, however, specifies that flowers were also embroidered on the skirts of this robe (LXX Exod. 28:30). Philo includes the latter in his exegesis.

> Now such was the raiment of the high priest; and both it and its parts have a meaning which must not be passed over in silence. For the whole is in fact a representation and copy of the cosmos, and the parts are representations of its several portions. We must begin with the robe which reaches to the feet. This tunic is completely violet, a model of the air. For the air is black by nature, and in a certain manner is like a robe reaching to the feet, stretching from above, from the regions below the moon, to the ends of the earth, spreading out everywhere. Therefore the tunic also spreads from the breast to the feet, around the whole body. And from it around the ankles there come forth pomegranates and embroidered flowers and bells. The embroidered flowers are a symbol of earth, for from this comes all that flowers and grows. The pomegranates are a symbol of water, appropriately so called because of their flowing juice. The bells are a symbol of the harmony and unison of these things, for neither earth without water nor water without substance of earth is sufficient in itself for generation of life, but the combination and mixture of the two. And their place is a most clear witness of what has been explained. For just as the pomegranates, the flowers, and the bells are on the skirts of the robe, so everything of which they are symbols, earth and water, are assigned to the lowest region, and in harmony with the All they echo together, and show their particular powers at fixed periods of time and at the appropriate seasons. The robe with appendages at the ankles is displayed as a symbol of three elements, air, water, and earth, out of which and in which all mortal and perishable things exist – fittingly: for just as the robe is one, and the said three elements are of one sort

since everything below the moon is subject to turnings and changes, and just as the pomegranates and flowers hang from the robe, so also in some manner earth and water are suspended on air; for air is a vehicle of these things.

(De Vit. Mos. II. 117–121)

The full-length robe of violet with its flowers, pomegranates, and bells, is given an almost identical explanation in *De Spec. Leg.* I. 84–85, 93–94, except that the bells are there said to represent the harmony of the different parts of the cosmos, not simply the harmony of water and earth. In *De Migratione Abrahami* 102–103, however, Philo considers not so much the cosmic significance of the high priest as his symbolizing the Logos, and its activity in the realm of human soul and intellect. Some of the vestments, he says, like the head-dress with the Divine Name inscribed upon it, belong to the realm of pure intellect; others, like the flowers and bells of the full-length robe, correspond to sensible realities tested by sight and hearing. In this instance, the bells also express in sound the harmony which exists between sensible things and mind or thought. Thus in the person of the high priest both mind and senses enter the sanctuary in complete harmony.

Over the full-length violet robe, the high priest wore the ephod, a garment resembling a waistcoat, curiously fashioned out of gold, blue, purple, and scarlet with a band for tying it made of the same colours and fine linen, and having in its shoulder-pieces two emerald stones, each engraved with six names of the twelve tribes of Israel (Exod. 28:5–12). This garment, says Philo, symbolizes the heaven.

Reason ... represents the ephod as a symbol of heaven. For first of all the two round stones of emerald on the shoulder-pieces reveal, as some suppose, the rules of the stars for day and night, the sun and the moon; but if one were to speak approaching nearer the truth, each of the two hemispheres. For just as the stones are equal in size, so are the hemispheres above and below earth; and neither is made to wane or wax like the moon. And the colour is also a witness to this, for the appearance of the whole heaven seems like an emerald as it meets the sight of men. Also six names had to be engraved on each of the stones, since each of the hemispheres also splits the zodiac into two and takes over six zodiacal signs.

(De Vit. Mos. II. 122–123)

The emeralds again feature as representing the hemispheres and the divided zodiac in *Quis Heres* 176; *QE* II.109. Set into the ephod is a breastplate, Hebrew *ḥôšen*. According to *De Spec. Leg.* I. 86, 94, both these items symbolize the heaven. The breastplate contained twelve precious stones in four rows of three. These are of different colours, and symbolize the circle of the zodiac, each group of three stones indicating the four seasons which recur according to stable principle (*De Vit. Mos.* II. 124; *De Spec. Leg.* I. 87). LXX had referred to this breastplate as *logeion*, 'place of reason'; and Philo explains that the stones were fixed there since

> the transitions and seasons of the year take place through reason (*logos*) which is ordered and steadfast. Here is a fact most strange: through the change of seasons is demonstrated their eternal duration.
>
> (*De Vit. Mos.* II. 125)

The breastplate–*logeion* itself is made doubled (Exod. 28:16), and represents the fact that reason is two-fold both in the universe and in human beings. In the former, reason deals with both the archetypal ideas from which the sensible world was made, and with the visible things which are copies of the intelligible world. In human beings, reason may both immanent in thought, and expressed in rational speech (*De Vit. Mos.* II. 127). The Bible orders that the mysterious oracle called Urim and Thummim be placed in the breastplate–*logeion* (Exod. 28:30). LXX rendered this oracle as *dēlōsis kai alētheia*, 'clear-showing and truth', allowing Philo to comment that these particular qualities are appropriate for the breastplate which is made four-square. For in each person reason is both immanent as thought and expressed as speech: 'clear-showing' is the quality proper for thought, 'truth' that most applicable to uttered speech (*De Vit. Mos.* II. 128–129; cf. *De Spec. Leg.* I. 89–92, where 'truth' and 'clear-showing' are explained as earthly representations of celestial bodies and heavenly realities; see also *Legum Allegoria* III. 118f.). Once more, the cosmos and the rational element in human beings are brought together in Philo's exposition of this ancient oracle.

On his head the high priest wears a tiara (*kidaris*), signifying that while he acts as priest he is superior to all, even kings (*De Vit. Mos.* II. 131). Already ben Sira had alluded to the royal aspects of the high priest's office, with special reference to his attire; it seems that

Philo has further developed these traditional notions.[14] Above the tiara is the golden plate bearing the Name of God, for nothing can subsist without invocation of His Name, since His goodness and merciful power constitute the harmony of all things (*De Vit. Mos.* II. 132). Philo sums up the meaning of the high priest's attire as follows:

> In this way the high priest is adorned (*diakosmêtheis*) and sent forth for his holy task, so that whenever he enters (the sanctuary) offering the ancestral prayers and sacrifices the whole universe (*kosmos*) may enter with him by means of those copies which he bears upon himself: the ankle-length robe being a copy of the air, the pomegranate of water, the flowery border of earth, the scarlet of fire, the ephod of heaven, the circular emeralds ... of the two hemispheres according to their form, the twelve stones on the breastplate in four rows of threes a copy of the zodiac, the *logeion* a copy of what holds together and governs everything. For it was necessary that the one consecrated as priest to the Father of the world should need the son [i.e., the world], most perfect in virtue, as advocate, both so that there should be no remembrance of sins, and an abundance of plentiful good things.[15] Perhaps, again, he is teaching the worshipper of God in advance that, even if he is not worthy of the Maker of the universe, he should at any rate try without ceasing to be worthy of the universe, a copy of which he wears: he is thus obliged to carry as an image the pattern in his heart, and so in some manner be changed from man into the nature of the universe and ... himself be a little universe.
>
> (*De Vit. Mos.* II. 133–135)

More succinctly, in *De Spec. Leg.* I. 95–96 he remarks that the garments are a copy of the universe, an 'icon' of the All which the high priest wears, so that by contemplation of it he may make his own life worthy of the sum total of things, and that in the Temple Service the whole cosmos may perform the liturgy with him. Being consecrated to the Father of the world, the high priest takes with him the world, which is the Father's son, for the worship (*therapeia*) of the creator and begetter of all things.

In *De Spec. Leg.* I, Philo offers a general overview of the sacrificial system. The sacrifice of a goat of sin offering at each festival he explains as symbolizing the removal from the soul of sin and the passions: Jewish feasts are sober affairs (cf. Josephus, *Cont. Ap.* II. 195), and the worshipper, seeking freedom from sin, is less inclined to return to it (190–193). Philo describes the rituals of the three basic form of animal offering, the whole burnt sacrifice, the peace offering, and the sin offering, along with the offerings for praise and guilt which are variants of the peace offering and sin offering respectively (194, 198–199, 212–215, 224–233, 234–241). In general, there are two reasons for sacrifice: it is offered to give honour to God, and to procure for human beings a share in God's good things and riddance from evils. The three basic forms of sacrifice he conforms to this scheme: the God-directed whole burnt offering is single, as God is one, all of it being offered to God; while the peace offerings and sin offerings, concerned with people, are two in number, the peace offering being offered to seek God's blessings, the sin offering for release from sin (195–197).

In this same work, Philo explains the significance of the rituals in accordance with his understanding of how human beings are composed, and the parts which body and soul ought to play in an approach to God. Thus the male animal required for the whole burnt offering signifies completeness, and corresponds to the rational principle in mankind: it is the offering to God alone of the highest sacrifice (200–201). By laying hands on the victim, the offerer expresses a good mind and blameless character (this is developed at length, 202–204), the blood of the animal being poured at the altar in a circle, the perfect figure: for blood is life, and the ritual action expresses the will of the mind to serve God completely (204–205). The entrails of the victims are washed, a symbol of the purification of lusts and appetites from the offerer: the feet are washed, signifying that they now are to tread the 'upper air', the soul of the offerer passing from earth to heaven to be in company with the harmonious movements of the sun, moon, and stars over whom God reigns as king (206–207). The divided portions of the victim indicate that all things come from and return to One: when creatures meditate on the One God, they perceive his powers to be many, and the division of the animal signifies this and man's thanksgiving for it (208–211).

The peace offering does not, however, consign heart and brains, the seat of the ruling principle in man, to the altar. Why should this be? Because, says Philo, the ruling principle can initiate sin, foolishness, and injustice, and no one would wish these to be remembered through an act of sacrifice (212–215). The offering of the kidneys, liver-lobe, and fat, however, symbolize the offering to God of what is richest (i.e., fat), the generative principle (i.e., kidneys), and the producer of blood which is life (i.e., liver), this last organ also acting as a sieve removing impurities and being closely related to the prophetic mind (216–220). Being now God's property, the peace offering must not be allowed to go rotten: it preserves the body and the soul, these two parts; thus it must be consumed within three days (222–223). The praise offering, a variant of the peace offering, gives thanks to God for his benefits, and must be consumed in one day (224–225). As for the guilt offering, its flesh is consumed by the priests to honour the givers of the sacrifice, and to reassure them that they are forgiven; for God would not implicate the priests in sin, and their eating of the victim is a sure sign that the sin has been pardoned (242–243).

A section on the Nazirite vow (247–254) leads to discussion of purity: in offering sacrifice, the body must be free of defilement, and the soul of passions. The soul is purified by the sacrifices, the body by ablutions. Indeed, the unblemished nature of the animal, and the careful scrutiny of it to ascertain its fitness for sacrifice, suggests the self-examination of the offerer and rigorous purification of soul (257–260). As regards purification of the body, Philo concentrates on the ritual of the red heifer, which is slaughtered and burnt, and whose ashes are mixed with water to purify persons of corpse-uncleanness (see Num. 19). In this instance Philo explains the meaning of the rite before he describes it: man is made of earth, ashes, and water, of things of little worth. He should recognize this, and turn from self-deception to know himself and who he is. This ritual expresses most eloquently Philo's sense of the need for human beings realistically to appraise their true character and make-up as they come into the divine presence (262–266).

THE TAMID LAMBS AND ASSOCIATED OFFERINGS

The daily Service was made up of a complex of rites, which included the sacrifice of the lambs, the offering of incense, and the preparation of the lamps on the seven-branched candlestick. The meaning of the two lambs, one offered in the morning and the other at evening, is unambiguous as far as Philo is concerned. They act as thanksgiving for the benefits which God bestows by day and night. He does not allude to the idea that they might atone for sins committed in the day and in the night (see Targum PJ of Num. 28:4; *Num. Rabb.* 21:17). Indeed, the Tamid seems to be part of that universal thanksgiving which Philo regards as characteristic of the Temple Service: most probably, therefore, he believed that it should derive from the public revenues of the Temple, as stipulated by *m. Sheq.* 4:4; *Sifre Num.* 142; *b. Men.* 65a; PJ of Num. 28:2, and given by Josephus (*Ant.* III. 237) as standard practice in the first century AD.[16]

> But since some of the sacrifices are on behalf of the whole nation, or, if one must speak the truth, on behalf of the whole race of men; and others are on behalf of each person among those who think it fit to perform the sacred rites, we must speak first about the public sacrifices. The order of these is marvellous. For some are offered day by day, others on the seventh days, others at new moons and at the sacred months, others at fasts, others on the three occasions of festivals.
>
> So then, day by day two lambs are prescribed for offering, the one at dawn, the other at the latter part of the evening. Both are for thanksgiving, the one for the benefits of the day, the other for those granted by night, which God supplies to the race of men never-endingly and continuously.
>
> (*De Spec. Leg.* I. 168–169)

The Tamid also illustrates, for Philo, the radical importance of equality as a virtue. He records how Moses demonstrates that it is essential for true justice, and lists many examples contained in the Torah which he gave to Israel. These include God's division of time into night and day and the human race into man and woman. Likewise, there are two cherubim on either side of the Ark, and the Ten Commandments are equally distributed on two tablets of stone. He then turns to the Tamid.

> Otherwise, you perceive that the continual sacrifices as well are divided into equal parts, both in respect of the offering of fine flour which the priests present for themselves, and as regards the sacrifice of the two lambs which it is prescribed to offer on behalf of the nation. The law orders that one should sacrifice one half of the said offerings in the morning, and the other in the late evening, so that God be thanked for

the good things which are showered on all both by day and by night.

(Quis Heres 174)

Leaving the lambs themselves, we may turn to the offering of incense on the golden altar in the Holy Place, which formed an essential element of the daily Service. The Mishnah (*Yoma* 2:4; *Tamid* 5:2) states that priests were chosen by lot to offer the incense, a duty which seems to have been especially coveted. The offerer would necessarily draw close to the curtain separating the Holy of Holies from the Holy Place, and might thus be privileged to receive a message from God or from an angel, like the priest Zechariah according to Luke 1:9–23.

> And twice each day the sweetest-smelling of all incenses is offered within the veil at the rising and setting of the sun, both before the sacrifice offered at dawn and after the evening sacrifice. So the offerings with blood are a thanksgiving for the blood-element in ourselves (*or*: . . . a thanksgiving for us, who have blood in ourselves), while the incense offerings are a thanksgiving for the guiding principle, the rational spirit in us which was formed according to the archetypal model of the divine image.
>
> *(De Spec. Leg.* I. 171)

(The altar of burnt-offering was of stone.) But the other was constructed of the purest gold, and fixed in the inmost shrine within the first veil. It is visible to none of the others, but only to those of the priests who are purified; and it does service for the incense offerings. From this it is evident that God considers even the smallest grain of incense offered by a holy man more worthy than myriads of beasts, which someone may offer when he is not at all proper. For I believe that in the same measure as gold is better than common stones, and the things in the inmost sanctuary more holy than those outside, so the thanksgiving made through the incense offerings is superior to that made through creatures with blood in them.

Wherefore the altar of incense is honoured not only in the great expense of its material, its construction, and its position, but also in serving first each day the thank offerings of men to God. For it is not permitted to offer the whole burnt offerings outside (that is, in the court) before the incense is offered at first light. Now this is a symbol of nothing other than this: what is dear in God's sight is not the number of sacrificed beasts, but the purest, rational spirit of the one who offers sacrifice.

(ibid. I. 274–277)

The matter of equality, which Philo had illustrated in the case of the two Tamid lambs, is also exemplified in the composition of the incense offered daily; and further number symbolism is invoked to explain the proportions of the ingredients.

Equality, indeed, is nobly displayed in the composition of the incense offerings. For it is said: 'Take for yourself sweet-smelling things, stacte, cloves, and sweet galbanum and clear frankincense, an equal weight of each; and they shall make it into incense, a perfume work of the perfumer of pure composition, a holy work.' For he says that each of the parts must come together to each other equally to make the blending of the two. And I believe that these four, of which the incense is made up, are symbols of the elements out of which the whole universe was completed. For he compares stacte with water, and cloves with earth, and galbanum with air, and clear frankincense with fire. For stacte is like water because of its drops; cloves are dry and like earth; 'sweet' is added to galbanum to refer to the air, for there is a sweet smell in air; and 'clear' is added to frankincense to demonstrate light.

(Quis Heres 196–197)

Philo continues (ibid. 198) by noting how Moses carefully uses language in describing the assembly of the ingredients, so as to set the heavy components stacte and cloves, representing water and earth, apart from the light ones galbanum and frankincense:

So it turns out that the orderly composition and mixture of these things is the oldest and most perfect work, holy, truth to tell – namely the universe. This, he believes, ought to give thanks to the One who has made it by means of the symbol of the incense offering; so that the composition prepared by the perfumer's art is in principle offered as incense, but in fact the whole universe, wrought by divine wisdom, is offered in the morning and evening as a whole burnt offering. For it is a suitable life for the universe, to give thanks to its father

121

and maker unremittingly and continuously by burning itself
as incense and resolving itself into a single substance as
proof that it treasures up nothing, but sets forth itself completely as a votive offering to the God who begot it.

(Quis Heres 199–200)

In the following passage, Philo incorporates the altar of incense
into his understanding of the ritual:

the altar (of incense), as was shown earlier, is reckoned as
thanksgiving for the elements, since it actually possesses parts
of the four. The wood is of the earth, the incense offering is
of water (for first it is melted and then dissolved into liquids),
the vapour is of air, and what is kindled is of fire; and the
composition of frankincense, galbanum, cloves, and stacte is
a symbol of the elements.

(ibid. 226)

Philo contrasts the altar of burnt offering in the outer court with
the altar of incense set in the inner sanctuary. Moses wished to
symbolize virtues of both body and soul, and to indicate thereby
their perfections. The outer altar, visible to all, pays attention to
things of the body which are good, but of secondary
importance.

But when he (the wise man) is present at the inner altar, he
will be familiar with all things bloodless, without flesh, without body, with things deriving from reason alone, which are
represented by frankincense and the incense offerings. For
just as these fill the nostrils, so those things fill the whole
region of the soul.

(De Ebrietate 87)

The positioning of the furniture in the inmost sanctuary is also
symbolically significant:

In the middle is the altar of incense, a symbol of thanksgiving for earth and water which it is fitting should be made for
the things which come from both of these. For these have
been allotted the middle position of the universe.

(De Vit. Mos. II. 101)

The symbols of heaven and earth are set in line (with the
table) . . ., the candlestick a symbol of heaven, the burner of

vapours, as it is literally called, a symbol of the earthy things
from which arise vapours.

(ibid. II. 105)

Philo refers the incense and incense altar to the cosmos, which
under these symbols gives thanks to God: the altar may also represent earth and water in their thanksgiving. The incense may also
signify the intellect and the moral sense in their giving of thanks.
Thus while much of what is said about the incense may derive
from Philo's principles set out in his general understanding of the
Temple Service, earlier Jewish writers of Second Temple times had
already closely associated the incense with the wise who are occupied in study of the Torah, and with Wisdom itself. Thus ben Sira,
who places Lady Wisdom in the sanctuary on Zion ministering in
the holy tabernacle before the Lord, had directly compared her
with incense and its component spices galbanum, onyx, and stacte
(24:15), and urged his pupils, no doubt students of the Torah
which is Wisdom, to give out a smell like that of incense (39:14). In
this connection, it should be emphasized that the Bible explicitly
notes that the incense is to be offered in the sanctuary directly in
front of the place where God meets with Moses (Exod. 36:6).
Incense, therefore, is in close proximity to the Divine Presence, and
comparison with it of Wisdom and her students who give out a
smell like incense places them at but a single remove from the
Almighty Himself. Similarly, the document from Qumran Cave 4
formerly called Florilegium, now more often styled A Midrash on
the Last Days (4Q174), speaks of the mysterious *mqdš 'dm* (meaning probably 'a sanctuary of men') which God has ordered to be
built for Himself, in which they offer up before Him like incense
(*mqṭyrym*) deeds of Torah.[17] The association of the Sages occupied
in Torah study with incense is attested also in Rabbinic texts such
as *b. Men.* 110a (R. Samuel bar Nahmani in the name of R. Jonathan) and PJ of Exod. 40:5. It is therefore possible that the already
existing idea that incense has some affinity with study and intel-
lectual activity may have influenced Philo's exegesis of the daily
ritual.

The ordering of the seven-branched candlestick (Menorah) and
its seven lamps also took place each morning, and thus formed an
integral part of the priests' duties for the Tamid (*m. Tamid* 3:1, 6).
Once more, the candlestick symbolizes heaven (*De Vit. Mos.* II.
105). Philo stresses the sacrificial significance of the lights kindled

123

and their cosmic affinities: they are compared with the stars, themselves ministers in 'the temple of the universe', as noted above, *De Spec. Leg.* I. 66–67. Again, in another passage (*De Spec. Leg.* I. 114) quoted earlier, we learn that the high priest is the taxiarch, 'commander' of the heavenly *taxis*, the host or rank of celestial armies: these are clearly related to the stars in the material quoted below. It should be noted how in this way Philo relates the high priest in his ministry to things super-terrestrial in a manner recalling the description of the high priest as 'another man from outside the world' in *Aristeas* 99.

> Again he orders that lamps on the holy candlestick within the veil be burning from evening until early morning, for several reasons. One is so that the holy places should be lighted from the succession of the daily light in the likeness of the stars, never being partakers of darkness. For these, when the sun has set, show forth their own light, not leaving the order (*taxin*) in which they are stationed (*etachthēsan*) in the universe.
>
> There is another reason also: that at night something of a brother and kinsman to the daily sacrifices might be ritually discharged for the purpose of pleasing God, and that no time or occasion should neglect thanksgiving. So the sacrifice of thanksgiving most suitable and most fitted for the night (for it is fitting to call it a sacrifice) is the gleam of the most sacred light in the inmost sanctuary.
>
> And a third and very compelling reason is the following. For not only when we are awake are we well treated, but also when we are asleep; since the bountiful God supplies for our mortal race a great assistance, sleep, as an advantage for both body and soul. The body is freed from daily toils, and the soul relieves itself of cares and retires into itself from the crowd and noise of the senses; and then, at any rate, can it be private and keep company with itself. The law judged appropriately that the thank offerings be portioned out, those for waking-time through the sacred victims which are offered, and those for sleep and the advantages arising from it through the kindling of the sacred lamps.
>
> (*De Spec. Leg.* I. 296–298)

These explanations of the lights and candlestick are of a piece with what Philo has said already about the incense and its altar, especially in so far as all these things express thanksgiving to God.

Somewhat different, however, is the extended discussion in *QE* II. 73–81. There, the several parts of the candlestick are referred to heavenly objects in turn. The pure gold of which the candlestick is made refers to the heavenly quintessence: it is of 'turned work', figuring the periodic cycles; like heaven, it is a unit with many members. Its oblique branches resemble the zodiac: the centre branch represents the sun, with three planets above it, and three below. The decorative cups, balls, and flowers represent respectively the zodiac signs of each season, the cosmic sphere, and the seasons. The seven lamps symbolize the seven planets, whose paths are in the south whence they give light, their shadow falling in the northern region. Their light derives from the celestial sphere.

All this, suggests E. R. Goodenough, derives not from Philo himself, but from 'allegorists' to whom he has earlier referred (*QE* II. 71), the latter indebted to Chaldean or Stoic astronomy.[18] In addition, we may note a reference to 'natural philosophers' in his comments on the candlestick in another place, which again includes mention of the south as the place where the planets have their courses:

> He placed the candlestick in the south, through which he hints figuratively at the movement of the light-bearing stars; for the sun and moon and the rest make their courses in the south, very far removed from the north. From there, then, six branches, three from either side, issue forth from the central lampstand to make up the number seven. And on all of them are seven lamps and candlesticks, symbols of the planets so-called by the natural philosophers. For the sun, just like the candlestick, is ordered in fourth place as the middle of the six, and gives light equally to the three above and to those below it, governing that musical instrument which is in truth divine.
>
> (*De Vit. Mos.* II. 102–103)

It is indeed possible that Philo has derived some of these ideas from non-Jewish sources, although Jewish texts later than Philo's time attest the idea that the paths of the planets are in the south (PJ of Exod. 40:4; cf. *b. Baba Bathra* 25b). With *QE* II. 73–81, Goodenough contrasts what Philo says in *De Congressu* 8. There, the candlestick gives light only from that part which looks towards God, the seventh part, placed in the midst of the other six branches: it sends its rays upwards to God, as if the light were too bright for human sight. The setting for these remarks is a discussion of Sarai's change of name to Sarah, the latter signifying one who is virginal in respect of both God and man; and it should be pointed out that Philo here states explicitly that the heavenly archetype of the candlestick, not its earthly replica in the Temple, is under consideration. This may go some way to explaining the differences between the various passages, although Philo is elsewhere capable of slight variations in his explanations of the Temple furniture.

Goodenough also comments on a lengthy section in *Quis Heres* 216–228 which is informed by Philo's theory of creation by bisection.[19] His concern with the equal division of things leads him to a consideration of opposites, and the fact that 'oppositeness' is a constant fact of creation: see further ben Sira 33:14–15; 42:24. Philo can attribute the 'theory of opposites' expounded by the philosopher Heracleitus to Moses (*Quis Heres* 213–214), since the candlestick which he constructed illustrates how six is divided into two opposite groups of three by the central lamp-holder in the Menorah which represents the Logos, itself both a divider and the cohesive force in the universe. When God made a covenant with Abraham, Gen. 15:9–10 records how three sacrificial beasts were divided into two parts and placed opposite each other, the mysterious light walking between these six pieces (Gen. 15:17) being the seventh, the Logos who divides the victims. The candlestick represents the same truth for Philo, the middle branch making a seventh which divides equally the other six branches into two threes on either side of it (*Quis Heres* 207, 219). Once more its lamps represent the planets, the central lamp being the sun, the rest serving this: above it are lights representing Saturn, Jupiter, and Mars, with Mercury, Venus, and the Moon below (*Quis Heres* 221–224). Finally, Philo returns to a well-worn theme:

> And the candlestick represents thanksgiving for all the things in heaven, so that no part of the universe incur guilt of unthankfulness; but that we may know that all the parts which are in it give thanks – the elements and the full-formed creatures, not only the ones on earth, but also those in heaven.
>
> (*Quis Heres* 226)

Philo's lengthy exposition of the candlestick's various meanings contrasts with the near silence of his Jewish predecessors about this object, prompting the question of why he should be so concerned with it? The candlestick seems to inform several of Philo's concerns. Thus it speaks of light as a divine gift; of a cosmos ordered in all its parts giving thanks to its creator; of illumination of the rational element in the human soul by divine action; and of God's presence in the created world along with His Logos, the active principle in creation. It is also possible that Philo found the symbolism of the candlestick useful for apologetic purposes. Thus it proves that Moses anticipated the theory of opposites later embraced by Heracleitus (*Quis Rerum* 214), and shows that Jews, no less than Gentiles, are *au fait* with the astronomical knowledge of their day. One writer earlier than Philo, however, had alluded to the Menorah. Hecataeus of Abdera, in a work no doubt intended for Gentile readers, had spoken of 'an inextinguishable light' in the Temple; and it is possible that Philo felt called to elaborate and explain this statement.[20] That he was aware of the work attributed to Hecataeus is suggested by *De Spec. Leg.* I. 74, which like the former refers to the lack of any grove (*alsos*) in the Temple, and seeks to explain this curiosity.[21] His evident high regard for the candlestick may also be connected with the growing importance of this object in the Diaspora, as a recognizable symbol of Jewish religion and national identity.

THE TAMID OFFERING OF THE SABBATH

The Torah orders that the two lambs for the Tamid are to be supplemented by two further lambs each Sabbath (Num. 28:9–10). Philo regards the Sabbath as a festival of the universe, not of a single city or country, which alone of festivals may properly be called 'public' (*pandêmos*): it is, indeed, the 'birthday of the cosmos', *tou kosmou genethlion* (*De Opificio Mundi* 89). This is explained further in *De Spec. Leg.* II. 59: the seventh day was that on which the world, God's handiwork of six days, was revealed as fully completed. Israel in the desert wanderings rediscovered this truth when the manna was supplied to them in *double* measure on Sabbath (*De Vit. Mos.* I. 207). The Sabbath, indeed, was a privileged day even before the beginning of heaven and all sensible things (ibid. II. 263). All this is presupposed in what follows:

> But on the seventh day he doubles the number of the victims by adding like to like, since he regards the seventh day (which

indeed he publicly recorded as the birthday of the universe) as equal in honour to eternity. For this reason he intended to make the sacrifice of the seventh day like the 'perpetuity' of the daily sacrifice of lambs.

(De Spec. Leg. I. 170)

Confirming the Sabbath's privilege was the provision on that day of new Bread of the Presence on the golden table in the sanctuary, the removal of the old bread, and its consumption by the priests: incense accompanied this bread, and was offered on the altar as its 'memorial' (Lev. 24:5–9). The table on which these things lay was covered with pure gold and provided with plates, dishes, and bowls, likewise of pure gold (Exod. 25:23–30; 37:10–16). The table and its bread do not feature prominently in post-biblical writings earlier than Philo; from him, however, they merit special treatment, for which some explanation is required. We may begin with the cosmic significance which Philo attributes to the bread, which will not strike the reader as wholly unexpected. To this explanation, however, he appends a more 'philosophical' understanding of the loaves as symbolic of a particular virtue.

And loaves are set forth on the seventh days upon the holy table, equal in number to the months of the year, in two settings of six (twelve), each setting by analogy with the equinoxes: for there are two in each year, both spring and autumn, which are reckoned as six months. For this reason ... [in the spring] all that has been sown comes to completion when the trees begin to bear fruit; and in the autumn also the fruit of the trees comes to perfection, at the same time as sowing again begins to take place. So nature runs her course through the ages and gives in turn some gifts, then others, to the human race. The double groupings of the loaves in sixes are set forth as symbols.

They also indicate in a figure self-control (*enkrateia*), the most advantageous of the virtues, which keeps guard upon thrift, contentment, and frugality against the most harmful fortress of licentiousness and greed. For bread is sufficient nourishment for a lover of wisdom, furnishing bodies without disease and reason healthy and sober in the highest degree.

(De Spec. Leg. I. 172–173)

Mention of 'self-control' permits Philo immediately to indulge in polemic against luxurious foods (*De Spec. Leg.* I. 174); but he will return to this virtue many times, finally extolling its practice by the Therapeutae (see below, p. 131), whom he regards as living the very life of self-control and frugality which the Bread of the Presence symbolizes. For the present, however, he resumes the theme of self-control in relation to the table:

> And on the loaves are set together incense and salt. The first is a symbol that there is no seasoning more sweet-smelling than frugality and self-control (*enkrateia*) when wisdom is acting as judge. And the salt is a symbol of the durability of all things (for it preserves whatever it is sprinkled upon), and of a sufficient relish.
>
> (*De Spec. Leg.* I. 175)

The Hebrew Bible does not order salt to be placed on the table. Philo here follows LXX, who do so order in their version of Lev. 24:7. They were probably moved to include salt in the arrangements because the bread is among 'the most holy things' (Lev. 24:9), that is, in the category of sacrificial offerings of the highest degree of sanctity; and all sacrifices must be salted with salt (Lev. 2:13). The bread also constitutes a kind of covenant (Lev. 24:8), which some Scriptural verses associate with salt (Lev. 2:13; Num. 18:19). These matters, however, appear not to interest Philo at this point, who concentrates his attentions on incense as a symbol of fragrant frugality, and on salt as representing durability. The latter, however, is also a relish, a point he will reiterate in his treatise on the Therapeutae.

In other passages Philo makes the loaves represent the twelve tribes, in each adding points of further information.

> This unleavened food is so holy, that in the oracles it is ordained that twelve unleavened loaves, equal in number to the tribes, should be set forth on the golden table in the inmost shrine; and they are called 'the bread of setting forth'.
>
> (*De Cong.* 168)

The setting forth of twelve loaves on the holy table, equal in number to the tribes, confirms most clearly what has been said already. For they are all unleavened, the clearest example

of unmixed food which has been prepared not by artifice for
pleasure, but by nature for what is necessary for use.

(De Spec. Leg. II. 161)

You see also the loaves set forth on the holy table, how the
twelve are distributed by number into equal parts and placed
in groups of six, memorials of the twelve tribes. Leah, representing virtue, is mother of six tribal leaders and in possession of half of these; the children of Rachel and the illegitimate children of the concubines represent the other half.

(Quis Heres 175)

The first of these passages seeks to explain the LXX's description
of the loaves as 'bread of the setting forth': it translates the
Hebrew 'bread of arrangement', that is, the bread set out in order
upon the table (see LXX Exod. 40:23) and 'Bread of the Presence',
that is, bread laid before the Holy of Holies where God's earthly
Presence dwells (see LXX Exod. 39:17). The second states that the
bread was unleavened, a detail not found explicitly in Scripture, but
made clear by the Mishnah (*Men.* 5:1–3). Philo makes much of this:
it is the purest, simplest, most sincere and unmixed of foods, appropriate for the priestly class, who represent those whose souls
have advanced to the noblest practice of virtue and are attuned to
the divine world. Indeed, he links the unleavened bread of the
Passover festival, which represents a return to the simple, frugal,
and austere life of the world's original population, with the Bread
of the Presence:

The setting forth of the twelve loaves on the holy table,
which are equal in number to the tribes, particularly confirms
what has been said. For they are all unleavened, the clearest
example of unmixed food which has been prepared not by
artifice for pleasure, but by nature for necessary use.

(De Spec. Leg. II. 161)

Again commenting on the unleavened bread of Passover, called
'bread of affliction' in Deut. 16:3, he remarks that unleavened
bread has a particular sanctity:

This unleavened food is so holy that it is prescribed by the
oracles that twelve unleavened loaves, equal in number to the
tribes, be set forth on the golden table in the innermost
shrine; and they are called 'bread of setting forth'.

(De Cong. 168)

Philo holds in highest regard a group of Jewish ascetic contemplatives resident in Egypt and called Therapeutae, speaking of them as living 'in soul alone', 'citizens of heaven and of the world', united to the creator by virtue and possessed even now of the highest happiness (*De Vit. Cont.* 90). For the most part solitaries, they met on Sabbaths and festivals to share the simplest of foods: water, bread, salt as an additional course, and hyssop for the fastidious.[22] On the annual feast most dear to them (in all probability Pentecost), this meal assumes special significance, Philo relating it directly to the Bread of the Presence ritual in the Temple:

> The young ones . . . bring in a table on which is the most holy food, leavened bread with an additional course of salt, with which hyssop has been mixed, out of respect for the holy table set forth in the sacred hall of the temple. For on the latter are loaves and salt without seasoning, the loaves being unleavened, and the salt unmixed. For it was fitting that the simplest and sincerest things (*heilikrinestata*) should be allotted by portion to the highest class of the priests as a reward for ministry; but that others should emulate what is similar, while abstaining from what is exactly the same so that their betters might have their privilege.
>
> (*De Vit. Cont.* 81–82)

Whether the association of this meal with the Bread of the Presence represents the opinion of the Therapeutae themselves, or is founded on Philo's own interpretation, is impossible to tell. As we have seen, salt is not included in the ritual as ordered by the Hebrew Bible, but is introduced by the LXX translators. Hyssop nowhere features in comments about the bread elsewhere; and here Philo is at pains to point out that the Therapeutae eat leavened bread and mixed salt. This may well suggest that he himself is responsible, if not for linking this meal to the Bread of the Presence, then at least for the individual details of the comparison. In any event, Philo hereby indicates a belief in a kind of replication of Temple ritual by persons outside the Temple. That he should entertain such a notion is quite logical, since we have seen how often he is able to suggest meanings for aspects of the Service which are drawn from the interior development and activity of the virtuous human soul. His interpretation of the incense offering discussed earlier well illustrates the point.[23]

Despite these elevated and solemn interpretations of the bread,

Philo does not lose sight of the more mundane, yet ultimately fundamental significance which they bear. In this, he is at one with tradition committed to writing after his time, preserved in PJ of Exod. 40:4; *b. Baba Bathra* 25b.

> Now the table is set towards the north, on which are loaves and salt, since the north winds are most productive of nourishment, and because victuals issue from heaven and earth, the first giving rain, the second bringing to full growth the seeds with the help of the streams of water.
>
> (*De Vit. Mos.* II. 104)

> And the table represents the thanksgiving for completely formed mortal creatures; for loaves and libations, which things having need of nourishment necessarily require for use, are placed on it.
>
> (*Quis Heres* 226)

Once more, Philo has devoted time and space to a matter which his predecessors hardly noted. There can be little doubt that his interest in ascetic practice and mystical contemplation has played its part in this: the bread represents *enkrateia*, that 'self-control' which, he tells us, is characteristic of the Therapeutae (*De Vit. Cont.* 34–36). It evokes simplicity, being *heilikrinestatos*, 'most sincere, most simple, most unmixed (ibid. 82) in exactly the manner of the *heilikrinestatos* God the Therapeutae worship (ibid. 2). This God is the active cause of all things, the *heilikrinestatos* and most unsullied mind of the universe, surpassing virtue, knowledge, and the good (*De Op. Mun.* 8). In their great annual meal, consuming loaves suggestive of the Bread of the Presence, the Therapeutae emulate the priests: as Philo reminds us, robed in his vestments, the high priest bears the cosmos into God's presence to offer *therapeia*, 'worship', to the Creator of All (*De Spec. Leg.* I. 96). As he constantly asserts, this privilege is accorded only to the virtuous soul which advances through ascetic practice to a knowledge of the Divine; and the Bread of the Presence provides Philo with a powerful symbol for one of the most important elements in his philosophy.

Yet the symbolic significance of the loaves as representing God's gift of food brought by the north wind is recorded elsewhere in Jewish tradition, and may suggest that Philo owes this perception to a commonly held belief. The twelve loaves also serve as a bridge between the twelve tribes of Israel and the twelve months of the year, since in Philo's view they symbolize both. The association of the twelve months with the tribes, however, is attested earlier by Jubilees, which asserts this as a necessary prerequisite for the full establishing of Israel's priestly service.[24]

THE SERVICES FOR FESTIVALS

Passover and unleavened bread

The spring festival of Pesaḥ (Passover) is described in detail in *De Spec. Leg.* II. 144–175. Philo sometimes expounds Pesaḥ, rendered in Greek as Pascha, by calling it *ta diabatêria* (so *De Spec. Leg.* II. 145, 147; *De Vit. Mos.* II. 224), a technical term drawn from Greek religion referring to sacrifices made by persons about to cross a boundary or a river. Sometimes he calls the feast *diabasis* (so *Legum Allegoria* III. 94; *De Abrahamo* 25), 'a crossing over, a passing over'. Both literal and allegorical senses are explored. On the one hand, the feast (as in the biblical account) celebrates Israel's departure from Egyptian slavery into freedom under divine protection (*De Spec. Leg.* II. 146); on the other hand, this crossing is easily allegorized into a separation from the passions of Egypt (*Leg. All.* III. 94). It thus symbolizes the turning away of the mind from enslaving passions to give thanks to God who has saved it and brought it to freedom (*De Mig. Abr.* 25). It symbolizes purification of the soul, and its passing from the body and the passions (*De Spec. Leg.* II. 147, where this opinion is explicitly attributed to allegorists; *De Cong.* 106).

The Bible indicates that, in Second Temple times, non-priests retained the privilege of slaughtering the Passover victim, while the priests sprinkled the blood (2 Chr. 30:15–16). Philo makes much of this, noting that on this day the whole people (*ho leôs hapas*) is counted worthy of priestly office (*De Spec. Leg.* II.145; *De Vit. Mos.* II. 224) and permitted to do what is normally reserved for priests alone.[25] His explanation of this otherwise extraordinary procedure leads him to contradict the Bible, according to which the Passover victims were killed before Israel's departure from Egypt (Exod. 12). Philo, on the contrary, asserts that the multitude of Israelites who had fled Egypt were so eager to give thanks that they offered sacrifice without the priests, and the law ordered them to do likewise for the future as a reminder of thanksgiving (*De Spec. Leg.* II. 146). For this occasion, the ordinary house assumes the form and dignity of the Temple, those taking part in the meal being in a state of purity (*De Spec. Leg.* II. 148).

Following the biblical narrative (Exod. 12:14–20), he naturally considers the Feast of Unleavened Bread (Maẓẓot) along with Passover, noting its association with the Exodus, but also relating the feast to the harmony of the whole universe (*De Spec. Leg.* II. 150). In this latter connection Philo notes that Maẓẓot is celebrated in what Scripture terms 'the first month', even though in the Jewish calendar of his and our day it is actually the seventh month.[26] It occurs at the spring equinox: he also notes that Pesaḥ falls then (*De Vit. Mos.* II. 222). Philo perceives in this time of year a 'representation and copy' of the beginning, when the world was created (*De Spec. Leg.* II. 151). God reminds people of the creation; and the month is styled 'first' by Scripture because it is like an image of the first beginning, as if impressed from an archetypical seal (*De Spec. Leg.* II. 152; and see also *QE* I.1). Philo therefore appears to be an early representative of the view that the world was created in Nisan, which R. Joshua upholds against the opinion of R. Eliezer that it was created in Tishri (*b. Rosh Ha Shanah* 11a; *Ber. Rab.* 22:4; and cf. *De Spec. Leg.* II. 153–154).[27]

The seven days of Maẓẓot reflect the seven days of creation (*De Spec. Leg.* II. 156), the first and last of these being called holy. Philo once more draws on musical imagery to expound this detail, suggesting that thereby harmony may be achieved between these days and the intermediate ones. This leads him to speculate on the feast's significance for past and future, the first day marking the end of a completed time, the seventh the end of the feast and the beginning of the future (*De Spec. Leg.* II. 157). It is possible that Philo's words on this subject echo tradition found in the Palestinian Targumim of Exod. 12:42, where the night of Pesaḥ commemorates both the past creation of the world, along with the advent of the Messiah and the future redemption.[28] At the very least, they indicate that his thoughts on Passover and Unleavened Bread have a future as well as a past reference. Indeed, the unleavened bread itself may refer to the future: having stated that the Jews left Egypt in such haste that their bread was unleavened, and that the feast recalls this event, Philo remarks that the corn at this time of year is still unripe. The unleavened, that is, 'immature' bread reflects this and encourages thoughts of future growth and maturity (*De Spec. Leg.* II. 158).

Finally, however, Philo returns to thoughts of the unleavened bread as symbolic of simplicity. The exegetes of Scripture tell him that unleavened bread is a gift of nature; and, since Pesaḥ and Maẓẓot recall the time of creation, he pictures the earliest human beings living on simple and unaltered foods, in the days before pleasure took control. Each year this original simplicity is recalled in the unleavened bread, as a summons to frugality in everyday life. As proof of this he adduces the unleavened loaves set on the holy table within the sanctuary (*De Spec. Leg.* II. 159–161).[29]

The offering of the sheaf

Philo follows LXX of Lev. 23:11 in understanding that the first sheaf of the new corn harvest was to be offered in the Temple on the morrow of first day of Pesaḥ.[30] This is an offering of first-fruits of the Jews' own land and of the whole earth; again, therefore, Jews and the whole world are united in one action, giving thanks to God. Philo drives the point home: what the priest is to the city, the nation of the Jews is to the whole world (*De Spec. Leg.* II. 162–163). This leads Philo to a critique of polytheism with its worship of created things, a common error rectified by the Jews in their service of the uncreated and the eternal (164–166). The reason for this soon appears: he is concerned to refute accusations of dislike of the human race (*apanthrôpia*) brought against Jews. Such charges, he asserts, are astonishing when Jewish prayers, festivals, and first-fruits accomplish the religious duties which the whole of humanity is obliged to carry out, but so often shirks (167). The sheaf also represents the Jews' thanksgiving that they possess their own fertile land, owned formerly by a large population: because of its wicked-ness, the latter was dispossessed, a reminder to Jews that obedience to virtue is a condition of possessing the land (168–170). Reiterat-ing humanity's obligation to thank God for the harvest (171–174), Philo records that the offered sheaf is of barley (175). This is nowhere stated in Scripture, but is attested by Josephus, *Ant.* III. 250. Wheat, in Philo's estimation, is a superior grain to barley; the latter is offered to show that this 'secondary' food is not inappropriate for first-fruits offerings, representing the necessities of life, whereas wheat is appropriate for luxury. Indeed, it is improper to consume food of any kind before due thanks has been given for it (175).

Feast of Pentecost

The sheaf-offering begins a period of counting fifty days to reach Shabu'ot, the Feast of Weeks or Pentecost. Philo regards fifty as a highly significant number, and discourses on it accordingly.[31] Most important is its association with the Therapeutae, who keep as their greatest feast that which has allotted to it the number fifty, made up of the right-angled triangle 'which is the beginning of the origin of all things'.[32] Two leavened wheat loaves are offered as first-fruits, and the name of the feast Philo understands as 'feast of first-fruits, first-products':[33] the loaves are not gifts to God, but serve as a symbol of gratitude for His bounty (*De Spec. Leg.* II. 179–180). The feast's name may also be explained as connected with wheat as the 'best' food for the best of living things (181). Leaven was normally forbidden in sacrificial offerings (see Lev. 2:11); thus Philo explains that these loaves are *sui generis*, indeed being offered at the altar, but immediately returned for the consumption of the priests on the festival day.[34] For leaven represents food in its most complete and entire form, and is appropriate for offering alongside wheat, the most superior of grains: it also rises, and is thus symbolic of rejoicing associated with thanksgiving (182–185). The two loaves represent thanksgiving for the past provision of food, and for the future hopes of God's bounty (187).

Feast of Trumpets

The day of New Year, better known as Rosh Ha-Shanah (1st Tishri), Philo calls 'feast of trumpets' (*De Spec. Leg.* I. 186; II. 188) after its description as *zikrôn terû'âh* ('memorial of a trumpet blast': Lev. 23:24), rendered by LXX as *mnêmosunon salpingôn*, 'memorial of trumpets'. He notes that the trumpet blast accompanies the sacrifices of that day, and that the day has a two-fold significance. First, for Jews it celebrates the gift of the Torah at Mount Sinai, which was accompanied by a terrifying trumpet blast (cf. Exod. 19:13, 16, 19) to the corners of the earth (*De Spec. Leg.* II. 188–189). This interpretation differs from that of the later Rabbis, who regard the Feast of Weeks as commemorating the giving of the Torah (*b. Pes.* 68b; *Shab.* 88a; *Seder 'Olam Rabbah* 5), while the first day of Tishri represents the Day of Judgement of all mankind (*m. Rosh Ha-Shanah* 1:2; *b. Rosh Ha-Shanah* 16b, 18a) and recalls the binding of Isaac (*b. Rosh Ha-Shanah* 16a). It cannot be determined whether

Philo depends on earlier tradition for the meaning he ascribes to this day, or whether he himself is responsible for linking it with the giving of the Torah.[35] Second, however, he gives a more general sense to the feast. The trumpet, he says, is used in war to signal advance to battle and retreat. Nature can make war on herself: enemies can destroy crops, and nature can equally wreak havoc with bad weather. The latter, Philo suggests, may be caused by human impiety (190–191). This feast uses the instrument of war to serve as a thanksgiving to God 'the peace-maker and peace-keeper, who destroys divisions both in the cities and in the parts of the universe and produces well-being and prosperity and abundance of other good things . . .' (192).

The Day of Atonement

Philo refers to this day (10th Tishri) as 'the Fast'. It is listed among the feasts, even though those revelries commonly associated with the latter are forbidden on this day (*De Spec. Leg.* II. 193). It is indeed the greatest of feasts, a Sabbath of Sabbaths (so LXX Lev. 16:31; 23:32), or in Greek parlance a seven of sevens (194). Philo gives three explanations of the name. The feast requires self-control (*enkrateia*) in respect of food and drink; it is entirely given over to entreaties and supplications to propitiate God and to seek pardon for voluntary and involuntary sins; and it is held when harvest is complete as a brief voluntary abstinence from the new produce, demonstrating that human beings depend on God for their sustenance rather than on food. God's miraculous gifts of food for Israel when she wandered in the desert are thus recalled (195–199). A lengthy disquisition on the significance of the number ten as all-perfect and its relationship to this temporary abstinence from food follows (*De Spec. Leg.* II. 200–204).

In *De Spec. Leg.* I. 186–189 Philo lists the sacrifices offered on this day, noting its two-fold character as feast and purification, the latter described as 'a flight from sins' (*phugê hamartêmatôn*), the merciful God granting to repentance an honour equal to non-commission of sin (187). It is here that he offers brief remarks on the best known ceremony of the day, the selection of two goats by lot, one 'for the Lord', the other (the famous so-called scapegoat) 'for Azazel' (see Lev. 16:5, 7–10). What is striking here is his complete silence about the confession of sins made by the high priest as he lays his hands on the head of the goat for Azazel (Lev. 16:21). The goat

> was sent out into pathless and untrodden wilderness, carrying upon it the curses which had been upon those who had sinned, who had been purified by changing to what is better, having washed off old lawless behaviour with new good order.
>
> (188)

LXX of Lev. 16:8, 10, 26, do not represent Azazel as a proper name. In the first two instances, they translated it as *apopompaios*, 'carrying away, sending away'; in the third, 'the goat for Azazel' becomes 'the goat that has been set apart for sending forth'.[36] Philo seems to follow LXX's understanding, the oldest post-biblical interpretation we have: the goat is both sent forth and carries away the curses. In describing the goat's destination as 'pathless and untrodden wilderness', however, Philo goes beyond LXX, and may be indebted to an early form of tradition extant in Rabbinic literature. According to *b. Yoma* 67b, *Sifra Aḥare Mot* Pereq 2:8, and PJ of Lev. 16:10, Azazel is associated with a rough and craggy place.[37] Likewise, Philo's words about repentance for sins and a change to what is better find no place in the biblical narrative; nor do we find there any suggestion that Israel has been washed, even metaphorically. Both these themes, however, find a place in Rabbinic tradition, which insists on the importance of repentance along with the Day of Atonement (*m. Yoma* 8:8–9), and declares in the name of R. Aqiba:

> Happy are you, O Israel. Before whom are you made pure? Who purifies you? Your Father who is in heaven, as it is said: 'And I shall sprinkle upon you pure water, and you shall be clean' (Ezek. 36:25). And it says, 'The hope *miqwêh* of Israel, the Lord' (Jer. 17:13). Just as the immersion-pool (*miqweh*) purifies the unclean, so the Holy One, Blessed be He, purifies Israel.
>
> (*m. Yoma* 8:9)

Feast of Tabernacles

A brief note in *De Spec. Leg.* I. 189 lists the number of victims sacrificed during the seven days of this feast, and singles out the additional eighth day (Shemini Azeret) as deserving of special discussion in the future. Philo's detailed observations may be found at *De Spec. Leg.* II. 204–213. This extended disquisition is completely silent about the rites observed in the Temple. It is possible that Philo has limited his observations to comments on the mode of celebration known to him among Alexandrian Jews, and to customs which may have been known to the Gentiles among whom they lived.[38]

New Moons and ceremony of 'the basket'

In *De Spec. Leg.* II. 41, Philo states that the Torah lists ten feasts. The fourth to the tenth of these are Passover, the offering of the sheaf, Unleavened Bread, Pentecost, Trumpets (which he calls the sacred month-day), the Day of Atonement, and Tabernacles. The first feast, 'every day', receives extended homiletic treatment in the paragraphs following the list (42–55), where no mention is made of the Tamid. Sabbath is the second feast, some of its laws and customs being set out in 56–70: to these, he appends lengthy notes on the laws of remission in the seventh ('Sabbatical') year and the year of Jubilee (71ff.), the powers and qualities of the number seven being impressed upon the reader throughout. In all this, the Temple Service is not discussed.

The third feast is New Moon. Sacrifices required for that day are set out in Num. 28:11–14. From that text, Philo (*De Spec. Leg.* I. 177) singles out first the two calves, the ram, and the seven lambs which must be offered: they add up to ten, which he regards as a perfect number, suitable for celebrating the moon's character. Two calves correspond to the moon's waxing and waning; one ram parallels the one law governing the waxing and waning; seven lambs indicate the seven changes of form which the moon undergoes each month (*De Spec. Leg.* I. 178). The meal and wine offerings associated with these sacrifices are ordered because of the moon's controlling influence over the growth and maturity of the fruits, corn, oil, and wine (179). These, and other benefits of the moon to mankind, are extolled further in *De Spec. Leg.* II. 14–144, but without reference to the Temple Service.

Although he does not list it as a feast, Philo discusses (*De Spec. Leg.* II. 215–222) the ceremony accompanying the presentation of first-fruits prescribed by Deut. 26:1–11. It is an offering of individuals, not of the nation, and the offerer, or the priest acting on his behalf, recites a special formula (Deut. 26:5–10) which Philo expands somewhat.[39] The offering of the fruits to God is tempered with the words 'if it be proper to bring what we receive' and an acknowledgement that they are gifts of God, unexpected and un-hoped for by the worshippers whom God has considered worthy of them (219).

CONCLUDING REMARKS

These can be brief, given the attention here devoted to Philo's work, and confined to three main observations. First, Philo's know-ledge of and faithfulness to Jewish tradition stands clearly revealed. Undoubtedly his wide knowledge of Greek thought, and especially his affection for the teachings of Plato and the Stoics as these were known to him, have profoundly affected his presentation of the Temple and its Service.[40] Jewish tradition, however, is never far away: even the cosmic and universal explanations of the Temple Service, so congenial to educated non-Jews, have their place in the writings of his Jewish predecessors such as Jesus ben Sira and the writer of *Aristeas*. Likewise, the union of earth and heaven in the worship of the Temple, often adduced by Philo, was a matter of moment for the Jews of Qumran.

Second, his concern with arithmology, while showing him to be a man of science well versed in the mathematical learning of the Greeks, may also have a specifically Jewish dimension as well. Here we may recall, for example, his discussion of the number fifty in respect of the Feast of Weeks and the ascetical Therapeutae: for some Jews in the land of Israel, the relationship of the number fifty to the calendar was a matter of supreme importance, as documents from Qumran have shown.[41]

Finally, Philo notes that the Service, its various rites and cere-monies, and the high priest's vestments can be understood as sym-bolic of the movement of the individual soul aided by the Logos towards its ultimate goal, the vision of God. The name Israel he understands as 'the man who sees God' (e.g., *De Somn.* I. 129, 171; *De Praem.* 27; *De Ebr.* 82; *De Conf. Ling.* 72); and Jacob, whose name was changed to Israel, is the source of the twelve tribes of Israel, called 'a royal dwelling and priesthood of God' (*De Sob.* 65–66). Certainly he comes close to the idea that the virtuous indi-vidual, freed from the confinement of the passions, expresses what is symbolized by the Temple and its Service: his understanding of

140

the incense offering as representing the offering of man's reason is a good illustration of this. Nor, it would seem, is he far removed from considering the whole assembly of the virtuous as constituting a Temple in themselves. For if the various items of the Service might properly be symbols of virtuous behaviour, might not those who exhibit such behaviour be properly a sort of Temple?

7

THE WRITINGS OF
JOSEPHUS

Flavius Josephus, whose Hebrew name was Joseph ben Mattathias, was born in the year 37/38 AD in Jerusalem. His father was a priest of the course of Jehoiarib (see 1 Chr. 24:7), and his mother was descended from the Hasmonean high priests and kings who had ruled in Jerusalem until the time of Herod. From an early age he took an interest and played a part in political life. His career, first as Jewish general, then as a client of the Flavian emperors, is known to us from his writings which include his *Life*, published around 95 AD. The date of his death is not precisely known, but is often given as around the year 100 AD. His account of the *Jewish War* (published towards the end of the 70s), his *Jewish Antiquities* (completed some twenty years after *War*), and his tract against the anti-Semitic Apion (*Contra Apionem*) written towards the end of his life, all provide information about the Second Temple which Josephus had known, and had possibly served as priest, during its final years.[1]

Josephus offers a good deal by way of description of the Temple as known to him, which Herod had begun to rebuild in 20/19 BCE. In *War* V. 184–247 the site, courts, gates, and outward form of the buidings are discussed, information is given about the interior of the sanctuary and its furniture, and the vestments of the high priest are described. Another account in *Ant.* XV. 380–425 supplements what is said in *War*. With Josephus' information it is usual to compare and contrast the description of the Temple buildings offered by *m. Middot*: there are several discrepancies between them. Recent archaeological work continues to add to our knowledge of Herod's project.[2] For the most part, what Josephus has to say here is descriptive, and does not dwell on his thoughts on the significance of the buildings. On occasions, however, he speaks of the symbolic meaning of individual items connected with the

Temple: these are of great interest, and are discussed further below.

The tabernacle which Moses constructed, and which accompanied Israel in her wanderings through the desert, was understood as a protoype of the later Temple. In *Ant.* III. 102–133 Josephus gives his own account of it, adding remarks on the Ark, the furniture in the sanctuary, and the altar of burnt offering (134–150). Extended discussion of the priestly vestments follows (151–178), leading to a section dealing specifically with the symbolism of all these things (179–187). The account of the consecration of tent and priests includes a description of God's appearing to dwell with His people (202–203). Description again dominates his account of the sacrifices prescribed by the Torah (224–257). Likewise, the first Temple built by Solomon and its appurtenances are described (*Ant.* VIII. 63–98), but nothing is said of their significance. This disappointing lack of comment on the meaning of the things he so lovingly describes may be attributed to his plans, never realized, to write another book devoted specifically to 'reasons' for the laws.[3]

Josephus does not, however, leave his readers entirely in the dark regarding the significance of the the Temple Service and its constituent parts. He occasionally states quite clearly what is the symbolic or deeper meaning of aspects of the Service, and recognizes the fascination it might hold for his non-Jewish readers. In what follows, it should be possible to trace his concern with the Temple's significance in the course of a literary career which spanned more than a quarter of a century. The material will be presented in chronological order of its publication.

NOTE ON THE TEXT

For the Greek text of Josephus, we have used *Josephus*, 9 volumes, Loeb Classical Library, trans. H. St J. Thackeray, R. Marcus, A. Wikgren, and L. H. Feldman (Heinemann: Harvard, 1963–1969). Translations are ours.

THE JEWISH WAR

The first year of the war against Rome led the Zealots, under the leadership of John of Gischala, to try to take control of affairs in Jerusalem. They enlisted the help of Idumaean forces, whom they introduced into the city: both parties proceeded to murder high-ranking Jews who up until then had commanded the war effort.

Among these were two former high priests, Ananus son of Ananus and Jesus son of Gamaliel, highly respected men whom Josephus goes out of his way to praise.[4] Their corpses were left unburied, an act of gross impiety which Josephus notes was almost unknown amongst Jews, even in the case of executed criminals (*War* IV. 316–317). His tribute to them reaches its climax with these words:

> So those who a little earlier had upon themselves the priestly raiment and were celebrating the cosmic worship, and who were revered by travellers to the city from the inhabited world, were seen perished, naked, as food for dogs and wild animals. I believe that Virtue herself groaned over those men, and lamented that she had been worsted by evil in such a way.
>
> (*War* IV. 324–325)

Josephus, like earlier writers, directly associates the priestly vestments with 'cosmic worship', *kosmikê thrêskeia*. The phrase may be understood as suggesting that the worship offered in the Temple was in some sense offered on behalf of the universe, or as part of a larger worship of God offered by the universe itself. Equally, Josephus may imply that the worship of the Temple symbolized the universe in its various parts, in such a way that the cosmos might be said to worship God in the course of Temple Service.[5] The respect accorded to the two high priests by visitors to the city from abroad also strengthens the impression that the universal significance of the Temple Service was known far beyond the homeland of the Jewish people, and that the deaths of these two men were in some sense universal tragedies. Interestingly, Josephus does not seek to explain or justify the link between these priests and 'cosmic worship' at this point, although it occupies his attention once he begins to describe the Temple in *War* Book V.

After describing the outward appearance of the Temple buildings, Josephus describes the great golden vine around the main gate into the building, and the golden doors which provided access. It is at this point that he begins to explain something of the inner significance of the place.

> Now in front of these was a veil ... of Babylonian woven cloth embroidered in blue and linen as well as scarlet and purple, worked in marvellous fashion. The combination of material it possessed did not lack theoretical significance, but was like an image of the universe. For it appeared that fire

was hinted at in the scarlet, the earth in the fine linen, the air in the blue, and the sea in the purple. Some of these things compare for reasons of similarity of colour; others, as in the case of the fine linen and the purple, because of their origin, since earth yields the former and the sea the latter. And the woven cloth was embroidered with the spectacle of the whole heaven, except for the signs of the Zodiac.

(War V. 212–214)

The veil was evidently one of the most eye-catching and memorable features of the Temple furniture: we know as much from *Aristeas* 86, where, however, nothing is said about its possible meaning. Philo gives no symbolic interpretation of the veil; rather, he explains the high priest's violet robe with its ornaments of embroidered flowers and pomegranates in terms of earth, air, fire, and water.[6] The Mishnah, too, says nothing about the meaning of the veil, although its excellent craftsmanship and lavish proportions are remarked upon (*Shek.* 8:4–5). What Josephus has to say is compatible with Philo's tendency to relate parts of the Temple or the priests' robes to individual parts of the universe, but evidently he has not been dependent on Philo for his interpretation of the veil. He is also keen to avoid any idea that the veil may have portrayed living creatures, contrary to the commandment of Exod. 20:4; Deut. 5:8. His account of the veil before the Holy of Holies in Solomon's Temple (*Ant.* IV. 72) is derived from 2 Chr. 3:14; Exod. 26:31, but carefully omits their reference to embroidered cherubim. Prominent in Solomon's Temple, the cherubim prove embarrassing for Josephus, who says that no one knew what they were like (*Ant.* VIII. 73). The signs of the Zodiac include creatures such as the ram, bull, and goat. Consequently, Josephus is careful to remark that the Zodiac was not figured on the veil. No doubt in saying this he was mindful of anti-Jewish calumnies against the Temple of a kind he reports in *Contra Apionem*, that the head of an ass, or an animal of some sort, was worshipped in the Holy Place.[7] Further, as a military commander in the war against Rome, he could not have been ignorant of the intense hostility displayed by ordinary Jews towards representations of living things: this very hostility had helped to fuel opposition to Roman rule.[8] He can therefore point to the ornamentation of the Temple veil as supporting evidence from within the most sacred building of the Jews, that his countrymen were profoundly antagonistic to idolatry.

Having earlier hinted at a cosmic dimension to the Temple worship, Josephus at last gives his readers an idea of what this might mean when he turns to describing the lampstand with its seven lamps, the table, and the altar of incense.

> The seven lamps represented the seven planets (for from the candlestick itself that number was divided), and the twelve loaves on the table the circle of the Zodiac and the year; and the altar of incense, because of the thirteen fragrant ingredients with which it is compounded from sea and land both uninhabited and inhabited, signified that all things are of God and for God.
>
> (*War* V. 217–218)

The symbolic interpretations of the three objects superficially recall remarks by Philo. Thus the latter tells how the seven lamps represent sun, moon, and planets (*De Vit. Mos.* II. 102–103; *QE* II. 75; *Quis Heres* 221–224). This detail, however, represents only one element in his otherwise intricate exegesis of biblical texts about the lampstand.[9] The note that the twelve loaves represent the circle of the Zodiac, however, is not directly stated by Philo, although he agrees with Josephus' interpretation associating them with the twelve months of the year (*De Spec. Leg.* I. 172). In this last passage, however, Philo goes further, comparing the two rows of the bread's arrangement with the two equinoxes, a point not made by Josephus. The latter understands the incense as meaning that everything comes from and is for God, which again corresponds more or less with one detail in Philo's elaborate explanation of it (*Quis Heres* 196–197); but Philo makes much of the spiritual significance of the incense offering, on which Josephus is silent.[10] Instead, he notes its thirteen ingredients, and takes the incense to be composed of items representing not only water and earth, but also air and fire (*Quis Heres* 196–197).[11]

The differences between Philo and Josephus as they explain the lampstand, Bread of the Presence, and incense make it improbable that the latter has borrowed material from the former, and they strongly suggest that, where the two writers agree on single points of detail, they are both dependent on traditional lore older than either of them. Indeed, this might be expected, given the relationship between the Temple Service and the cosmos expressed in writings like ben Sira's Wisdom and the Epistle of Aristeas.[12] What is striking about Josephus' words here is his concentration on the planets, the Zodiac, and the universe to the exclusion of matters considered important by earlier writers. Josephus seems determined to stress the cosmic aspects of the Temple's significance above all else. The same concern is evident in the final comment he makes in *War* about the high priest's vestments, which also tends to confirm his independence of Philo's work.

> He carried out his public ministry covering his thighs up to the loins with breeches; then he put on a linen undertunic, and a violet full-length robe over it, a garment well-rounded and fringed. Golden bells and pomegranates hung side by side from the fringes, the bells a symbol of thunder, the pomegranates of lightning.
>
> (*War* V. 231)

Unlike Philo, whose description of the violet robe follows that given by LXX, Josephus seems to abide by the Hebrew text of Exodus, which alludes only to bells and pomegranates on the skirts of the garment. These, says Josephus, represent thunder and lightning. This explanation differs considerably from that of Philo, for whom the bells signify the harmony of earth and water (*De Vit. Mos.* II. 119), the harmony of the different parts of the universe (*De Spec. Leg.* I. 84–85; 93–94), or the harmony betweeen sensible realities and the human mind (*De Mig. Abr.* 102–103). The pomegranates signify water (*De Vit. Mos.* II. 119; *De Spec. Leg.* I. 84–85; 93–94). In explaining these items, Josephus probably has in mind biblical verses which associate thunder and lightning with God's presence to redeem Israel at the Exodus (Ps. 18:13–14) and with God's voice (Isa. 30:30; Ps. 29:3; Job 37:4), in other words, with some form of divine revelation.[13] The appearance of the high priest in the Service, therefore, might be understood as an assurance of God's presence with Israel. This thought may not be without precedent, in that *Aristeas* may imply that the sound of the bells may point to the advent of one as it were 'from another world'.[14]

THE JEWISH ANTIQUITIES

Writing in *War*, Josephus confines explanations of the Temple and its parts to aspects of the priestly vestments, the Temple veil, the Menorah, the table, and the altar of incense. Much of this material is repeated in *Antiquities*, where, however, he offers additional comments on the significance of the Temple building. These are given as he sets out his version of Moses' construction of the tabernacle, in which Josephus finds that its three parts correspond to sea, earth, and heaven.

> For one will find that each of these is designed as a copy and configuration of the universe, if he is willing readily and with intelligence to make enquiry. For by apportioning the tabernacle, which is thirty cubits long, into three sections, giving over two portions to the priests as if it were a public place and permitted for human use, he signifies the earth and the sea, for indeed these are accessible to all. But he marks out the third portion for God alone, since heaven is also inaccessible to men. Then by placing on the table the twelve loaves he indicates that the year is divided into so many months; and by making the candlestick composed out of seventy portions he alluded to the decans of the planets, and by seven lamps upon it, for so many is their number, he hinted at the orbit of the planets.
>
> (*Ant.* III. 180–182)

Once more, similarities with Philo's discussion of the Temple as representing the universe come to mind. The three divisions corresponding to sea, earth, and heaven, however, draw attention to a matter which Philo does not emphasize. The waters of the sea recall the 'deep', the abysses where the waters under the earth (Gen. 7:11) are located.[15] Josephus may be hinting that the Temple in some manner holds together with the earth what is above it (the heaven) and what is below (the sea); if so, he obliquely alludes to the Temple as a stabilizing and unifying centre for the universe, a view expressed by earlier writers and by the so called Pseudo-Philo, who was most probably his contemporary.[16] The abysses or the deeps are parts of the universe: people may go down into them (*e.g.*, Ps. 107:26); and they would therefore be appropriately represented in the tabernacle. It must be admitted, however, that while Josephus' language permits such an understanding of the sea, it does not demand it.

As in *War* V. 217–218, the twelve loaves represent the months of the year; but reference to the Zodiac in the former is here omitted. By contrast, Josephus adds details about the Menorah. This not only bears the seven lamps symbolizing the order of the planets (so *War*): it is also made up of seventy parts representing the ten decans, the ten-degree portions of the Zodiac occupied and presided over by each planet. This detail again recalls Philo's interpretation of the Menorah, which may owe something to the astronomical ideas of the time, ideas of which Josephus may equally have been aware. Josephus then expounds the curtains of the tabernacle, attributing to their components the same sense he gave to the Temple veil (*War* V. 212–214), adding only that linen rightly represents earth since flax grows up from the ground, and that purple dye comes from fish, and may thus symbolize the sea where they live:

> The curtains woven of four components declare the nature
> of the elements: for the fine linen seems to indicate the earth
> since the flax grows up from it, and the purple seems to refer
> to the sea, since the colour is made purple by the blood of
> fishes; and the blue represents the air; and the scarlet would
> be a sign of fire.
>
> (*Ant.* III. 183)

He devotes greater space, however, to discussion of the high priest's vestments. Superficially, some of his comments again recall Philo: both authors 'breathe the same air', but give explanations of the robes which are not identical.

> The tunic of the high priest also signifies the earth since it is
> made of linen, and the blue colour signifies the vault of
> heaven; and it copies the lightnings with the pomegranates,
> and the thunder by the sound of the bells. And I believe that
> the ephod represents the nature of the universe which God
> thought good to make of four components; it was woven
> with gold signifying sunlight which beams upon all things.
> And he arranged the breastplate in the midst of the ephod
> after the manner of the earth, for it also has the most central
> place. And he surrounded it with a girdle, thereby signifying
> the ocean, for this too comprehends everything. Each of the
> two emeralds with which he fixed in place the robe of the
> high priest represents both the sun and the moon. Whether
> one wishes to think of the group of twelve stones as the
> months, or as the number of the stars which the Greeks call
> the circle of the Zodiac, he will not mistake the intention of
> that man. And the head-dress made of blue seems to me to
> betoken heaven; for otherwise it would not have had placed
> upon it the Name of God as an ornament upon the crown –

and this of gold, because of the brilliant rays of light in
which the Godhead most rejoices.

(*Ant.* III. 184–187)

The blue robe signifies both earth (being made of linen, like the
Temple and Tabernacle veils) and heaven, since it is blue in colour.
For Philo, however, this robe is symbolic of the air and of the
regions below the moon (*De Vit. Mos.* II. 117 ff.). The symbolism
of bells and pomegranates has already been discussed.[17] The
ephod, which Philo understood as representing heaven (*De Vit.
Mos.* II. 122 ff.), here indicates the universe made up of four elements, its golden parts symbolizing sunlight. No reason for this interpretation is given; but if the gold is taken to represent sunlight,
we find that the ephod was constructed out of four other materials,
blue scarlet, purple, and fine linen (Exod. 28:6). Josephus has probably been consistent in transferring to this vestment his understanding of the four materials expressed earlier (e.g., *Ant.* III. 183
in respect of the veils).

Contrasted with Philo's exposition of the breastplate, what
Josephus offers seems pedestrian; but it is consistent with his brief
and controlled explanations, which concentrate on the universal
significance of things to do with the Temple.[18] He thus presents
the earth set in the midst of the universe, surrounded by the great
ocean which has for its symbol the girdle of the high priest. The
two emeralds on the shoulder of the ephod allude to sun and
moon. For Philo, they signified the hemispheres, although he notes
that 'some suppose' they may represent sun and moon (*De Vit.
Mos.* II. 122–123). This last strongly suggests that Josephus drew
on ideas known to Philo, but espoused by others and already traditional in his day.

The twelve stones in the breastplate signify the months of the
year: the names of the twelve tribes are inscribed on them, and
tradition older than Josephus related them to the calendar (see
Jubilees 25:16; 32:3). Otherwise they may symbolize the Zodiac, a
notion shared by Philo (*De Vit. Mos.* II. 124; *De Spec. Leg.* I.87). At
this point Josephus says nothing of the oracle Urim and Thummim, nor of the names inscribed on the twelve stones. These he
has already described in great detail (*Ant.* III. 166–169, altering an
earlier description given in *War* V. 234); but of their significance he
remains silent. The head-dress of the high priest is interpreted as
referring to heaven, in that it bears the Name of God whose dwell-

ing is there: here again, gold symbolizes the light of the sun. Such explanation as Josephus gives of these things, therefore, culminates in a reference to the brilliant light in which God rejoices.

There is a coda, however, to this matter of light. Josephus describes (but does not explain) the ceremonies of Aaron's consecration as high priest, when he is robed in his vestments: this is followed by the account of the death of Aaron's sons, Nabad and Abihu (*Ant.* III. 204–211). The last sentence of this account notes that Aaron had been clothed with the priestly garments; interestingly, Josephus goes on to contrast him with Moses, who, dressed and behaving like a private citizen, was drawing up the laws under God's direction (*Ant.* III. 212–213). He then speaks of a matter omitted earlier, and states that the sardonyx on the right shoulder of the high priest's ephod would light up whenever God was present at the sacred rites, and that this light was visible from afar (*Ant.* III. 215). Furthermore, God would foretell victory to Israel's armies through the stones on the breastplate, which would flash forth brilliant light to indicate that God would help them (*Ant.* III. 216–217). Both these lights, however, ceased 200 years before his time, because of transgression of the laws (*Ant.* III. 218). He thus avoids uncomfortable questions about Urim and Thummim, the oracle which was associated with the breastplate and should have given advice to Israel in war (Exod. 28:30; Num. 27:21). The Jews had suffered defeat at Roman hands: Josephus exonerates the oracle, by indicating that it had ceased to function long ago. Before he gives this explanation, however, he is careful to contrast with this priestly oracle the laws composed by Moses wearing ordinary clothes. These will endure for all time, even though Urim and Thummim no longer function, and the sacred garments worn by Aaron (see *War* VI. 389) are now in Roman hands.[19]

CONTRA APIONEM

The two books which comprise this work are designed to refute slanders against the Jews, some of them quite extraordinary and fantastic in character, made by pagan authors under the guise of historical writing. Chief among these was one Apion, who attacked the Jews for (*inter alia*) sacrificing domestic animals, abstaining from pork, and practising circumcision: Josephus neatly turns to good effect Apion's Egyptian ancestry in his response to the attack (*Cont. Ap.* II. 137–142). Non-Jewish authors offering dispassionate accounts of Jews and their practices provide excellent supports for Josephus: one of these, Hecataeus of Abdera, Josephus quotes at length. His work has been discussed above.[20]

He again provides a brief description of the Temple and its courts (*Cont. Ap.* II. 102–111), which is designed especially to prove the impossibility of curious accusations brought against the Jewish cult.[21] Towards the end of the book, he makes a few observations about the Temple and its Service, which had ceased to operate some twenty-five years previously. There is one Temple for Jews, 'common for all, just as God is common for all' (*Cont. Ap.* II. 193). The 'all' in this statement probably refers to the Jews, although it is possible that Josephus refers to all humanity: he had, indeed, included the court of the Gentiles in his earlier description of the Temple (*Cont. Ap.* II. 103). He continues:

> We slaughter the sacrifices not to get ourselves into a drunken state, for this is disagreeable to God, but to produce a state of moderation in ourselves. And at the sacrifices it is first necessary to pray for the common safety, not for our own selves. For we were born for life in common (*koinôniai*), and he who honours this above his own personal concerns is especially favoured by God. Let supplication, then, be made to God, not so that he grant good things (for He Himself has given them voluntarily and set them forth in the midst for everyone), but so that we may be able to receive and accept and keep them.
>
> (*Cont. Ap.* II. 195–197)

SUMMARY

Josephus wrote after the ghastly events of 66–70, which witnessed the collapse of the Jewish state and Temple, and the atrocities which accompanied these things. It is therefore not surprising that he strongly brings to the fore the cosmic significance of the Temple, the high priest, and the Service. In a manner redolent of Philo, he explains to his non-Jewish readers that the worship offered in Jerusalem had a beneficial effect for the whole world: perhaps he implies that the destruction of the sanctuary augurs no good for the future. Sacrifices, which had been offered by the Jewish community even for the Emperor (*Cont. Ap.* II. 77), were offered for the common safety of the nation, and with regard to moderation (*sôphrosunê*), that greatest of all virtues extolled by all the great philosophers of Greece and Rome. Above all, the Jewish Temple and its rites make clear that Jews do not suffer from *apanthrôpia*, 'hatred of mankind', since the whole created order is mysteriously represented in the ordered and temperate workings of the Service.[22] In this, Josephus strongly agrees with Philo (see *De Spec. Leg.* II. 167 on the offering of the sheaf of new corn): at the end of his life, he seeks to defend his people against slander, and his defence of the Temple Service relies on its universal character.

8

PSEUDO-PHILO'S *LIBER ANTIQUITATUM BIBLICARUM*

This unusual writing survives in a Latin translation of what was almost certainly a Hebrew original. Falsely ascribed to Philo of Alexandria, its author is unknown, although there is general agreement that it was composed by a Jew living in the land of Israel. *Liber Antiquitatum Biblicarum* (*LAB*), the Latin title by which it is commonly known, offers a 're-written' version of the Bible beginning with the opening of Genesis and extending to the death of King Saul. Most students of the book concur in dating it to the first century AD; there is, however, no agreement whether it had reached its present form before or after the year 70 of that century. Some scholars detect an allusion to the end of the sacrificial Service and capture of Jerusalem by Titus in XIX. 7, which would indicate a final date of composition in the last quarter of the century. Be this as it may, the several exegetical and aggadic traditions which combine to make up the book appear in many instances to have originated before the destruction of the Temple; and it is not impossible that the unkown author witnessed the last years of the Temple, as well as its profanation and destruction by the Romans.[1] Indeed, we shall see that *LAB* has a distinctive appreciation of the meaning of the Temple and its Service which closely compares with that of the other writings studied here.

NOTES ON THE TEXT

I have used the critical edition of the Latin text of *LAB* edited by Guido Kisch, *Pseudo-Philo's Liber Antiquitatum Biblicarum* (Notre Dame: Indiana, 1949). Translations are mine.

LAB XI. 15. The witnesses speak of the laver *et vase ejus* or *et vasis ejus,* 'and its vessel, dish', or 'and its vessels, dishes'. Scripture speaks of the laver and its base (Exod. 30:18; 38:8), vessels of the laver being otherwise unknown. We therefore follow M. R. James, *The Biblical Antiquities of Philo* (SPCK: London, 1917), p. 110 in reading *et base ejus,* 'and its base'.

LAB XIII. 8. All witnesses speak of 'the place of creation and the colour, *colorem'.* D. J. Harrington, 'Pseudo-Philo' in J. H. Charlesworth (ed.), *The Old Testament Pseudepigrapha,* vol. 2, p. 118 emends to *colubrum,* 'serpent', following James, op. cit., p. 116, which gives sense to an otherwise obscure clause.

COMMENTARY

Two figures in particular, those of Noah and Moses, dominate *LAB*'s presentation of Israel's sacrificial service. According to some writings from Second Temple times – Jubilees offers a good example – Adam acted as priest and offered sacrifice. It seems that the author of *LAB* knew that tradition, but drastically modified it: Adam is discussed in settings redolent of Temple Service, but is denied a priestly role.[2] The sacrifices of Cain and Abel are simply noted, without comment, in a poem attributed to David towards the end of the book.[3] For the author of *LAB*, the significance of sacrifice is first apparent in the offerings made by Noah after the Flood, a catastrophe which destroyed everything apart from the people and animals saved in Noah's ark (III. 3, 4, 7). All other things living prior to the Flood were absolutely destroyed.[4] The present world order, therefore, takes its beginning from Noah and those with him in the ark, whom he brought out at God's command (III. 8). According to Gen. 8:20–22, Noah's first act on leaving the ark was the offering of sacrifice. *LAB* III. 8–10 considerably expands these verses.

> 8. And it happened on the ninetieth day that God dried up the earth and said to Noah: Go out of the ark, you and all who are with you, and increase and multiply on the earth. And Noah went out from the ark, he and his sons and his sons' wives, and all the beasts and reptiles and birds and cattle he led out with him, as God had commanded him. Then Noah built an altar to the Lord, and took some of all the clean cattle and clean birds, and offered a whole offering upon the altar; and it was received by the Lord as a savour of

rest.   9. And God said: I will not again curse the earth on account of man, because the nature of man's heart has left off from his youth; and so I shall not again utterly ruin all the living things I have made. But it shall happen, that when those living on the earth have sinned, I shall judge them by famine or sword or fire or death, and there shall be earthquakes, and they shall be scattered into uninhabited places. But the earth I shall not again ruin with the water of a flood. And in all the days of the earth, seed and harvest, cold and heat, summer and autumn, day and night, shall not cease, until I remember those who dwell on the earth, until the times be completed.   10. But when the years of the world (or: age) shall have been completed, then the light shall cease and darkness shall be put out; and I shall give life to the dead, and raise up from the earth those who sleep. And hell shall repay its debt, and destruction shall restore its portion, so that I may render to everyone according to their deeds and according to the fruit of their devices, until I pass judgement between soul and flesh. And the world shall rest and death shall be put out, and hell shall shut its mouth. And the earth shall not be without young ones, nor barren for those who dwell on it; and no one who has been justified in me shall be defiled. And there shall be another earth and another heaven, an everlasting dwelling.

No hint is given how Noah knew which victims would be acceptable for sacrifice, nor how he knew what might be the correct procedures in the act of service. In this, as in other matters already noted, the author seems aware of earlier traditions, perhaps of the sort still extant in Jubilees. The meaning of Noah's sacrifice, not given in the Bible, is understood to be 'a savour of rest'. God accepts it as such, and its consequences are spelled out. Noah's name is interpreted as deriving from Hebrew root *nwḥ*, 'to rest', *LAB* I. 20 further explaining the name as

> this man will give rest to us and to the earth, from those which are upon it; on whom punishment shall come because of the wickedness of their evil deeds.

The rest which follows this offering means that God will never again curse the earth or destroy all living things indiscriminately. Sinners will be judged in differing ways; but never will the whole earth be subjected to a universal flood. Times and seasons will recur regularly.

But all this is determined only for a limited time-span. Noah, the man whose name means 'rest', offers a sacrifice which inaugurates and guarantees a period of rest, the present world order which the author enjoys. This order owes nothing to Adam: Noah's sacrifice marks a fresh start for the universe, with God's approval. When the years of the present world 'shall have been completed', however, all this will come to an end. Light and darkness, the 'day and night' of Gen. 8:22, shall no longer have dominion. Then the dead will be raised, the underworld disgorge its inhabitants, and the people will be judged. The world will then enjoy a 'rest' different in quality from the temporary rest granted by Noah's 'savour of rest'.

The world order established upon Noah's sacrifice, although transitory, is divinely guaranteed. *LAB* III. 11 stresses the covenant which God made with Noah (Gen. 9:8–11), that he would never destroy the world with a flood. According to Gen. 8:12–13, the sign of this covenant 'for everlasting generations' (*dôrôt 'ôlâm*) would be the rainbow. *LAB* III. 11–12 does not allow this to stand, and modifies the promise:

> 11. And God again said to Noah and his sons: Behold, I shall make my covenant with you and with your descendants after you, and shall not again ruin the earth with the water of a flood. And all that moves and lives shall be for you as food. But you shall not eat flesh with the blood of the life. For whoever sheds man's blood, his blood shall be shed by the hand of God, because God made man in His own image. But you, increase and multiply and fill the earth like the multitude of fish which multiply in the waves (of the sea). 12. And God said: This is the covenant which I have made between Me and you. And it shall happen that when I cloud (the sky) with clouds, My bow shall appear in the cloud; and it shall be for a memorial of the covenant between Me and you and all who live upon the earth.

The rainbow is now proclaimed as a 'memorial', a notion which the author links closely with the Temple Service of the present world order (IV. 5; XIII. 4, 6, 7; XIV. 4; XXVI. 12) and which will presently feature in discussion again. No longer is it assured 'for everlasting generations': for *LAB*, the end of the present world will bring another heaven and another earth in which Noah's covenant will no longer apply. In the meantime, however, the rainbow's validity remains important to the author's thoughts about sacrifice. In a section not derived from Scripture, he tells of the increase and dissemination abroad of human beings after Noah's death:

> And then they began to work the land and to sow seed upon it. And when the land was parched, those who dwelt upon it called out to the Lord; and God heard them, and increased the rain. And it happened that when the rain came down upon the earth, that the rainbow appeared in the cloud. And those who lived on the earth saw the memorial of the covenant, and fell on their faces and slew victims, offering whole burnt offerings to the Lord.
>
> (IV. 5)

Here the rainbow assures human beings that the rain does not betoken another flood. But rain is also needed for growth of crops. Thus the rainbow assures people not only of the stability of the present world inaugurated after Noah's whole burnt offerings, but also of its fertility.[5] The association of the Temple Service with the fertility of the land is a matter the author will address later at greater length, when he considers the annual festivals. The memorial of the covenant elicits a sacrifice from the people. It is not said that the offerings were made in thanksgiving, although such an understanding may be implied. What is clear, however, is that the rainbow reminds the people of God's covenant with Noah, which itself was granted after Noah's sacrifice of whole burnt offerings to the Lord.

Nothing further is said of sanctuary or sacrifice until the account of Moses' reception of the Torah, which culminates in the commands to make the tabernacle and its furnishings.

> And (God) commanded him directly about the Tabernacle and the ark of the Lord, and about the sacrifice of whole offerings and of incense, and concerning the care of the table and the candlestick, and concerning the laver and its base, and concerning the ephod and the breastplate, and the most precious stones, that they should make them in this way among the children of Israel. And He showed him their likeness, so that they should make them according to the pattern which he had seen. And He said to him: Make for Me a sanctuary, and the Tabernacle of My Glory shall be among you.
>
> (XI. 15)

This drastically summarizes extensive portions of Scripture (Exod. 25:1–28:43). We must therefore suppose that the author has retained for mention only commandments he holds in special regard, which God gave directly (*in faciem*, 'to his face') to Moses, showing him that things should be made according to their heavenly pattern. The command that Moses make the tabernacle and its furniture according to a heavenly pattern is given twice, Exod. 25:9, 40; and Pseudo-Philo evidently regards it as of special significance. The sanctuary exists so that the tabernacle of God's glory might be present with Israel. Indeed, Moses is expected exactly to replicate on earth items which properly belong in heaven itself. The author's thought is not far removed from those Rabbinic texts which speak of the earthly Temple corresponding to the heavenly dwelling place of God, in such as way that the throne of God's glory corresponds to the earthly sanctuary (see *b. Ber.* 33b; *Mekhilta de R. Ishmael Shirta* 10:24–28; *Gen. Rab.* 55:8; *Exod. Rab.* 33:3; PJ of Exod. 15:17).

The full force of this distinctive presentation of the commandments about the tabernacle and its Service is appreciated only when it is understood that the author elsewhere strongly contrasts Moses with Adam. *LAB* XXVI. 6 states that God had showed to Adam everything: this is reported in a lengthy discussion of mysterious precious stones, some of which are superabundant light-bearers granted by God's own special favour a place in the Holy of Holies in Solomon's Temple (XXVI. 7–15). As such, it should be noted (XXVI. 12), these stones will be placed above the two cherubim in God's sight 'as a memorial to the house of Israel'.[6] But Adam had sinned, losing thereby knowledge of the precious stones and other secrets. Moses, it would seem, is responsible for restoring (at least in part) privileges granted to Adam before he sinned. This theme will recur presently.

The episode of the golden calf prevents for a time the realization of God's commands about the sanctuary. After punishing the apostates, Moses prays (XII. 8–9) to God for mercy on Israel, the latter now being represented as a vine which links the abyss, earth, and heaven.[7]

8. So then Moses went up on to the mountain, and prayed, saying: Behold now, Thou art God who hast planted one vine, and hast set its roots in the abyss, and hast stretched out its branches up to Thy highest seat. See – at this time – that

that vine hath lost its fruit and hath not known its husband-man. And now, if Thou be angry with Thy vine, and uproot it from the abyss and dry up its branches from Thy highest and everlasting seat, never again shall the abyss come to nourish it, nor shall Thy throne come to refresh that vine of Thine which Thou hast burned. 9. For Thou art He who art all light, and hast decorated Thy house with precious stones and with gold, and also with perfumes, spices and balsam-wood, and cinnamon, and with roots of myrrh and costum Thou hast decorated Thy house; and Thou hast filled what Thou hast created with different foods and with the sweetness of different drinks. If therefore Thou hast no pity on Thy vine, O Lord, all things have been made for nothing, and Thou shalt no have anyone to glorify Thee. For even if Thou shouldst plant another vine, this one would not believe in Thee, because Thou hadst ruined the first. For if Thou shouldst abandon the world completely, then who will per-form for Thee what Thou hast spoken as God? And now let Thy anger be restrained from Thy vine; rather, let what was said by Thee beforehand, and what is to be said, be per-formed; and let not Thy labour be for nothing, nor Thy in-heritance be pulled asunder in humiliation.

Should God destroy the vine, the link between abyss, earth, and heaven will cease to exist: everything will have been made for noth-ing, to no purpose. Israel, God's vine, is the unifying force in the created order. *LAB* XVIII. 10; XXIII. 12; XXVIII. 4; XXX. 4; XXXIX. 7 also speak of Israel as a plantation which links earth and heaven. This imagery is bound up with the sanctuary, since God has *planted* Israel on His mountain, the sanctuary which His hands have made according to Exod. 15:17, the very verse which the Rabbis took to mean that the earthly and heavenly dwelling places of God correspond to one another. And the language which the author of *LAB* XII. 8–9 employs to speak of God's house refers not only to His heavenly dwelling, but to the earthly sanctuary with its precious stones, its light (see *LAB* XI. 15; XIII. 1; XXVI. 12–15), its incense, food of animal sacrifices and wine of drink offer-ings. If Israel is uprooted, the earthly sanctuary which Moses has been ordered to construct according to an heavenly exemplar will never be built, and then creation will have been in vain, to no purpose, for God will have no one to glorify Him. The vine-symbol belongs firmly in the realm of beliefs about the Temple: if the author of *LAB* lived in the last days of the second Temple, he would have known, and possibly have seen, the golden vine which decorated the entrance to the sanctuary (Josephus *War* V. 210–211; *Ant.* XV. 395; *m. Middoth* 3:8). The earthly sanctuary, which Moses was shown in a pattern, is inextricably bound up with Israel as vine, holding together the component parts of the universe. For God to forsake this vine is tantamount to his forsaking creation; by showing mercy to the vine, He ensures that His work has not been in vain.[8]

God acceded to Moses' request, and the tabernacle with all its furnishings and the high priestly robes are made, as he had been shown (XIII. 1). Both at XI. 15 and XIII. 1 the laver and its base are named, no doubt because of its association with the sea (1 Kings 7:23, 39) and the author's interest in the abysses.[9] A brief note then informs us that the priests were consecrated, and that when all was completed the cloud covered everything.

From this completed tabernacle, God gave Moses commandments concerning sacrifice and festivals. According to XIII. 2, God said to Moses:

> This is the law of the altar (lit.: 'thurible') on which you shall sacrifice to me and pray for your souls. Now concerning these things from which you shall make offering to me, offer from the flock calf, sheep and she-goat, and from the birds turtle-dove and dove.

Sacrifice and prayer are here conjoined. This is particularly appropriate, in that the author elsewhere gives symbolic meanings to the animals and birds listed above. Thus the calf is said to be symbolic of the multitude of Abraham's descendants (XXIII. 7); the sheep represents both the assembly of Israel and the priests selected from it (XVII. 4) as well as the sages who shall enlighten Abraham's children (XXIII. 7); the she-goat alludes to the barren matriarchs granted children by God; the turtle-dove, the prophets born of Abraham; and the dove the city of Jerusalem (XXIII. 7). In these animal victims, the whole of Israel as descendants of Abraham thus finds itself figuratively offered to God in sacrifice.

The sheep, however, holds a special place. It was a male sheep which God granted to Abraham as a substitute for his son Isaac when his father bound him on the altar and went to sacrifice him at God's command (Gen. 22:13). The degree of importance *LAB* attaches to this event is indicated by no fewer than three references (XVIII. 5; XXXII. 2–4; XL. 2) to the sacrifice of Isaac.[10] In the second of these, words are put into Isaac's mouth stating what may have been a commonly held view of lamb offering in the first century AD:

> If a lamb out of the flock be accepted as an offering to the Lord as a savour of sweetness, and if flocks are appointed to the slaughter for the iniquities of mankind, and moreover man is set to inherit the world.
>
> (XXXII.3)

Not only is the sacrifice one of sweetness; it deals with iniquities, and is thus a sin offering effecting atonement. The goat offering was more often associated with this function, a fact which did not escape the author of Jubilees and which he heavily emphasized; but the sheep or lamb also has atoning significance through its use in the Tamid, as the author of Jubilees had been aware.[11]

The law of leprosy follows (XIII. 3), and festivals are listed. First is Maẓẓot, the Feast of Unleavened Bread (XIII. 4):

> And it shall happen, that when the times come round for you, you shall sanctify me on a festival day and be joyful in my sight on the Feast of unleavened bread; and you shall set bread before Me, celebrating the festival as a memorial, since on that day you came out of the land of Egypt.

The author's understanding of the feast is his own. It is a memorial of the day of the Exodus. Although the Bible associates the feast directly with the Exodus at Exod. 23:15; 34:18, it does not speak of it as a 'memorial'. This description is, however, applied to Pesaḥ (Exod. 12:14). *LAB* XLVIII. 3 and L. 2 refer to the Passover without describing or explaining it, or relating it to unleavened bread. In the first century AD it seems that Passover could be called 'the first day of unleavened bread' (*e.g.*, Mark 14:12; Luke 22:1), or the feast of unleavened bread could be defined as the Passover (*e.g.*, Josephus, *War* II. 10); thus unleavened bread itself might be assimilated to the Passover, and come to be regarded as a 'memorial'. But this does not fully explain *LAB*'s emphasis on the bread itself, set before God. Unleavened bread was not specially offered in the Temple Service at Pesaḥ: it was consumed by households in the Passover meal at their own tables. This meal is in any case a part of the sacrificial activity undertaken at Passover, and for the writer of

LAB this sacrificial character seems to be extended to the un-leavened bread.

For Pentecost, *LAB* XIII. 5 singles out the offering of the two loaves prescribed for the feast by Lev. 23:17. 'And on the feast of Weeks you shall set before Me bread, and you shall make unto Me an offering for your fruits.' It is not entirely clear what might be meant by the offering for your fruits, *pro fructibus vestris*. It may suggest that the offering is one of thanksgiving for the fruits already harvested. It may, however, be an offering to procure God's favour for the fruits, which are at a critical point in their maturing.[12]

Next (XIII. 6) we hear of New Year's Day (1st Tishri), which the author, like Philo, calls the Feast of Trumpets; to this he adds a note about the Fast of Yom Kippur, the day of Atonement.

> For the feast of Trumpets shall be for an offering for (or: to) your watchers, because I closely inspected the creation, so that you may be mindful of the whole world. And at the beginning of the years, when you show (them) forth to Me, I shall recognize the number of those who are dead and those who are born, and the fast of mercy. For you shall hold a fast to Me for your souls, that the promises of your fathers may be completed.

At first sight, no particular offering seems to be specified for the watchers, angels of high rank (see Dan. 4:13, 17, 23) who apparently act as Israel's guardians.[13] The name of the festival probably contains the clue to the nature of the offering: it may consist in the blowing of trumpets. They are, indeed, blown on this day precisely as a 'memorial' (Lev. 23:24), most likely to alert Israel's heavenly guardians to be ready to act at what is a time of judgement. For the author of *LAB*, like the later Rabbis, is in no doubt that God considers human deeds at this time.[14] It is the time when God oversaw or reviewed (*perspexi*) the creation; the author, therefore, seems to agree with other writers already encountered, that the world was created in Tishri. His thought seems to be that the trumpet-blasts are an offering to, or for Israel's angelic watchers, so that Israel may remember the whole world on the anniversary of its creation, on the day when judgement begins. On this day, Jews have the responsibility and privilege of 'remembering' the created order in union with their angelic counterparts. In the light of what has been said above about Israel's significance as a vine bridging the abyss, earth, and heaven, this responsibility is entirely comprehensible.

The New Year also involves a kind of census of the living and the dead, most likely in judgement. The Day of Atonement, on which this judgement is finally passed, is called a fast of mercy: as in the writings of Philo, it is given an entirely positive meaning. The author's interpretation of it, however, is *sui generis*: it enables the solemn promises made by God to the Patriarchs to find their fulfilment. The last festival considered is Tabernacles (XIII. 7).

> And bring near to Me the feast of Tabernacles: you shall indeed take for Me the beautiful fruit of the tree, and the bough of the palm and of willows and of cedars, and branches of myrtle. And I shall remember the whole earth with rain, and the rhythm of the seasons shall be established; and I shall set in order the stars and command the clouds, and the winds shall sound, and the lightnings shall run to and fro, and there shall be a storm of thunder. And this shall be for an everlasting sign, and the nights shall yield dew, as I spoke after the flood of the earth.

The theme of 'memorial' recurs, God remembering the whole earth in respect of rain: the promise is universal, and is not restricted to the Jews. In short, the whole order of things promised by God to Noah for the universe is here recalled. Seasons, stars, clouds and all natural phenomena necessary for the welfare of the human race occur according to God's ordinance set forth after the Flood, when Noah offered his sacrifice. Tabernacles in particular seems to be an annual evocation of the covenant with Noah.

What follows leaves the reader in no doubt that the order of the festivals is bound up with the order of the seasons of the year, the fruitfulness of the crops, and the stability of the world.[15] The solemn cataloguing of the festivals brings the author once more to mention of Noah, to whom God spoke after the flood, and to the losses sustained by Adam (XIII. 7–9)

> 7. ... and the nights shall yield dew, as I spoke after the flood of the earth, 8. at the time when I gave command about the year of the life of Noah and said to him: These are the years which I established after the weeks in which I visited the city of men, at the time when I showed to them the place of creation and the serpent. And He said: This is

the place about which I taught the first-formed man when I said: If you do not transgress what I have commanded you, all things shall be under your control. But he transgressed my ways, and was persuaded by his wife; for she was seduced by the serpent. And then death was established for the generations of men. 9. And the Lord said further: Still I showed (him) the ways of paradise, and said to him: These are the ways which men have lost by not walking in them, since they sinned against Me.

Here the insights about the meaning of the festivals, particularly the Feast of Tabernacles, are firmly anchored in the life of Noah. The author goes further, linking his teaching about the festivals to Adam who was promised authority over all things, only to lose it through sin. Even so, he was shown the ways of paradise, which it seems the celebration of the festivals in some measure restores. Adam's sin unleashed disorder in the world, an instability which found its climax in the Flood. After that Flood, the world is ordered anew through Noah's sacrifice, 'the savour of rest', with its promise of ordered seasons and fruitful rain for the whole world. The festivals commanded to Moses, especially Tabernacles, are of a piece with Noah's covenant, and are intended to ensure the same result.[16] Thus God commanded Moses

about the salvation of the souls of the people and said: If they walk in My ways, I shall not abandon them, but have mercy upon them always, and bless their seed; and the earth shall hasten to yield its fruit, and there shall be for them rains and benefits, and the earth shall not be barren.

(XIII. 10)

Finally, to leave the reader in no doubt that Moses' work in ordering the tabernacle and its Service is directly related to Noah's covenant ordering the world after his sacrifice, and that it goes some way to restoring what was lost by Adam's sin, the author tells (XIX. 10–11) how Moses before his death was shown by God

10. . . . the measurements of the sanctuary, and the number of the offerings, and the signs by which they shall begin to examine the heavens. And He said: These are the things which were forbidden to the race of men after they had sinned. 11. And now your rod, by which signs were performed, shall be for a witness between Me and My people;

and it shall be that, when they sin, I shall be angry with them. Then I shall remember My rod, and spare them according to My mercy. And your rod shall be in My sight as a remembrance for all days, and it shall be likened to the rainbow by which I made My covenant with Noah when he came out of the ark, saying: I shall set My bow in the cloud, and it shall be for a sign between Me and mankind, so that the water of a flood never again be upon the whole earth.

As ever, the author draws attention to God's solemn promises and the memorials of these things. Yet even these arrangements for Israel's sanctuary and worship as revealed to Moses are of limited duration, an interim arrangment lasting only until God visit the world: then He will shorten the times, and change the rules which at present govern the motions of stars, sun, and moon, before raising the dead (XIX. 13). Thus, the reader might understand, God Himself in those days would 'change the time and the law', and bring to proper effect what the monstrous fourth beast of Daniel's vision had blasphemously presumed to do (Dan. 7:25).

SUMMARY

Writing at some time in the first century AD, the author of *LAB* re-presents biblical history as it were from a period in the remote past: from the point of view of the written work, the Temple of Solomon has not yet been built. This writer clearly restricts the significance and efficacity of the Temple and its Service to what we might call 'ordinary history', where times and seasons were the times and seasons that he knew and that we still know. In the future, 'times and seasons' will be changed by God, the dead will be raised, and another order of things will come into being: Temple and sacrifice do not appear to belong to this future with its other world and other heaven. *LAB* is emphatic that the present order of things takes its beginning from Noah, and from the covenant God made with him. The sacrificial service which Noah performs is a vital element in that covenant, guaranteeing a fertile world with predictable times and seasons directed towards the well-being of the whole human race.

The instructions given to Moses regarding the tabernacle and its furniture build directly on God's covenant with Noah. These commandments, however, are directed not to humanity in general, but to Israel, described by the author as a 'vine'. This vine turns out to be a kind of *axis mundi*, holding together the abyss, earth, and the heaven where God has his house. The Tabernacle is made in accordance with a heavenly blueprint, and reproduces on earth the heavenly reality of God's dwelling. Once more, the sense of the Temple as providing stability and order in creation is strongly marked. God's instructions to Moses also allude to Noah and to Adam, the latter being responsible for losing privileges which human beings should properly have retained. Among these are the ways to Paradise: these and other gifts are, it would seem, partly restored to Israel with the building of the tabernacle and the conduct of its Service. The due celebration of the annual festivals, in particular, give Israel some part in the divinely appointed order of things which themselves directly affect the whole human race.

Almost everything which this author has to say about the Temple is attested in earlier writings. What comes clearly to the fore, however, is the importance of this institution for preserving and guaranteeing the continuing order of the world known to the writer and his contemporaries – all of them, Jew and non-Jew alike. The end of the Temple would mean the end of the world as they knew it: while it stands, and the Service is maintained, Jews provide for non-Jews an order providing the food and sustenance without which human life would be impossible. The end of the Temple will mean resurrection to eternal life for the righteous in a new order of things. The place of non-Jews in this 'new order' is not one which the author discusses in any detail; but one is left wondering if it will be quite so assured as it was in the days when Noah's covenant, assured by the regular offering of the sacrifices, held undisputed sway.

NOTES

1 HECATAEUS OF ABDERA

1 The complexities of the debate are made clear by C. R. Holladay, 'Pseudo-Hecataeus', in *Fragments from Hellenistic Jewish Authors vol. I: Historians* (Scholars Press: Chico, 1983), pp. 277–297, and effectively summarized by E. Schürer, *The History of the Jewish People in the Age of Jesus Christ*, rev. and ed. G. Vermes, F. Millar, and M. Goodman (Clark: Edinburgh, 1986), vol. 3.1, pp. 671–675. For a detailed survey of opinion, see Holladay, article on 'Hecataeus, Pseudo-', *Anchor Bible Dictionary*, vol. 3, pp. 108–109, who lists scholars accepting or denying the authenticity of the fragments. Holladay himself doubts that they are genuine, but is scrupulously judicious in indicating that the question is still open (see *Fragments*, pp. 282–283). By contrast, analysis of recent scholarship offered by M. Pucci ben Zeev, 'The Reliability of Josephus Flavius: The Case of Hecataeus' and Manetho's Accounts of Jews and Judaism: Fifteen Years of Contemporary Research (1974–1990)', *JSJ* 24 (1993), pp. 215–234, concludes that the fragments are most likely genuine, although Josephus may have derived his information from Hecataeus via an intermediary source. R. Doran, 'Pseudo-Hecataeus', in J. H. Charlesworth (ed.) *The Old Testament Pseudepigrapha* (Darton, Longman & Todd: London 1985) vol. 2, pp. 905–919, also argues for the authenticity of the fragments.
2 See further Schürer, op. cit., vol. 3, pp. 672–673; and Doran, op. cit., pp. 905, 909–910.
3 See Holladay, *Fragments*, p. 279; Schürer, op. cit., vol. 3, pp. 674–675; and Doran, op. cit., pp. 909, 912–913.
4 Here we can only give the briefest selection of difficulties raised by the fragments, of which even the number and extent are matters of disagreement. For full discussion, the reader is referred to works listed above in note 1.
5 See M. Stern, *Greek and Latin Authors on Jews and Judaism*, vol. 1. *From Herodotus to Plutarch* (The Israel Academy of Sciences and Humanities: Jerusalem, 1974), p. 24.
6 See Schürer, op. cit., vol. 3, p. 673.
7 See Stern, op. cit., p. 24, Holladay, *Fragments*, p. 282, and Schürer, op.

cit., pp. 673–674.

8 See B. Z. Wacholder, *Eupolemus: A Study of Judaeo-Greek Literature* (Jewish Institute of Religion: Cincinnati, 1974), pp. 183–205.

9 See N. Walter, *Der Thoraausleger Aristobulos. Untersuchungen zu seinen Fragmenten und zu pseudepigraphischen Resten der jüdisch-hellenistischen Literatur*, Texte und Untersuchungen 86 (Akademie Verlag: Berlin, 1964), pp. 172–187; and 'Pseudo-Hekataios I und II', in *Jüdische Schriften aus hellenistisch-römischer Zeit*, I.2 (Mohn: Gütersloh, 1976), pp. 144–160.

10 See Holladay, *Fragments*, pp. 288–290. It should be noted that, if the fragments are not genuine, additional complications arise in assessing their date, since Aristeas 31 refers to the writings of Hecataeus. Much then depends on the date of Aristeas, itself disputed, and on resolution of the question whether Aristeas was at all dependent on (Pseudo-)Hecataeus.

11 See O. R. Sellers, *The Citadel of Beth-Zur* (Westminster: Philadelphia, 1933), p. 73; O. R. Sellers, R. W. Funk, J. L. McKenzie, P. Lapp, and N. Lapp, 'The 1957 Excavation at Beth-Zur', *Annual of the American Schools of Oriental Research* 38 (1968), p. 2; N. Avigad, 'A New Class of Yehud-Stamps', *IEJ* 7(1957), pp. 148; Stern, op. cit., pp. 40–41; and Holladay, *Fragments*, pp. 325–326. The second Hebrew word is read as *phh*, to yield 'Hezekiah the governor', by F. W. Funk in *Encyclopedia of Archaeological Excavations in the Holy Land*, ed. M. Avi-Yonah (Oxford University Press: London) vol. 1 (1975) pp. 263–267.

12 See Doran, op. cit., p. 915, Holladay, *Fragments*, p. 326, and for a later period Schürer, op. cit., vol. 2, pp. 233–236.

13 For the date of Jubilees, see below, p. 85.

14 So J. G. Gager, 'Pseudo-Hecataeus Again', *ZNW* 60 (1969), p. 137, as quoted by Doran, op. cit., p. 915. But for a contrary view see Holladay, *Fragments*, p. 326.

15 See Doran, ibid.

16 On this see particularly Stern, op. cit., p. 42.

17 For details, see Schürer, op. cit., vol. 2, pp. 188–196.

18 See Schürer, op. cit., vol. 2, pp. 197–198.

19 Other ancient estimates of Jerusalem's size and population may be found in Holladay, *Fragments*, p. 331, nn. 36, 37.

20 For the significance of this in arguments about the genuinness of the fragments, see Doran, op. cit., p. 918, and Holladay, *Fragments*, p. 331, n.38.

21 Cf. Holladay, *Fragments*, p. 331, n. 39, who notes that Ezra 6:3 gives the breadth as sixty cubits.

22 By contrast, the Chronicler has a particular interest in the table and the Bread of the Presence: see 1 Chr. 28:16; 2 Chr. 4:19; 13:11; 29:18, indicating their importance in early Second Temple times. If the writer of the Hecataeus fragment were a Jew, one might have expected a reference to the table.

23 Cf. Doran, op. cit., p. 915, noting how the whole description of the Temple and the note about the lack of an image point to a writer steeped in the Greek tradition of ethnography. Contrast Holladay, *Fragments*, p. 332, n. 43.

24 Doran, op. cit., pp. 915–916, believes Hecataeus to be Plutarch's authority (*De Iside et Osiride* 6) for saying that the priest-kings of Heliopolis

in Egypt were but moderate drinkers of wine. On abstinence from wine in paganism, see references in Holladay, *Fragments*, p. 332, n. 44.

25 On the purity system, and the absolute necessity of maintaining it at all times, see F. Schmidt, *La Pensée de Temple. De Jérusalem à Qoumrân* (Seuil: Paris, 1994), pp. 77–87, and J. Neusner, *The Idea of Purity in Ancient Judaism (with a Critique and a Commentary by Mary Douglas)* (Brill: Leiden, 1973).

2 ARISTEAS

1 For Aristeas and the origins of the Septuagint, see especially A. Pelletier, *Lettre d'Aristée à Philocrate*, Sources Chrétiennes 89 (Cerf: Paris, 1962), pp. 78–98; S. Jellicoe, *The Septuagint and Modern Study* (Oxford University Press: Oxford, 1968), pp. 29–58; and E. Schürer, *History of the Jewish People*, rev. and ed. G. Vermes, F. Millar, and M. Goodman (Clark: Edinburgh, 1986), vol. 3.1, pp. 677–684.

2 Cf. Schürer, *History*, vol. 3, p. 684; Pelletier, op. cit., p. 56; G. W. E. Nickelsburg, *Jewish Literature between the Bible and the Mishnah* (SCM: London, 1981), p. 168; and R. J. H. Shutt, 'Aristeas, Letter of', *Anchor Bible Dictionary*, vol. 1, p. 381.

3 See Jellicoe, op. cit., p. 48, n. 1.

4 Schürer, op. cit., vol. 3, p. 684. Shutt, in the Introduction to his English translation of 'Letter of Aristeas' in J. H. Charlesworth (ed.), *Old Testament Pseudepigrapha* (Darton, Longman & Todd: London, 1985), vol. 2, p. 9, agrees with Jellicoe (op. cit., p. 49) on a date of around 170 BC.

5 See especially Jellicoe, op. cit., pp. 47–52; Schürer, op. cit., vol. 3, pp. 679–684; Shutt, op. cit., pp. 8–9; and the summary discussion by G. W. E. Nickelsburg in 'Stories of Biblical and early Post-Biblical Times', in M. E. Stone (ed.), *Jewish Writings of the Second Temple Period, CRINT* Section 2 (Van Gorcum: Assen, 1984), pp. 77–78.

6 See below, p. 89. In respect of what *Aristeas* has to say, it should be noted that LXX translated Hebrew *ṭabbûr* as *omphalos*, 'navel' at Judg. 9:37; Ezek. 38:12.

7 See A. Pelletier, op. cit., pp. 146–147. On the city of Jerusalem and the Temple buildings as described by Aristeas, see particularly M. Hadas, *Aristeas to Philocrates (Letter of Aristeas)* (Harper for the Dropsie College: New York, 1951), pp. 12–15. He also (pp. 14–15) discusses the theory that the Temple curtain, called *katapetasma* by Aristeas 86 and meaning a curtain which was drawn downward from above, may have been that spoken of by Pausanias (5.12.14) as that presented by Antiochus IV to the temple of Zeus at Olympia.

8 See below, p. 49.

9 See *b. Sukk.* 49a, commenting on Isaiah's parable of the vineyard (Isa. 5:1 ff.): R. Jose said, The cavity of the Pits (*šytyn*) descended to the Abyss ... 'and planted it with the choicest vine' (Isa. 5:2) refers to the Temple; 'and built a tower in the midst of it' (ibid.) refers to the altar; 'and also hewed out a winepress therein' (ibid.) refers to the Pits. See

also *t. Sukk.* 3:15; *yer. Sukk.* 4:6.18; *t. Me'ilah* 1:16; and below on Greek ben Sira 50:15.

10 See especially Pseudo-Philo's *Liber Antiquitatum Biblicarum* XII:8–9, and the commentary by C. T. R. Hayward, 'The Vine and its Products as Theological Symbols in First Century Palestinian Judaism', *Durham University Journal* 82 (1990), pp. 11, 14–15.

11 *m. Tamid* 3:8 reads:

From Jericho they used to hear the noise of the Great Gate as it was being opened; from Jericho they used to hear the noise of the musical instrument shaped like a shovel; from Jericho they used to hear the sound of the wood which ben Qatin made as a machine for the laver; from Jericho they used to hear the voice of Gebini the herald; from Jericho they used to hear the sound of the flute; from Jericho they used to hear the sound of the cymbal; from Jericho they used to hear the sound of the (Levites') song; from Jericho they used to hear the sound of the trumpet, and, some say, even the voice of the High Priest, when he proclaimed the Divine Name on Yom Kippur.

12 But see further below, comments on 95.

13 For the Hebrew text, see C. Newsom, *Songs of the Sabbath Sacrifice: A Critical Edition*, Harvard Semitic Studies 27 (Scholars Press: Atlanta, 1985), p. 303. The translation is mine: for Newsom's, see ibid., pp. 306–307.

14 See Newsom. op. cit., p. 4.

15 Cf. G. Vermes, *The Dead Sea Scrolls in English* (2nd edn, Penguin Books: Harmondsworth, 1975), pp. 210–211. This point is noted, to good effect, by D. C. Allison, 'The Silence of Angels: Reflections on the Songs of the Sabbath Sacrifice', *RQ* 13 (1988), pp. 189–197.

16 On the inscription of the *petalon* and the form of Hebrew letters used, which do not directly concern us, see Pelletier, op. cit., pp. 151–152.

17 See below, pp. 51–55.

18 See H. T. Andrews, 'The Letter of Aristeas', in R. H. Charles (ed.), *The Apocrypha and Pseudepigrapha of the Old Testament*, vol. 2 (Oxford University Press: Oxford, 1913), p. 104.

19 See R. J. H. Shutt, 'Letter of Aristeas', in *The Old Testament Pseudepigrapha*, vol. 2, p. 19; Pelletier, op. cit., p. 153.

20 Cf. M. Hadas, *Aristeas to Philocrates*, pp. 48–52.

3 THE WISDOM OF JESUS BEN SIRA IN HEBREW

1 See M. Hengel, *Judaism and Hellenism*, vol. 1 (SCM: London, 1974), p. 131; M. Gilbert, 'Wisdom of Ben Sira', in M. E. Stone (ed.), *Jewish Writings of the Second Temple Period*, in *CRINT* Section 2 (Van Gorcum: Assen, 1984), p. 291; E. Schürer, *The History of the Jewish People in the Age of Jesus Christ*, rev. and ed. G. Vermes, F. Millar, and M. Goodman (Clark: Edinburgh, 1986), vol. 3.1, p. 202; and P. W. Skehan and A. A. di Lella, *The Wisdom of ben Sira*, Anchor Bible 39 (Doubleday: New York, 1987), pp. 8–10; cf. A. A. di Lella, 'Wisdom of ben Sira', in *Anchor Bible*

Dictionary, ed. D. N. Freedman, vol. 6 (Doubleday: New York, 1992), p. 932 (who suggests a date *c*.180 BC); D. S. Williams, 'The Date of Ecclesiasticus', *VT* 44 (1994), pp. 563–565.

2 It is sometimes suggested that ben Sira himself was a priest: see Schürer, op.cit., vol. 3, pp. 201–202; Skehan and di Lella, op.cit., p. 518. He was very likely a Zadokite sympathizer (so, for example, Schürer, ibid.); but for a different view, see S. M. Olyan, 'Ben Sira's Relationship to the Priesthood', *HTR* 76 (1983), pp. 261–286.

3 For the Qumran and Masada fragments, see details in Skehan and di Lella, op. cit., pp. 53, 61; and for knowledge of ben Sira among the Rabbis and early Christians, see Gilbert, op. cit., pp. 300–301; cf. Skehan and di Lella, op. cit., pp. 18–20.

4 For the place of the Zadokites among the Qumran group, see J. Liver, 'The "Sons of Zadok the Priests" in the Dead Sea Sect', *RQ* 6 (1967), pp. 3–30, and, for a rather different view, P. R. Davies, 'Sons of Zadok', in *Behind the Essenes. History and Ideology in the Dead Sea Scrolls*, Brown Judaic Studies 94 (Scholars Press: Atlanta, 1987), pp. 51–72. For continuing Zadokite influence at Leontopolis see C. T. R. Hayward, 'The Jewish Temple at Leontopolis: A Reconsideration', in *Essays in Honour of Yigael Yadin*, ed. G. Vermes and J. Neusner, *JJS* 33 (1982), pp. 429–443; and R. T. White, 'The House of Peleg in the Dead Sea Scrolls', in P. R. Davies and R. T. White (eds), *A Tribute to Geza Vermes*, (Academic Press: Sheffield, 1990), pp. 67–98, esp. pp. 82–89.

5 For details, see Schürer, op. cit., vol. 3, p. 202. Ptolemy Physcon VII Euergetes reigned with his brother from 170–164 BC, and then alone from 145–117 BC, reckoning his regnal years from 170. On the question of whether ben Sira's grandson produced the translation before or after Ptolemy's death in 117 BC, see discussion in Skehan and di Lella, op. cit., pp. 8–9; 134–135; its resolution does not affect our comments.

6 See Schürer, op. cit., rev. and ed. G. Vermes and F. Millar (Clark: Edinburgh, 1973), vol. 1, pp. 200–215 for a convenient critical account of his reign, which ended in his famous breach with the Pharisees (Josephus, *Ant.* XIII. 288–298; cf. *b. Qidd.* 66a). The Jews of Qumran, deeply hostile to the Hasmoneans, were also active in his reign.

7 The military strength of the Jews of Heliopolis, and surviving inscriptional evidence from the settlements, are discussed by Schürer, op. cit., vol. 3.1, pp. 47–49.

8 Skehan and di Lella, op. cit., p. 550, speak of the word as a *mot crochet*, a catchword linking two sections of the poem.

9 See further J. R. Levison, *Portraits of Adam in Early Judaism from Sirach to 2 Baruch* (Academic Press: Sheffield, 1988), pp. 33–48 for discussion of the figure of Adam in ben Sira's writings.

10 See S. P. Brock, 'Some Aspects of Greek Words in Syriac', in A. Dietrich (ed.), *Synkretismus im syrisch-persischen Kulturgebiet* (Abhandlungen der Akademie der Wissenschaften: Göttingen, 1975), pp. 98–104; 'Jewish Traditions in Syriac Sources', *JJS* 30 (1979), pp. 222–223.

11 Cf. P. Wernberg-Møller, *The Manual of Discipline* (Brill: Leiden, 1957), p. 87; and A. R. C. Leaney, *The Rule of Qumran and its Meaning* (SCM: London, 1966), p. 160. But see further J. Marböck, 'Henoch – Adam –

der Thronwagen: Zur frühjüdischen pseudepigraphischen Traditionen bei Ben Sira', *Bib. Zeit.* n.s. 25 (1981), pp. 103–111.

12 On Jubilees and its date, see below, p. 85.

13 Unfortunately the Hebrew text of 44:7 is damaged. It forms part of the introduction to the poem, and speaks of the ancestors of Israel: 'All these were honoured in their generations, and from their days . . . their beauty, *tp'rtm.*' For the damaged portion, the Greek reads: 'and in their days they were a glory'.

14 Many authorities date Tobit to around 200 BC: see Schürer, op.cit., vol. 3.1, pp. 223–224. But it may derive from an earlier period: see G. W. E. Nickelsburg, 'Stories of Biblical and Early Post-Biblical Times', in *Jewish Writings of the Second Temple Period*, p. 45. On the contrasting attitudes of Tobit and ben Sira to Jerusalem and the Second Temple, see C. T. R. Hayward, 'The New Jerusalem in the Wisdom of Jesus ben Sira', *SJOT* 6 (1992), pp. 124–128.

15 Building operations seem characteristic of the Zadokite house: see Hayward, 'The New Jerusalem', pp. 128–130, and 'The Jewish Temple at Leontopolis: A Reconsideration', *JJS* 33 (1982), pp. 429–443.

16 For the view that ben Sira 50 describes Yom Kippur, see J. G. Snaith, *Ecclesiasticus* (University Press: Cambridge, 1974), pp. 251–252.

17 See B. G. Wright, *No Small Difference. Sirach's Relationship to its Hebrew Parent Text* (Scholars Press: Atlanta, 1989), p. 177.

18 The case against ben Sira's poem as a description of Yom Kippur is compellingly argued by F. Ó Fearghil, 'Sir 50, 5–21: Yom Kippur or the Daily Whole-Offering?', *Biblica* 59 (1978), pp. 301–316, and accepted by Skehan and di Lella, op. cit., pp. 550–552. For discussion of the curtain (*prkt* and *msk*), see Ó Fearghil, op. cit., pp. 308–311.

19 See Ó Fearghil, op. cit., pp. 302–306 for detailed comparison of ben Sira with the Mishnah; Skehan and di Lella, op. cit., p. 551; and below, pp. 54–55.

20 Later Jewish tradition certainly interpreted this star as a king: see *jer. Ta'an.* 4.68d; PJ, TN, FT(P), FT(V), and TO of Num. 24:17; and G. Vermes, 'The Story of Balaam', in *Scripture and Tradition in Judaism*, 2nd edn (Brill: Leiden, 1973), pp. 165–166; M. McNamara, 'Early Exegesis in the Palestinian Targum (Neofiti 1) Numbers Chapter 24', *PIBA* 16 (1993), pp. 57–79.

21 On ben Sira's understanding of Aaron, see below, pp. 66–71.

22 See above, pp. 6–8. For the Temple Service as guarantor of the stability of the universe, see further under Jubilees and Pseudo-Philo.

23 Cf. ben Sira 1:4–9; 24:3–9; G. von Rad, *Wisdom in Israel* (SCM: London, 1972), pp. 245–246; and Hengel, op. cit., pp. 159–162.

24 For this observation, see L. G. Perdue, *Wisdom and Cult* (Scholars Press: Missoula, 1977), pp. 189–190; J. L. Crenshaw, *Old Testament Wisdom. An Introduction* (SCM: London, 1981), p. 153, and C. T. R. Hayward, 'Sacrifice and World Order: Some Observations on ben Sira's Attitude to the Temple Service', in S. W. Sykes (ed.), *Sacrifice and Redemption. Durham Essays in Theology* (University Press: Cambridge, 1991), pp. 22–34.

25 See above, p. 52.

26 Verse 14 ends with the word *'lywn*, 'Most High': the same word

concludes verse 16, and also probably was found in verse 15, where the Greek has 'the Most High, King of all'. The scribe has omitted verse 15 by homoioteleuton, his eye passing straight from '*lywn* at the end of verse 14 to the '*lywn* of verse 15. See also Skehan and di Lella, op. cit., p. 549.

27 In this connection, note that some Rabbinic sources regard *pqd*, 'visit', as equivalent in meaning to *zkr*, 'remember': cf. *b. Rosh Ha-Shanah* 32b; TO, PJ, and TN of Gen. 50:24; Exod. 4:31; and Hayward, op. cit., p. 129. On the note in 1 Chr. 16:4 that the Levites 'invoked', see S. Japhet, *I and II Chronicles*, SCM Old Testament Library (SCM: London, 1993), p. 315.

28 See the list of references to Isaiah quoted by Skehan and di Lella, op. cit., p. 553.

29 For detailed discussion, see Japhet, op. cit., pp. 302–304; 439–448.

30 See Japhet, op. cit., pp. 925–931 for the whole ritual, and p. 928 for the temporal sequence of events.

31 See Japhet, op. cit., pp. 497–498 for the textual difficulties of this verse, which she renders: 'All this in writing, from God, as he made me/him (*sc.* David) understand.'

32 See op. cit., p. 547: 'and over the throng sweet strains of praise resound', with note on p. 549.

33 See A. Z. Idelsohn, *Jewish Liturgy and Its Development* (Schocken: New York, 1960), pp. 110–111.

34 See Skehan and di Lella, op. cit., pp. 420–423; Idelsohn, op. cit., pp. 20–22.

35 See *m. Yoma* 7:1; *Soṭah* 7:7; *Tamid* 5:1.

36 See Skehan and di Lella, op. cit., pp. 547, 554.

37 The root may also be connected with *nâdîb*, 'nobleman': see J. A. Goldstein, *I Maccabees*, Anchor Bible 41 (Doubleday: New York, 1976), p. 237.

38 TO has: 'to Him belong strength and exaltation'. See Vermes, op. cit., p. 153.

39 See Wright, op. cit., p. 179.

40 See above, p. 51, on verses 5–11.

41 On these divinely engraved stones of supernatural origin, and their relationship to the stones in the high priest's breastplate, see C. T. R. Hayward, 'Pseudo-Philo and the Priestly Oracle', *JJS* 46 (1995), pp. 43–54.

42 *theia grammata estêliteumena theiôn phuseôn hupomnêmata.*

43 See R. de Vaux, *Ancient Israel. Its Life and Institutions* (Darton, Longman & Todd: London, 1961), pp. 350–352; M. Haran, *Temples and Temple Service in Ancient Israel* (Oxford University Press: Oxford, 1978), pp. 213–214; and W. Dommershausen, article 'gôrâl', in *Theological Dictionary of the Old Testament*, vol. 2 (Eerdmans: Grand Rapids, 1977), pp. 453–454.

44 According to *b. Yoma* 73b, the Urim and Thummim spelled out divine messages using the letters of the tribal names inscribed on the precious stones. PJ of Exod. 28:30 indicates that the letters shone forth from the stones. The breastplate also gave notice of Israel's victories in battle, according to PJ of Exod. 28:15. With all this, compare Josephus, *Ant.* III. 214–218. According to him (*Ant.* III. 218), the stones ceased to

shine forth about 200 years prior to his writing the *Antiquities*, completed around 93/94 AD. This would mean that Josephus believed that they still operated in the time of the Zadokite priesthood, ceasing around 104/103 BC, probably with the death of John Hyrcanus I: see H. St J. Thackeray, *Josephus Jewish Antiquities Books I–IV* (Harvard University Press: Cambridge, Mass., 1967), pp. 420–421.

45 See Skehan and di Lella, op. cit., p. 514.

46 On the significance of *ẓedeq* in the heavenly realm, as depicted in other Jewish writings, see J. M. Baumgarten, 'The Heavenly Tribunal and the Personification of Sedeq in Jewish Apocalyptic', *Aufstieg und Niedergang der römischen Welt*, Teil 11 Principat, Band 19,1. Halbband: Religion (Judentum: Allegemines; Palästinisches Judentum), ed. W. Haase (de Gruyter: Berlin, 1979), pp. 219–239.

4 THE WISDOM OF JESUS BEN SIRA IN GREEK

1 See E. Schürer, *History of the Jewish People*, rev. and ed. by G. Vermes and F. Millar (Clark: Edinburgh, 1973), vol. 1, pp. 603–605.

2 Greek has *par' escharai bômou*. In LXX, *eschara* is the word used at Exod. 27:4–5 for a kind of grating arranged around the altar.

3 See further B. G. Wright, *No Small Difference* (Scholars Press: Atlanta, 1989), pp. 179–181.

5 THE BOOK OF JUBILEES

1 So E. Schürer, *The History of the Jewish People*, rev. and ed. G. Vermes, F. Millar, and M. Goodman (Clark: Edinburgh, 1986), vol. 3.1, pp. 312–314, where different opinions of its date and provenance are rehearsed: see also G. W. E. Nickelsburg, *Jewish Literature between the Bible and the Mishnah* (SCM: London, 1981), pp. 78–79; and, 'The Bible Rewritten and Expanded', in M. E. Stone (ed.), *Jewish Writings of the Second Temple Period, CRINT* Section 2 (Van Gorcum: Assen, 1984), pp. 101–103; K. Berger, *Das Buch der Jubiläen: Jüdische Schriften aus hellenistisch-römischer Zeit*, Band II, Lieferung 3 (Mohn: Gütersloh, 1981), pp. 295–301; and J. VanderKam, 'The Putative Author of the Book of Jubilees', *JSS* 26 (1981), pp. 209–217. The most recent critical discussion of the date and place of origin of Jubilees, by J. C. VanderKam, article 'Jubilees', *Anchor Bible Dictionary*, vol. 3, pp. 1030–1031, dates the work sometime between 170 and 140 BC. For the relationship between Jubilees and 11QTemp., see VanderKam, 'The Temple Scroll and the Book of Jubilees', in G. J. Brooke (ed.), *Temple Scroll Studies* (Academic Press: Sheffield, 1989), pp. 211–236.

2 For details of the Jubilees calendar, see Schürer, op. cit., vol. 1, pp. 599–601; J. van Goudoever, *Fêtes et Calendriers Bibliques* (Beauschene: Paris, 1967), pp. 93–103; A. Jaubert, 'Le Calendrier des Jubilées et de la Secte de Qumrân. Ses Origines Bibliques', *VT* 3 (1953), pp. 250–264; and 'Le Calendrier des Jubilées et les jours liturgiques de la Semaine', *VT* 7 (1957), pp. 35–61; M. Testuz, *Les Idées religieuses du Livre des Jubilées* (Minard: Paris, 1960),

pp. 121–137; and J. M. Baumgarten, 'Some Problems of the Jubilees Calendar in Current Research', *VT* 32 (1982), pp. 485–489.

3 All quotations from Jubilees are taken from the translation of R. H. Charles, *The Book of Jubilees* (Black: London, 1902).

4 See further J. C. Endres, *Biblical Interpretation in the Book of Jubilees* (Catholic Biblical Association of America: Washington, 1987), p. 82.

5 See above, pp. 53, 56–58, 61–62.

6 See Charles, op. cit., pp. 22–24, who notes the same tradition in Philo (*QG* II.25), *The Book of Adam and Eve*, *Midrash Tadshe* 15, and various Christian authors.

7 Charles, op. cit., p. 69, notes Ezek. 38:12 and compares Ezek. 5:5; I Enoch 26:1, as representing the Land of Israel as the centre of the earth. The expression *ṭabbûr hâ'âreẓ* in Ezek. 38:12 has sometimes been understood as 'the navel of the earth'; and A. J. Wensinck, *The Idea of the Western Semites Concerning the Navel of the Earth* (Verhandelingen der K. Akademie van Wetenschappen: Amsterdam, 1917) argued for the existence of an *omphalos* motif in ancient Hebrew thinking about Mount Zion. But see now S. Talmon, article 'har', in G. Botterweck and H. Ringgren (eds) *Theological Dictionary of the Old Testament*, vol. 3, (Eerdmans: Grand Rapids, 1978), pp. 437–438.

8 See above, pp. 45–47.

9 See further C. T. R. Hayward, 'Heaven and Earth in Parallel', in *Christ, The Sacramental Word*, ed. D. Brown and A. Loades (SPCK: London, 1996), pp. 57–74.

10 See below, pp. 109–118.

11 For Adam as a pious man in Rabbinic Literature, see *b. Erub.* 18b. He is depicted as priest also in *Apocalypse of Moses* 29:3–6; PJ Gen. 8:20; *b. Abodah Zarah* 8a; *Shabb.* 28b; *Gen. Rab.* 34:9; *PRE* 31:3. The Talmud and Midrash state that he offered an ox, in accordance with Ps. 69:32.

12 Note that Jubilees 6:3 lists four animal victims, ox, goat, sheep, and kids: PJ of Gen 8:20 states that Noah offered four whole offerings.

13 See Charles, op. cit., p. 49.

14 See above, pp. 51–52.

15 See further J. M. Baumgarten, '*4Q HALAKAH*ᵃ 5, The Law of *ḤADASH*, and the Pentecontad Calendar', *JJS* 27 (1976), pp. 36–46.

16 See above, pp. 52, 53, 56, 78.

17 See Charles, op. cit., p. 117, citing also *jer. Yoma* 4:5 and *b. Ker.* 6ab as listing the seven ingredients of the incense.

18 The presentation of the ritual of Sukkoth by Jubilees is odd, in that the participants are said to wear wreaths on their heads, and process around the altar seven times each day in the morning (16:30–31). The first of these requirements is unknown to the halakhah; the second seems to predicate of each of the seven days a rite required by the Mishnah (*Sukkah* 4:5) only on the seventh. See further Charles, op. cit., p. 118.

19 For attempts to set Jubilees' presentation of Isaac's sacrifice at Sukkoth, and their refutation, see R. le Déaut, *La Nuit Pascale* (Institut Biblique Pontifical: Rome, 1963), pp. 179–184.

20 See above, pp. 87–88.

21 Charles, op. cit., pp. 186–188, dating Jubilees in the Hasmonean period,

compares this passage with Testament of Levi 8–9. But the date of Testament of Levi is disputed; see Schürer, op. cit., vol. 3.2, pp. 774–775. Parallels with Jubilees are undoubted.

22 See Hayward, 'Angels and Worshippers'.

23 On this episode, see further J. Schwartz, 'Jubilees, Bethel, and the Temple of Jacob', *HUCA* 56 (1985), pp. 63–86.

24 For the way way in which the thought of Jubilees 'writes' Jacob into the story of the creation, and the associations which can then be made between the Sabbath and Jacob–Israel, see also J. VanderKam, 'Genesis 1 in Jubilees 2', *Dead Sea Discoveries* 1 (1994), pp. 300–321, and Hayward, 'Heaven and Earth . . .'.

25 J. B. Segal, *The Hebrew Passover from Earliest Times to* AD *70* (Oxford University Press: Oxford, 1963), p. 20, seems to regard the description as purely historical; but Jubilees' treatment of the other festivals can differ from Biblical and other descriptions, as already noticed. In the case of Passover, however, the angel gives directions to Moses both for the Exodus and for future generations; the assumption might be, therefore, that the regulations do represent something of historical actuality.

26 See Segal, op. cit., p. 233, who suggests that the account of Hezekiah's Passover in 2 Chr. 30 already presupposes more use of daylight hours to accommodate the large numbers of pilgrims offering victims.

6 THE WRITINGS OF PHILO OF ALEXANDRIA

For a comprehensive introduction to Philo's thought and writings, with excellent bibliography, the reader is referred to E. Schürer, *The History of the Jewish People*, rev. and ed. G. Vermes, F. Millar, and M. Goodman (Clark: Edinburgh, 1986), vol. 3.2, pp. 816–889. Extensive introductions include E. R. Goodenough, *An Introduction to Philo Judaeus* (Yale University Press: New Haven, 1940); H. A. Wolfson, *Philo*, 2 vols (Harvard University Press: Cambridge, Mass., 1947); J. Daniélou, *Philon d'Alexandrie* (Librairie Arthème Fayard Paris, 1958); S. Sandmel, *Philo of Alexandria: An Introduction* (Oxford University Press: Oxford, 1979); and P. Borgen, 'Philo of Alexandria' in M. E. Stone (ed.), *Jewish Writings of the Second Temple Period, CRINT* Section 2 (Van Gorcum: Assen, 1984), pp. 233–282. See now also N. G. Cohen, *Philo Judaeus. His Universe of Discourse* (Peter Lang: Frankfurt, 1995).

1 See P. Borgen, article 'Philo of Alexandria', in *Anchor Bible Dictionary*, vol. 5, pp. 333–334, for the most recent summary discussion of Philo's life and family, and Schürer, op. cit., vol. 3.2, pp. 814–816 for further discussion and extensive bibliographical information.

2 For studies of Philo's attitude to the Temple Service in general, see H. A. Wolfson, *Philo*, vol. 2, pp. 237–259. P. Borgen, 'Philo of Alexandria', in *Jewish Writings of the Second Temple Period*, pp. 269–272. I. Baer, 'The Service of Sacrifice in Second Temple Times', *Zion* 40 (1975), pp. 95–153 (in Hebrew), compares Philo's writing on sacrifice with ideas expressed in Rabbinic literature, and discerns in both sets of writings the

understanding that the offerings are intended to establish harmony between God's attributes of mercy and justice. For harmony as a key element in Philo's view of sacrifice, see below, pp. 110–111, 116, 134.

3 See further J. Laporte, 'The High Priest in Philo of Alexandria', *Studia Philonica Annual* 3 (1991), p. 71, quoting also *De Vit. Mos.* II.5 and *De Praem.* 56.

4 For an exhaustive study, see J. Laporte, *Eucharistia in Philo*, Studies in the Bible and Early Christianity 3 (Edwin Mellen: Toronto, 1983).

5 On the Man-in-Reality as the perfect man attuned to the most profound self-offering in worship, see Laporte, 'The High Priest', pp. 80–81.

6 On the high priest as a cosmic and mystical symbol, see further J. Laporte, 'The High Priest', pp. 74–77.

7 On the high priest as Logos, see Laporte, 'The High Priest', pp. 74–77. The Logos is both the architect of the cosmos, and a divine attribute active in and upon the soul of the virtuous man.

8 For this, see *De Somn.* II. 185–189. The progressive purification of the high priest reaches it climax on the Day of Atonement when, robed only in a garment made entirely of white linen representing incorruption and most brilliant light, he enters the Holy of Holies. There he offers the highest offering of all, namely himself, free of all passions and earthly constraints (*De Somn.* I. 214, 216–218).

9 See above on ben Sira, pp. 52–54. On the 'interiorization' of worship in Philo's thought, see V. Nikiprowetzky, 'La Spiritualisation des Sacrifices et le culte sacrificiel au Temple de Jérusalem, chez Philon d'Alexandrie', *Semitica* 17 (1967), pp. 97–116.

10 See Jubilees 4:26; 2:7; 3:12; 8:19, all discussed above, pp. 88–91.

11 For discussion of the date and provenance of Wisdom, see E. Schürer, op. cit., vol. 3.1, pp. 572–573; G. W. E. Nickelsburg, *Jewish Literature between the Bible and the Mishnah* (SCM: London, 1981), 184–185; D. Winston, article, 'Solomon, Wisdom of', in *Anchor Bible Dictionary*, vol. 6, pp. 122–123. The work was most likely composed either in the latter half of the first century BC, or in the opening decades of the first century AD.

12 See D. Winston, *The Wisdom of Solomon*, The Anchor Bible 43 (Doubleday: New York, 1979), pp. 321–322. Thus he notes Philo, *De Spec. Leg.*. I. 66ff., quoted in part above (p. 99), to the effect that the universe is God's temple, a notion expressed by Pseudo-Heracleitus and others. See further J. Vilchez, *Nueva Biblia Española Sapiencales V Sabiduria* (Verbo Divino: Estella, 1990), pp. 449–451, who notes Aaron's universal priesthood interceding for the whole world, the symbolism of his vestments, and the use made of these notions by the Church fathers.

13 See above, pp. 49–55, 66–70. The image of the rainbow describing Simon in his priestly vestments is particularly instructive, as is also the use of the verb *kosmein* and related forms in the Greek translation of ben Sira's Wisdom.

14 On ben Sira, see above, pp. 51, 63.

15 For Philo's moral and symbolic ideas regarding atonement and the

system of purity, see J. Laporte, 'Sacrifice and Forgiveness in Philo of Alexandria', *Studia Philonica Annual* 1 (1989), pp. 34–39.

16 There were those who thought that the expenses of the Tamid should be borne by the high priest himself. Possibly they represented a 'Sadducee' point of view which did not prevail in the Jerusalem Temple, although this is far from certain: *Meg. Ta'an.* 1 refers to the period 1st to 8th Nisan as settling the debate that the Tamid should be provided out of the treasury.

17 4Q174 (Flor.) I. 6–7. On the meaning of *mqdš 'dm*, see G. J. Brooke, *Exegesis at Qumran. 4QFlorilegium in its Jewish Context* (Academic Press: Sheffield, 1985), pp. 184–186; D. Dimant, '4QFlorilegium and the Idea of the Community as Temple', in A. Caquot, M. Hadas-Lebel, and J. Riaud (eds), *Hellenica et Judaica. Hommage à Valentin Nikiprowetzky* (Peeters: Paris, 1986), pp.165–189. For further discussion of Philo's treatment of the incense, see E. R. Goodenough, *Jewish Symbols in the Greco-Roman Period*, vol. 4 (Pantheon Books: New York, 1954), pp. 199–208; and for modern critical discussions of the altar of incense see the literature cited by Schürer, *op. cit.*, vol. 2, pp. 296–297, n.17.

18 See further E. R. Goodenough, *Jewish Symbols*, vol. 4, pp. 82–88, and D. M. Hay, 'Philo's References to other Allegorists', *Studia Philonica* 6 (1978–1979), pp. 41–75.

19 See *Jewish Symbols*, vol. 4, pp. 85–87.

20 For Hecataeus on the light, see above, pp. 23–25. A full-scale treatment of the Menorah and its symbolism is to be found in L. Yarden, *The Tree of Light. A Study of the Menorah, the Seven-Branched Lampstand. Agdistis, Attis, and the Almond Tree. Another Look at Movers' Etymology* (Skriv Service: Uppsala, 1972).

21 As suggested already by F. H. Colson, *Philo*, LCL, vol. 7 (Harvard University Press: Cambridge, Ma., 1968), p. 142. For further possible links between Philo and Hecataeus, see ibid., pp. 258–259, 621–622. The Menorah appears on coins of Mattathias Antigonus the Hasmonean (*c.*37 BC): see Schürer, op. cit., vol. 2, pp. 297–298, n. 18, and literature cited there. It was therefore possibly more important as a symbol before 40 AD than is suggested by D. Barag, 'The Menorah in the Roman and Byzantine Periods: A Messianic Symbol', *Bulletin of the Anglo-Israel Archaeological Society* (1984–1985), pp. 44–47.

22 *De Vit. Cont.* 73. On the Therapeutae, see Schürer, op. cit., vol. 2, pp. 591–597; C. T. R. Hayward, article 'Therapeutae', *Encyclopedia of the Dead Sea Scrolls* (Clarendon Press: Oxford, forthcoming); and R. Beckwith, 'The Vegetarianism of the Therapeutae, and the Motives for Vegetarianism in Early Jewish and Christian Circles', *RQ* 13 (1988), pp. 407–410.

23 See above, pp. 120–123, noting how he may have called on earlier, existing tradition.

24 See above, pp. 100–101.

25 For the Chronicler, see S. Japhet, *I and II Chronicles* (SCM: London, 1993), pp. 948–951, 1038–1054. Philo does not say who handled the blood: see further J. B. Segal, *The Hebrew Passover from the Earliest Times to*

AD 70 (Oxford University Press: London, 1963), p. 29 and the literature there cited.

26 Counting, that is, from Tishri, which is the month of the New Year. For a list of months and discussion of the calculation of the year, see Schürer, Appendix III, 'Principal Features of the Jewish Calendar', in op. cit., vol. 1, pp. 587–601.

27 Philo goes on to say that the month of the autumnal equinox (Tishri) is not named by the Torah as first month, even though it is first in the calendar (*De Spec. Leg.* II. 153: Josephus calls Marcheshvan the second month, thus making Tishri the first; *Ant.* I. 80–81). The Mishnah states in a well known passage that there are four New Years: see *m. Rosh Ha Shanah* 1:1, and cf. *Mekh. de R. Ishmael* Pisḥa 2: 13–34. See further R. le Déaut, *La Nuit Pascale* (Institut Biblique Pontifical: Rome, 1963), pp. 218–221, and pp. 224–225 for Philo's association of Pesaḥ with creation.

28 See le Déaut, op. cit. For a summary of issues involved in the Targumim and their 'Poem of the Four Nights' at Exod. 12:42, see M. McNamara and C. T. R. Hayward, *Targum Neofiti 1: Exodus*, The Aramaic Bible 2 (Liturgical Press: Collegeville, 1994), pp. 51–53.

29 For discussion of this last point, see above, pp. 128–130. On unleavened bread as symbolic of the ascetic life, see also *De Sac.* 62 and *De Cong.* 161, cited by Segal, op. cit., p. 28.

30 A literal rendering of the Hebrew of this verse places the offering of the sheaf 'on the morrow after the Sabbath', a famous phrase variously interpreted in antiquity. LXX agree with the interpretation ascribed elsewhere to the Pharisees, understanding 'Sabbath' in this verse to mean 'festival day', that is, Passover (see *m. Men.* 10:1–4; *b. Men.* 65b-66a; *Sifra Emor* Pereq 10:5). For the interpretations of other Jewish groups, see J. van Goudoever, *Fêtes et Calendriers Bibliques* (Beauchesne: Paris, 1967), pp. 31–48; J. le Moyne, *Les Sadducéens* (Gabalda: Paris, 1972), pp. 177–189; Schürer, op. cit., vol. 2, p. 410; and J. M. Baumgarten, 'The Pharisaic–Sadducean Controversies about Purity and the Qumran Texts', *JJS* 31 (1980), p. 169. On Philo and sheaf, see also Goodenough, *Jewish Symbols*, vol. 5.1 pp.87–88.

31 See *De Spec. Leg.* II. 176–178. Philo says (177) that it is made up of 'the most elemental and eldest of things encompassing existing objects', namely the right-angled triangle. This figure is 'the beginning of the origin of all things'; and fifty in number are pillars supporting the Tabernacle proper, prototype of the Temple which represents the universe (*De Vit. Mos.* II. 79–80).

32 *De Vit. Cont.* 65. The festival, though not named, is almost certainly Pentecost. The description of the right-angled triangle as 'the beginning of the origin of all things', *archê tês tôn holôn geneseôs*, is almost verbatim that found in *De Vit. Mos.* II. 80, quoted above, note 31.

33 See also *De Spec. Leg.* I. 183–185, where the feast has already been explained in terms of thanksgiving, and the special sacrifices for the day (two calves, one ram, seven lambs, following Num. 28:27; Lev. 23:18 lists seven lambs, one bull, two rams) are listed along with two lambs consumed by the priests. These last are required by Lev. 23:19, where

they are called *zebaḥ šᵉlâmîm* (festal offerings), a term translated by LXX as *thusia sôtêriou*, 'sacrifice of preservation'. Philo interprets the latter as a thanksgiving for God's preservation of the corn from natural disasters or from war (185).

34 For the priestly dues, and Philo's understanding of them, see *De Spec. Leg.* I. 131–140; and Goodenough, op. cit., vol. 5.1, p. 88.

35 See further J. Potin, *La Fête juive de la Pentecôte*, vol. 1 (Cerf: Paris, 1971), pp. 136–140, where *De Spec. Leg.* II. 188–192 is quoted and discussed, and a theory of a development of a feast of the giving of the Torah in Rabbinic tradition is outlined.

36 Presumably the LXX translators divided the name Azazel into two words, *'ēz*, 'goat', and *'âzal*, 'it went': the Vulgate (Lev. 16:8, 10, 26) similarly interprets it as *caper emissarius*, 'the he-goat sent out'. The same principle of interpretation seems to underlie the version of Symmachus, 'the departing goat' (Lev. 16:8), 'the goat sent out' (Lev. 16:10): Aquila has 'the released goat' at Lev. 16:10, but at 16:8 a rare form *kekratêmenon* or *kekrataiômenon*, derived from Hebrew *'ōz*, 'strength' and possibly meaning 'the seized one'. See further A. Salvesen, *Symmachus in the Pentateuch* (University of Manchester: Manchester, 1991), p. 117.

37 See Rashi on Lev. 16:8, where he derives the name from *'zz*, 'to be strong', and *'l*, 'mighty'. He speaks of it as a steep, flinty, and high summit: so also PJ of Lev. 16:8, which specifies the place as Soq (precipice), Beth Haduri (cf. *m. Yoma* 6:8). See further M. Maher, *Targum Pseudo-Jonathan: Leviticus*, The Aramaic Bible 3 (Liturgical Press: Collegeville, 1994), p. 167.

38 So Goodenough, op. cit., vol. 4, p. 161. See ibid., pp. 158–161 for discussion of *De Spec. Leg.*. II. 204–213, which says nothing of lulab and ethrog; the water-drawing ceremony and the water libation; the perambulation of the altar with willow branches; the chanting of Hallel; the playing of flutes; the illuminations in the court of the women; the blowing of trumpets; and the general carefree rejoicing of the populace. All these things are regarded as integral elements of the feast by *m. Sukkah* 4:1–5:4.

39 See further Goodenough, op. cit., vol. 5.1, pp. 88–89, who notes an allegorical interpretation of the basket ceremony in *De Somn.* II. 272–273, according to which the fruits represent the abundant produce (*euphoria*) of the soul and the harvest of the mind offered in the cosmic Temple.

40 For the influence of Plato and the Stoa on Philo's interpretation of the Bible, see R. Arnaldez, 'L'influence de la traduction des Septante sur le commentaire de Philon', in *Etudes sur le judaisme hellénistique. Congrès de Strasbourg (1983)*; publié sous le direction de R. Kuntzmann et J. Schlosser, Lectio Divina 119 (Cerf: Paris, 1984), pp. 251–266; and Y. Amir, *Die hellenistische Gestalt des Judentums bei Philon von Alexandrien* (Neukirchener-Verlag: Neukirchen-Vluyn, 1979).

41 Note, for example, the use of Philo's numerological evidence in J. M. Baumgarten, '4Q *HALAKAH*ᵃ 5, The Law of *ḤADASH*, and the Pentecontad Calendar', *JJS* 27 (1976), pp. 36–46. The Temple Scroll

(11QTemp) in particular appears to embrace a calendar which not only puts a distance of fifty days between the sheaf-waving and Pentecost, but also between Pentecost (fifteenth day of the third month) and festival of new wine (third day of the fifth month), and between the latter and the festival of oil (twenty-second day of the sixth month). See Y. Yadin, *The Temple Scroll*, vol. 1 (The Shrine of the Book: Jerusalem, 1983), pp. 99–122; J. C. VanderKam, article 'Calendars', *Anchor Bible Dictionary*, vol.1, pp. 818–820.

7 THE WRITINGS OF JOSEPHUS

1 There is a vast literature on the life and writings of Josephus. For an excellent recent introduction to these, see the article by L. H. Feldman, 'Josephus', *Anchor Bible Dictionary*, vol. 3 (Doubleday: New York, 1992), pp. 981–998. Discussion in greater detail, with substantial bibliography, is given in E. Schürer, *The History of the Jewish People*, rev. and ed. G. Vermes, F. Millar, and M. Goodman (Clark: Edinburgh, 1973), vol. 1, pp. 43–63. See also particularly S. J. D. Cohen, *Josephus in Galilee and Rome* (Brill: Leiden, 1979), and T. Rajak, *Josephus. The Historian and his Society* (Duckworth: London, 1983).

2 On the architecture and building of the Temple in general the standard work is T. Busink, *Der Tempel von Jerusalem von Salomo bis Herodes. Eine archäologisch-historische Studie unter Berücksichtigung des Westsemitischen Tempelbaus*, 2 vols (Brill: Leiden, 1970, 1980): vol. 2, *von Ezechiel bis Middot*, deals with the Herodian period. For further bibliography, see C. Roth (ed.), *Encyclopedia Judaica* (Keter: Jerusalem, 1971–1972), vol. 15, pp. 942–988. On the rebuilding in Herod's reign, see Schürer, op. cit., vol. 1, pp. 308–309, n. 71; vol. 2, pp. 284–286; I. Singer (ed.), *The Jewish Encyclopedia* (Funk & Wagnall: New York, 1901–1906), vol. 13, pp. 85–97; C. Meyers, article 'Temple, Jerusalem', *Anchor Bible Dictionary*, vol. 6, pp. 364–365.

3 See *Ant.* I. 25 for reference to his proposed treatise on 'Customs and Causes', to which he refers his readers when discussing the Temple Service (*Ant.* III. 204–205, 223).

4 See *War* IV. 314–325. Ananus had held the high priesthood for three months in 62 (see *Ant.* XX. 197–203); Jesus held office sometime in 63–64 (*Ant.* XX. 213). See Schürer, op. cit., vol. 1, pp. 496–498; vol. 2, p. 232.

5 See also H. St J. Thackeray, *Josephus III. The Jewish War Books IV–VII* (Harvard University Press: Cambridge, Mass. 1968) LCL 210, pp. 96–97, noting that *kosmikê* may mean 'open to the whole world', or perhaps 'emblematic of the mundane system'.

6 See above, pp. 112–115.

7 See *Contra Apionem* II. 80–88, 114.

8 Note his comments on the attempt by Pontius Pilate to introduce busts of the Roman Emperor into Jerusalem, *War* II. 169–174; *Ant.* XVIII. 55–59; and see Schürer, op. cit., vol. 1, pp. 318, 384.

9 See above, pp. 123–127. On the supreme importance of scriptural

exegesis in Philo's writings, see D. T. Runia, 'How to Read Philo', *Nederlands Theologisch Tijdschrift* 40 (1986), pp. 185–198.

10 See above, pp. 121–123.

11 See above, p. 121.

12 See above, pp. 26–84.

13 Cf. also Apocalypse of John 4:5, where thunders may symbolize God's voice coming forth from his throne, before which the seer saw seven lamps (on a Menorah?).

14 See above, pp. 30, 35–36.

15 The laver of Solomon's Temple, a vast bronze vessel containing water, was indeed called 'the sea', 1 Kings 7: 23, 39, and in first temple times may have symbolized the primeval waters: for summary of modern discussion on this matter, see Carol Meyers, article 'Sea, Molten', in *Anchor Bible Dictionary*, vol. 5, pp. 1061–1062. In his account of Solomon's Temple, however, Josephus (*Ant.* VIII. 79–80) says only that the laver was called 'sea' on account of its size; nor does he offer any symbolic meaning for the laver in the Second Temple. Philo (*De Mig. Abr.* 98; *De Vit. Mos.* II. 136–140) emphasizes that the laver was made out of bronze mirrors, and that it symbolizes the blameless life of those who undertake self-examination, as it were looking at their minds in a mirror, removing perceived blemishes, and attaining to purity.

16 See above, pp. 31–32, 81 and below, pp. 159–161.

17 See above, p. 147.

18 See above, pp. 146–147.

19 See further C. T. R. Hayward, 'Pseudo-Philo and the Priestly Oracle', *JJS* 46 (1995), pp. 51–54.

20 See above, pp. 18–25.

21 These include the worship of an ass's head and the annual ritual murder of a well-fed Greek. The slander alleging Jewish hatred of Greeks in particular should be noted in conjunction with the following note.

22 Charges of Jewish dislike of other human beings and hatred of foreigners are found even in the writings of Hecataeus of Abdera, and Josephus was determined to refute them, not only in *Contra Apionem*, but also in *Antiquities*: see, on this point, L. H. Feldman, 'Josephus' Portrait of Balaam', *Studia Philonica Annual* 5 (1993), pp. 56–61.

8 PSEUDO-PHILO'S *LIBER ANTIQUITATIUM BIBLICARUM*

1 For discussion of the character, provenance, and date of *LAB*, see D. J. Harrington, J. Cazeaux, C. Perrot, and P.-M. Bogaert, *Pseudo-Philon: Les Antiquités Bibliques*, 2 vols, Sources Chrétiennes 229–230 (Cerf: Paris, 1976): vol. 2 of this work offers a detailed commentary on the text; G. W. E. Nickelsburg, *Jewish Literature between the Bible and the Mishnah* (SCM: London, 1981), pp. 265–268, 275; M. E. Stone (ed.), *Jewish Writings of the Second Temple Period*, *CRINT* Section 2, *The Literature of the Jewish People in the Period of the Second Temple and the Talmud* (Van Gorcum: Assen, 1984), pp. 107–110; D. J. Harrington, '*Pseudo-Philo*', in

J. H. Charlesworth (ed.), *The Old Testament Pseudepigrapha*, (Darton, Longman & Todd: London, 1983–1985), vol. 2 , pp. 297–303; E. Schürer, *The History of the Jewish People*, rev. and ed. G. Vermes, F. Millar, and M. Goodman (Clark: Edinburgh, 1986), vol. 3.1, pp. 325–331; and F. J. Murphy, *Pseudo-Philo. Rewriting the Bible* (Oxford University Press: Oxford, 1993), pp. 3–25, 223–270.

2 See C. T. R. Hayward, 'The Figure of Adam in Pseudo-Philo's Biblical Antiquities', *JSJ* 32 (1992), pp. 1–20. The author of *LAB* often modifies earlier traditions: see G. Vermes, 'The Story of Balaam – The Scriptural Origin of Haggadah', in *Scripture and Tradition in Judaism*, 2nd edn (Brill: Leiden, 1973), pp. 127–177; M. Wadsworth, 'The Death of Moses and the Riddle of the End of Time in Pseudo-Philo', *JJS* 28 (1977), pp. 12–19; C. T. R. Hayward, 'Pseudo-Philo and the Priestly Oracle', *JJS* 46 (1995), pp. 43–54.

3 *LAB* LIX. 4.

4 Before the Flood, God tells Noah (*LAB* III. 4) that He will establish His covenant with the latter 'to the end that I might destroy all those who dwell on the earth'. This is an unique and non-Biblical tradition: see J. P. Lewis, *A Study of the Interpretation of Noah and the Flood in Jewish and Christian Literature* (Brill: Leiden, 1968), p. 75.

5 See also Murphy, op. cit., pp. 35–36.

6 On these precious stones, granted to the judge Cenez, see further Hayward, 'Pseudo-Philo and the Priestly Oracle', pp. 47–49.

7 See further C. T. R. Hayward, 'The Vine and its Products as Theological Symbols in First Century Palestinian Judaism', *Durham University Journal* 82 (1990), pp. 9–18, which includes discussion of II Baruch, the Aramaic Targums, and Jewish coinage of the revolts against Rome.

8 Other writings of the period state openly what the author of *LAB* appears in this and other passages to take for granted, that *the world was created for the sake of Israel*: see Testament of Moses 1:12–13; IV Esdras 6:55, 59; 7:11; cf. II Baruch 14:19; 15:7; 21:24; PJ of Gen. 14:19, 22; PJ and TN of Num. 22:30; and discussion in Hayward, 'The Vine', p. 13. Note how *LAB's* version of Balaam's oracles (XVIII. 10–11) attaches cosmic significance to Israel as the vine, whose destruction would render God's creation vain.

9 For possible allusions to the abysses by ben Sira and *Aristeas*, see above, pp. 80–81, 31–32.

10 Perrot and Bogaert, in Harrington, Cazeaux, Perrot and Bogaert, *Pseudo-Philon*, vol. 2, p. 172 argue against the opinion that *LAB* understood Isaac's offering as somehow replacing the sacrifices of the Temple. They seem to be correct in this, and to their observations may be added what has been said here: Pseudo-Philo expects the Temple Service to continue until the present world order ends and the dead are raised, and this particular view of the Service suggests to me that *LAB* was indeed written before 70. For the author, Isaac's sacrifice has significance for the past. One of the reasons God chose Israel as His people was because of the blood of Isaac's sacrifice, XVIII. 5: see discussion in C. T. R. Hayward, 'The Sacrifice of Isaac and Jewish Polemic against Christianity', *CBQ* 52 (1990), pp. 301–302. The sacrifice

has force for the present in being related to other sacrifices offered on behalf of human beings, especially lamb offerings, XXXII. 3: see G. Vermes, 'Redemption and Genesis xxii', in *Scripture and Tradition*, pp. 199–201. It avails for the future: in XXXII.3 Isaac remarks that he had been born in the world to be offered as a sacrifice to his maker, and that his blessedness will extend to *all* people, such that the people will know that God has dignified man's life as having sacrificial value. On this Vermes (ibid., p. 201) remarks:

Ps.-Philo believed that by Isaac's unique example God conferred upon human nature its true diginity, the dignity of a divinely required and freely offered self-sacrifice. The blessing resulting from it would extend to all men for ever, and they would understand that they possess the same humanity which was made holy by Isaac's sacrifice.

11 See above, pp. 94–96.
12 M. R. James, *Biblical Antiquities*, pp. 114–115 compares XIII. 4–7 with a passage from Talmud Yerushalmi, according to which Pentecost is the time when God passes judgement on the fruit of trees. See further Perrot and Bogaert in Harrington, Cazeaux, Perrot, and Bogart, *Pseudo-Philon*, vol. 2 on XIII.5.
13 The phrase 'for/to your watchers' represents Latin *prospeculatoribus vestris*, the word *prospeculator* being otherwise unattested. M. R. James, *Biblical Antiquities*, p. 115, suggested reading *pro speculatoribus vestris*, 'to/for your watchers', which is probably correct: see L. T. Stuckenbruck, *Angel Veneration and Christology*, Wissenschaftliche Untersuchungen zum Neuen Testament, 2 Reihe 70 (Mohr: Tübingen, 1995), pp. 170–173, who also demonstrates convincingly that Pseudo-Philo was not opposed to offerings for good angels who serve God, but only to veneration of evil angels associated with magic. In a private communication, Dr Stuckenbruck has suggested to me that the author of *LAB* (in the original language) may have intended a play on words between *speculatoribus* and *perspexi*, such that the 'watchers' be seen as closely associated with God's 'watching over' the universe at New Year. From this, I venture to ask whether the 'watchers', as Israel's 'guardians', might not be prevailed upon by Israel's worship at New Year to implore God to exercise mercy with regard to the universe?
14 See above on Philo and the Feast of Trumpets, pp. 136–137. The New Year in Tishri is a time of judgement, as *m. Rosh Ha-Shanah* 1:2 attests.
15 See Murphy, *Pseudo-Philo*, pp. 73–75.
16 See also discussion in Murphy, *Pseudo-Philo*, pp. 92–94.

SELECT BIBLIOGRAPHY

Allison, D. C., 'The Silence of Angels: Reflections on the Songs of the Sabbath Sacrifice' *RQ* 13 (1988), pp. 188–197.

Amir, Y., *Die hellenistische Gestalt des Judentums bei Philon von Alexandrien* (Neukirchener-Verlag: Neukirchen-Vluyn, 1979).

Andrews, H. T., 'The Letter of Aristeas' in R. H. Charles (ed.), *The Apocrypha and Pseudepigrapha of the Old Testament*, vol. 2 (Oxford University Press: Oxford 1913), pp. 83–122.

Arnaldez, R., 'L'influence de la traduction des Septante sur le commentaire de Philon', *Etudes sur le judaïsme hellénistique. Congrès de Strasbourg (1983)*; publié sous le direction de R. Kuntzmann et J. Schlosser, Lectio Divina 119 (Cerf: Paris, 1984), pp. 251–266.

Avigad, N., 'A New Class of *Yehud*-Stamps', *IEJ* 7 (1957), pp. 146–153.

Baer, I., 'The Service of Sacrifice in Second Temple Times', *Zion* 40 (1975), pp. 95–153 (in Hebrew).

Barag, D., 'The Menorah in the Roman and Byzantine Periods: A Messianic Symbol', *Bulletin of the Anglo-Israel Archaeological Society* (1984–1985), pp. 44–47.

Baumgarten, J. M., 'The Heavenly Tribunal and the Personification of Sedeq in Jewish Apocalyptic', *Aufstieg und Niedergang der römischen Welt*, Teil 11 Principat, Band 19, 1. Halbband: Religion (Judentum: Allegemines; Palästinisches Judentum) ed. W. Haase (de Gruyter: Berlin, 1979), pp. 219–239.

Baumgarten, J. M., '4Q HALAKAH^{a}5, The Law of *HADASH*, and the Pentecontad Calendar', *JJS* 27 (1976), pp. 36–46.

———, 'The Pharisaic–Sadducean Controversies about Purity and the Qumran Texts', *JJS* 31 (1980), pp. 157–170.

———, 'Some Problems of the Jubilees Calendar in Current Research', *VT* 32 (1982), pp. 485–489.

Beckwith, R., 'The Vegetarianism of the Therapeutae, and the Motives for Vegetarianism in Early Jewish and Christian Circles', *RQ* 13 (1988), pp. 407–410.

Berger, K., *Das Buch der Jubiläen: Jüdische Schriften aus hellenistisch-römischer Zeit* Band II, Lieferung 3 (Mohn: Gütersloh, 1981).

Borgen, P., 'Philo of Alexandria', *Anchor Bible Dictionary*, vol. 5, pp. 333–342.

——, 'Philo of Alexandria', in M. E. Stone (ed.), *Jewish Writings of the Second Temple Period, CRINT,* Section 2 (Van Gorcum: Assen, 1984), pp. 233–282.

Brock, S. P., 'Some Aspects of Greek Words in Syriac', in A. Dietrich (ed.), *Synkretismus im syrischpersischen Kulturgebiet* (Abhandlungen der Akademie der Wissenschaften: Göttingen, 1975), pp. 98–104.

——, 'Jewish Traditions in Syriac Sources', *JJS* 30 (1979), pp. 212–232.

Brooke, G. J., *Exegesis at Qumran. 4QFlorilegium in its Jewish Context* (Academic Press: Sheffield, 1985).

Busink, T., *Der Tempel von Jerusalem von Salomo bis Herodes. Eine archäologischhistorische Studie unter Berücksichtigung des Westsemitischen Templebaus,* 2 vols. (Brill: Leiden, 1970, 1980).

Charles, R. H., *The Book of Jubilees* (Black: London, 1902).

Cohen, N. G., *Philo Judaeus. His Universe of Discourse* (Peter Lang: Frankfurt, 1995).

Cohen, S. J. D., *Josephus in Galilee and Rome* (Brill: Leiden, 1979).

Crenshaw, J. L., *Old Testament Wisdom. An Introduction* (SCM: London, 1982).

Daniélou, J., *Philon d'Alexandrie* (Librairie Arthème Fayard: Paris, 1958).

Davies, P. R., 'Sons of Zadok', in *Behind the Essenes. History and Ideology in the Dead Sea Scrolls,* Brown Judaic Studies 94 (Scholars Press: Atlanta, 1987), pp. 51–72.

de Vaux, R., *Ancient Israel. Its Life and Institutions* (Darton, Longman & Todd: London, 1961).

di Lella, A. A., 'Wisdom of ben Sira', *The Anchor Bible Dictionary,* ed. D. N. Freedman, vol. 6, (Doubleday: New York, 1992), pp. 931–945.

Dimant, D., '4QFlorilegium and the Idea of the Community as Temple', in A. Caquot, M. Hadas-Lebel, and J. Riaud (eds), *Hellenica et Judaica. Hommage à Valentin Nikiprowetzky,* (Peeters: Paris, 1986), pp. 165–189.

Dommershausen, W., 'gôrâl', *Theological Dictionary of the Old Testament,* vol. 2, G. J. Botterweck and H. Ringgren, (Eerdmans: Grand Rapids, 1977), pp. 450–456.

Doran, R., 'Pseudo-Hecataeus', in J. H. Charlesworth (ed.), *Old Testament Pseudepigrapha* vol. 2 (Darton, Longman & Todd: London, 1985), pp. 905–919.

Endres, J. C., *Biblical Interpretation in the Book of Jubilees* (Catholic Biblical Association of America: Washington, 1987).

Ó Fearghil, F., 'Sir 50, 5–21: Yom Kippur or the Daily Whole-Offering', *Biblica* 59 (1978), pp. 301–316.

Feldman, L. H., 'Josephus', *Anchor Bible Dictionary,* vol. 3, p. 981–998.

——, 'Josephus, Portrait of Balaam', *Studia Philonica Annual* 5 (1993), pp. 48–83.

Funk, F. W., 'Hezekiah the Governor', in M. Avi-Yonah (ed.), *Encyclopedia of Archaeological Excavations in the Holy Land* (Oxford University Press: London, 1975) vol. 1, pp. 263–267.

Gager, J. G., 'Pseudo-Hecataeus Again', *ZNW* 60 (1969), pp. 130–139.

Gilbert, M., 'Wisdom of Ben Sira', in M. E. Stone (ed.), *Jewish Writings of the*

Second Temple Period, in *CRINT* Section 2 (Van Gorcum: Assen, 1984), pp. 290–301.

Goldstein, J. A., *I Maccabees, Anchor Bible* 41 (Doubleday: New York, 1976).

Goodenough, E. R., *An Introduction to Philo Judaeus* (Yale University Press: New Haven, 1940).

———, *Jewish Symbols in the Greco-Roman Period,* 12 vols. (Pantheon Books: New York, 1953–1965).

Hadas, M., *Aristeas to Philocrates (Letter of Aristeas)* (Harper for the Dropsie College: New York, 1951).

Haran, M., *Temples and Temple Service in Ancient Israel* (Oxford University Press: Oxford, 1978).

Harrington, D. J., *Pseudo-Philo,* in J. H. Charlesworth (ed.), *The Old Testament Pseudepigrapha,* (Darton, Longman & Todd: London 1983–1985), vol. 2, pp. 297–377.

Harrington, D. J., Cazeaux, J., Perrot, C., and Bogaert, P.-M., *Pseudo-Philon: Les Antiquités Bibliques,* 2 vols., Sources Chrétiennes 229–230 (Cerf: Paris, 1976).

Hay, D. M., 'Philo's References to other Allegorists', *Studia Philonica* 6 (1978–1979), pp. 41–75.

Hayward, C. T. R., 'The Jewish Temple at Leontopolis: A Reconsideration', in *Essays in Honour of Yigael Yadin,* ed. G. Vermes and J. Neusner, *JJS* 33 (1982), pp. 429–443.

———, 'The Sacrifice of Isaac and Jewish Polemic against Christianity', *CBQ* 52 (1990), pp. 292–306.

———, 'The Vine and its Products as Theological Symbols in First Century Palestinian Judaism', *Durham University Journal* 82 (1990), pp. 9–18.

———, 'Sacrifice and World Order: Some Observations on ben Sira's Attitude to the Temple Service', in S. W. Sykes (ed.), *Sacrifice and Redemption. Durham Essays in Theology* (Cambridge University Press: Cambridge, 1991), pp. 22–34.

———, 'The Figure of Adam in Pseudo-Philo's Biblical Antiquities', *JSJ* 32 (1992), pp. 1–20.

———, 'The New Jerusalem in the Wisdom of Jesus ben Sira', *SJOT* 6, (1992), pp. 123–138.

———, 'Pseudo-Philo and the Priestly Oracle', *JJS* 46 (1995), pp. 43–54.

———, 'Angels and Worshippers in an Ancient Jewish Perspective' (forthcoming).

———, 'Therapeutae', *Encyclopedia of the Dead Sea Scrolls* (Clarendon Press: Oxford, forthcoming).

Hengel, M., *Judaism and Hellenism,* vol. 1 (SCM: London, 1974).

Holladay, C. R., *Fragments from Hellenistic Jewish Authors vol. 1: Historians* (Scholars Press: Chico, 1983), pp. 277–335.

———, 'Hecataeus, Pseudo-', *Anchor Bible Dictionary,* vol. 3, pp. 108–109.

Idelsohn, A. Z., *Jewish Liturgy and Its Development* (Schocken: New York, 1960).

James, M. R., *The Biblical Antiquities of Philo* (SPCK: London, 1917).

Japhet, S., *I and II Chronicles,* SCM Old Testament Library (SCM: London, 1993).

Jaubert, A., 'Le Calendrier des Jubilées et de la Secte de Qumrân. Ses Origines Bibliques', *VT* 3 (1953), pp. 250–264.

———, 'Le Calendrier des Jubilées et les jours liturgiques de la Semaine', *VT* 7 (1957), pp. 35–61.

Jellicoe, S., *The Septuagint and Modern Study* (Oxford University Press: Oxford, 1968).

Laporte, J., *Eucharistia in Philo*, Studies in the Bible and Early Christianity 3 (Edwin Mellen: Toronto, 1983).

———, 'Sacrifice and Forgiveness in Philo of Alexandria', *Studia Philonica Annual* 1 (1989), pp. 34–42.

———, 'The High Priest in Philo of Alexandria', *Studia Philonica Annual* 3 (1991), pp 71–82.

Leaney, A. R. C., *The Rule of Qumran and its Meaning* (SCM: London, 1966).

le Déaut, R., *La Nuit Pascale* (Institut Biblique Pontifical: Rome, 1963).

le Moyne, J., *Les Sadducéens* (Gabalda: Paris, 1972).

Levison, J. R., *Portraits of Adam in Early Judaism from Sirach to 2 Baruch* (Academic Press: Sheffield, 1988).

Lewis, J. P., *A Study of the Interpretation of Noah and the Flood in Jewish and Christian Literature* (Brill: Leiden, 1968).

Liver, J., 'The "Sons of Zadok the Priests" in the Dead Sea Sect', *RQ* 6 (1967), pp. 3–30.

McNamara, M., 'Early Exegesis in the Palestinian Targum (Neofiti 1) Numbers, Chapter 24', *PIBA* 16 (1993), pp. 57–79.

McNamara, M., and Hayward, C. T. R., *Targum Neofiti 1: Exodus*, The Aramaic Bible 2 (Liturgical Press: Collegeville, 1994).

Maher, M., *Targum Pseudo-Jonathan: Leviticus,* The Aramaic Bible 3 (Liturgical Press: Collegeville, 1994).

Marböck, J., 'Henoch – Adam – der Thronwagen: Zur frühjüdischen pseudepigraphischen Traditionen bei ben Sira', *Bib. Zeit.* n.s. 25 (1981), pp. 103–111.

Meyers, C., 'Sea, Molten', *Anchor Bible Dictionary*, vol. 5, pp. 1061–1064.

———, 'Temple, Jerusalem', *Anchor Bible Dictionary*, vol. 6, pp. 350–369.

Murphy, F. J., *Pseudo-Philo. Rewriting the Bible* (Oxford University Press: Oxford, 1993).

Neusner, J., *The Idea of Purity in Ancient Judaism (with a Critique and a Commentary by Mary Douglas)* (Brill: Leiden, 1973).

Newsom, C., *Songs of the Sabbath Sacrifice: A Critical Edition*, Harvard Semitic Studies 27 (Scholars Press: Atlanta, 1985).

Nickelsburg, G. W. E., *Jewish Literature between the Bible and the Mishnah* (SCM: London, 1981).

———, 'Stories of Biblical and Early Post-Biblical Times', in M. E. Stone (ed.), *Jewish Writings of the Second Temple Period, CRINT* Section 2 (Van Gorcum: Assen, 1984).

Nikiprowetzky, V., 'La Spiritualisation des Sacrifices et le culte sacrificiel au Temple de Jérusalem, chez Philon d'Alexandrie', *Semitica* 17 (1967), pp. 97–116.

Olyan, S. M., 'Ben Sira's Relationship to the Priesthood', *HTR* 76 (1983), pp. 261–286.

Pelletier, A., *Lettre d'Aristée à Philocrate*, Sources Chrétiennes 89 (Cerf: Paris, 1962).

Perdue, L. G., *Wisdom and Cult* (Scholars Press: Missoula, 1977).

Potin, J., *La Fête juive de la Pentecôte*, 2 vols (Cerf: Paris, 1971).

Pucci, M. ben Zeev, 'The Reliability of Josephus Flavius: The case of Hecateus' and Manetho's Accounts of Jews and Judaism: Fifteen Years of Contemporary Research (1974–1990)', *JSJ* 24 (1993), pp. 215–234.

Rajak, T., *Josephus. The Historian and his Society* (Duckworth: London, 1983).

Runia, D. T., 'How to Read Philo', *Nederlands Theologisch Tidjschrift* 40 (1986), pp. 185–198.

Salvesen, A., *Symmachus in the Pentateuch* (University of Manchester: Manchester, 1991).

Sandmel, S., *Philo of Alexandria: An Introduction* (Oxford University Press; Oxford, 1979).

Schmidt, F., *La Pensée de Temple. De Jérusalem à Qoumrân* (Seuil: Paris, 1994).

Schürer, E., *The History of the Jewish People in the Age of Jesus Christ*, 3 vols: vol. 1 rev. and ed. G. Vermes and F. Millar (1973); vol. 2 rev. and ed. G. Vermes, F. Millar, and M. Black (1979); vol. 3 rev. and ed. G. Vermes, F. Millar, and M. Goodman (1986–1987) (Clark: Edinburgh).

Schwartz, J., 'Jubilees, Bethel, and the Temple of Jacob', *HUCA* 56 (1985), pp. 63–86.

Segal, J. B., *The Hebrew Passover from Earliest times to AD 70* (Oxford University Press: Oxford, 1963).

Sellers, O. R., *The Citadel of Beth-Zur* (Westminster: Philadelphia, 1933).

Sellers, O. R., Funk, R. W., McKenzie, J. L., Lapp, P., and Lapp, N., 'The 1957 Excavation at Beth-Zur', *Annual of the American Schools of Oriental Research* 38 (1968).

Shutt, R. J. H., 'Aristeas, Letter of, *Anchor Bible Dictionary*, vol. 1, pp. 380–382.

———, 'Letter of Aristeas', in J. H. Charlesworth (ed.), *The Old Testament Pseudepigrapha*, vol. 2 (Darton, Longman & Todd: London, 1985), pp. 7–34.

Skehan, P. W., di Lella, A. A., *The Wisdom of ben Sira, Anchor Bible* 39 (Doubleday: New York, 1987).

Snaith, J. G., *Ecclesiasticus* (Cambridge University Press: Cambridge, 1974).

Stern, M., *Greek and Latin Authors on Jews and Judaism*, vol. 1, *From Herodatus to Plutarch* (The Israel Academy of Sciences and Humanities: Jerusalem, 1974).

Stone, M. E. (ed), *Jewish Writings of the Second Temple Period, CRINT* Section 2, *The Literature of the Jewish People in the Period of the Second Temple and the Talmud* (Van Gorcum: Assen, 1984).

Stuckenbruck, L. T., *Angel Veneration and Christology*, Wissenschaftliche Untersuchungen zum Neuen Testament, 2 Reihe 70 (Mohr: Tübingen, 1995).

Talmon, S., 'har', in *Theological Dictionary of the Old Testament*, vol. 3, ed. G. Botterweck and H. Ringgren (Eerdmans: Grand Rapids, 1978), pp. 427–447.

Testuz, M., *Les Idées religieuses du Livre des Jubilées* (Minard: Paris, 1960).

VanderKam, J. C., 'Calendars – Ancient Israelite and Early Jewish', *Anchor Bible Dictionary*, vol. 1, pp. 814–820.

——, 'Jubilees', *Anchor Bible Dictionary* vol. 3, pp. 1030–1032.

——, 'The Putative Author of the Book of Jubilees', *JSS* 26 (1981), pp. 209–217.

——, 'The Temple Scroll and the Book of Jubilees', in G. J. Brooke (ed.), *Temple Scroll Studies* (Academic Press: Sheffield, 1989), pp. 211–236.

——, 'Genesis 1 in Jubilees 2', *Dead Sea Discoveries* 1 (1994), pp. 300–321.

van Goudoever, J., *Fêtes et Calendriers Bibliques* (Beauschene: Paris, 1967).

Vermes, G., 'The Story of Balaam – The Scriptural Origin of Haggadah', *Scripture and Tradition in Judaism* (2nd edn, Brill: Leiden, 1973), pp. 127–177.

——, 'Redemption and Genesis xxii', *Scripture and Tradition in Judaism* (2nd edn, Brill: Leiden, 1973), pp. 193–227.

——, *The Dead Sea Scrolls in English* (2nd edn, Penguin Books: Harmondsworth, 1975).

Vilchez, J., *Nueva Biblia Española Sapiencales V. Sabiduria* (Verbo Divino: Estella, 1990).

von Rad, G., *Wisdom in Israel* (SCM: London, 1972).

Wacholder, B. Z., *Eupolemus: A Study of Judaeo-Greek Literature* (Jewish Institute of Religion: Cincinnati, 1974).

Wadsworth, M., 'The Death of Moses and the Riddle of the End of Time in Pseudo-Philo', *JJS* 28 (1977), pp. 12–19.

Walter, N., *Der Thoraausleger Aristobulos. Untersuchungen zu seinen Fragmenten und zu pseudepigraphischen Resten der jüdisch-hellenistischen Literatur* (Akademie Verlag: Berlin, 1964).

——, Pseudo-Hekataios I und II', in *Jüdische Schriften aus hellenistisch-römischer Zeit* I. 2 (Mohn: Gütersloh, 1976), pp. 144–160.

Wensinck, A. J., *The Idea of the Western Semites Concerning the Navel of the Earth* (Verhandelingen der K. Akademie van Wetenschappen: Amsterdam, 1917).

Wernberg-Møller, P., *The Manual of Discipline* (Brill: Leiden, 1957).

White, R. T., 'The House of Peleg in the Dead Sea Scrolls', in P. R. Davies and R. T. White (eds), *A Tribute to Geza Vermes* (Academic Press: Sheffield, 1990), pp. 67–98.

Williams, D. S., 'The Date of Ecclesiasticus', *VT* 44 (1994), pp. 563–565.

Winston, D., *The Wisdom of Solomon, The Anchor Bible* 43 (Doubleday: New York, 1979).

——, 'Solomon, Wisdom of', *Anchor Bible Dictionary*, vol. 6, pp. 120–127.

Wolfson, H. A., *Philo*, 2 vols. (Harvard University Press: Cambridge, Mass., 1947).

Wright, B. G., *No Small Difference. Sirach's Relationship to its Hebrew Parent Text* (Scholars Press: Atlanta, 1989).

Yadin, Y., *The Temple Scroll*, 3 vols. (The Shrine of the Book: Jerusalem, 1983).

Yarden, L., *The Tree of Light. A Study of the Menorah, the Seven-branched Lampstand. Agdistis, Attis, and the Almond Tree. Another Look at Movers' Etymology* (Skriv Service: Uppsala, 1972).

INDEX OF BIBLICAL AND OTHER TEXTS

SEPTUAGINT

RABBINIC LITERATURE

The Mishnah

INDEX OF MODERN
AUTHORS

209

INDEX OF NAMES

211